TOLKIEN AND THE CRITICS
Essays on J. R. R. Tolkien's *The Lord of the Rings*

TOLKIEN
AND THE CRITICS

Essays on J. R. R. Tolkien's
The Lord of the Rings

EDITED BY

Neil D. Isaacs and
Rose A. Zimbardo

UNIVERSITY OF NOTRE DAME PRESS
Notre Dame   London

FOR OUR HALFLINGS:
Ian, Jonathan, Daniel, Adam and Anne

FOREWORD

All quotations from *The Lord of the Rings* are taken from the revised edition (Boston, 1967), and we are grateful to Houghton Mifflin Company for their cooperation; citations will appear parenthetically in the text by volume and page numbers. All references to *The Hobbit* are to the Houghton Mifflin edition (Boston, 1938). References to Tolkien's essay "On Fairy-Stories" are to *Essays Presented to Charles Williams* (London, 1947), pp. 38-89, except in Burton Raffel's essay where, because of frequent cross-references to "Leaf by Niggle," citations are to *Tree and Leaf* (London, 1964). References to Tolkien's lecture "Beowulf: The Monsters and the Critics" are to *An Anthology of Beowulf Criticism*, ed. Lewis E. Nicholson (Notre Dame, Ind., 1963), pp. 51-103.

For permission to reprint we are grateful to the editors of *Time and Tide* for C. S. Lewis, "The Dethronement of Power," October 22, 1955; to Random House and Edmund Fuller for "The Lord of the Hobbits" from *Books with Men Behind Them* (New York, 1962), pp. 169-196; to the editors of *The Texas Quarterly* and W. H. Auden for "The Quest Hero," IV (1962), 81-93; to the editors of *Critique* and Patricia Meyer Spacks for material from "Ethical Patterns" in *The Lord of the Rings*," III (1959), 30-42; to the editors of *Niekas* and Marion Zimmer Bradley for "Men, Halflings, and Hero-Worship" in #16 (Summer, 1966); to the editors of *Thought* and Robert J. Reilly for "Tolkien and the Fairy Story," XXXVIII (1963), 89-106; to University of Florida Press and Charles Moorman for "The Shire, Mordor, and Minas Tirith" from *The Precincts of Felicity* (1966), pp. 86-100; and to the editors of *The Hudson Review* and Roger Sale for material from "England's Parnassus: C. S. Lewis, Charles Williams, and J.R.R. Tolkien," xvii (1964), 203-225. We are also grateful to all other contributors for their original essays and for their cooperation: Tom Gasque, Hugh Keenan, Mary Kelly, Burton Raffel, Roger Sale, and last but not least John Tinkler; and to Anne Kozak for her faithful editorial services.

TABLE OF CONTENTS

ON THE POSSIBILITIES OF
WRITING TOLKIEN CRITICISM

Neil D. Isaacs

THIS IS SURELY A BAD TIME FOR TOLKIEN CRITICISM. STO-
ries in *Holiday, Esquire, Saturday Evening Post, Saturday
Review*, and the Luce(fer) publications, to say nothing of
the feverish activity of the fanzines, do not produce a cli-
mate for serious criticism. Nor does the fact that *The Lord
of the Rings* and the domain of Middle-earth are eminently
suitable for faddism and fannism, cultism and clubbism encourage scholarly activity. Tolkien's enormous current popularity itself acts as a deterrent to critical activity, as it has
for other contemporary writers. Usually, when initial critical
reception has been so warm that it has contributed to great
popular success (as with Durrell, Cozzens, Salinger, Gold-
ing, Bellow, and even Mailer), the resultant popular success
has apparently occasioned critical second-thoughts, with
revaluations downward. But this recurrent phenomenon has
not really had any effect on Tolkien's reputation. One difference is that the Tolkien mass popularity was not fostered by
the mass media; it grew from the excellences and appeals of
the work itself and was simply reported in the media. There
never was any promotional bandwagon for Tolkien. But the
major difference is that there never was a critical bandwagon either.

The first reviewers were full of praise and awe but also
full of contradictions and questions, particularly about genre

and ultimate significance. Subsequent reviewers, with some egregious exceptions on both sides of the water, continued the praise and began proposing answers to some of the questions. But from the beginning critical studies appeared only occasionally, and though they have continued to appear, the occasions have not become more frequent. We have assembled here the best of the previously published work on Tolkien (with two exceptions) and added eight original pieces. The essays of C. S. Lewis, W. H. Auden, and Robert J. Reilly as well as the chapter from Charles Moorman's *Precincts of Felicity* appear without change. Patricia Meyer Spacks has revised her original article and Edmund Fuller has made some significant additions to his chapter from *Books with Men Behind Them*. Marion Zimmer Bradley's essay has been considerably revised.

The first exception is Roger Sale's "England's Parnassus: C. S. Lewis, Charles Williams, and J. R. R. Tolkien." Mr. Sale has completely reworked his material to provide a new cogent essay focused specifically on Tolkien. Touching on several of the points raised in this introductory essay, Sale's "Tolkien and Frodo Baggins" seems to me the *pièce de résistance* of the collection and incidentally answers Burton Raffel's charges of "not literature" with a careful case for "great literature." The second exception is the dissertation of Marjorie Evelyn Wright, "The Cosmic Kingdom of Myth: A Study in the Myth-Philosophy of Charles Williams, C. S. Lewis, and J. R. R. Tolkien" (University of Illinois, 1961). Because of Miss Wright's untimely death, the dissertation itself was never quite completed, and though it contains a great deal of valuable material we have decided, at least for now, not to extract and reorganize parts of it.

The purpose of this essay, and one purpose of the whole collection, is to demonstrate the great possibilities for Tolkien criticism, and the eight original essays in this collection

2

will perhaps urge the point with far greater effectiveness. This is not, I think, the place for an excursus on the function and value of criticism itself, but I would like to make some observations on the need for Tolkien criticism. As those few who reject *The Lord of the Rings* as a significant work of literature always say and as some who make the most extravagant claims for it demonstrate, the extraordinary popular success of Tolkien is the product of irrational adulation and is due to a variety of nonliterary cultural and social phenomena. It would be, then, one function of Tolkien criticism to shift the emphasis from extraliterary aspects of the trilogy and its audience to a consideration of the work itself. Such consideration might then answer some of the basic questions about such matters as genre, influences, sources, relationships, and the like.

But these, too, are more or less exterior approaches, and for all the insight they might contribute it seems to me that they would only add to the framework within which interior critical investigation might go on. Analytical and formalist, i.e. interior, procedures would have to be followed finally to illuminate the density of the material, the wealth of detail, and the integrity of the world of *The Lord of the Rings*. But the ultimate function of criticism is to render judgment on a work of art. The devices of criticism, the methods and approaches, furnish the means of arriving at a valid value judgment. And though the criteria for judging relative excellence will vary from critical system to critical system, the end of judgment remains always in view. In fact, one way of describing a critical system is to call it the explanation of a way to evaluation. Thus critical studies of Tolkien would provide the means for evaluative judgments. The emotionally-based impressions of *The Lord of the Rings* (and even the basis for the fanatic cultship) could then be checked against the findings of intellectually-based investigations. A by-product of this process might be the dispatching of such judgments as "literature for those who dislike literature" or "anti-intellectual escapism" or even "not literature."

Edmund Fuller, whose evaluation is quite high, justifies it with recourse to a wide variety of critical insights. Some of his suggestions might well be carried further; indeed, some have been. Patricia Meyer Spacks and Rose Zimbardo have dealt thoroughly and I think brilliantly with ethical patterns and moral vision, but there are other perhaps more obvious aspects of morality and related concerns which might profitably be examined. In the self-contained world of Middle-earth in the Third Age, aside from the stark polarities of the opposing forces, there may be seen in characters and peoples a variety of moral systems, political philosophies, and sociological patterns, perhaps even a variety of aesthetic, epistemological, and historical principles, which scholars of the appropriate disciplines or critics with appropriate interests could illuminate. I am confident that the results of such investigations would be interesting, not so much for their reflections of our paler (or more transparent) cultures, but for their further illuminations of the details of Tolkien's created world. While I am sure that no consistent allegorical pattern would be found, no one-for-one relationships between individuals or groups in Middle-earth and identifiable corresponding figures from life, I am equally confident that deliberate parallels would be discovered—oblique allusions, more direct evocations, and even parodies. In fact, the more I read Tolkien, the more convinced I am that the inside joke (which may of course be quite serious) is one of his favorite techniques. As in Joyce and Pound, the allusive nature of *The Lord of the Rings* is frequently borne in the linguistic texture of the work, but more like Eliot a vast polycultural background forms the raw material for points of reference. But beyond this we must not push, for unlike Joyce, Pound, and Eliot, the allusive nature of Tolkien's work is not designed with the elaborate high seriousness and super-intellectuality of a master puzzle-maker. The *game* of solution is turned by Tolkien to a *play* of nonsolution. Thus, it should be one pursuit of Tolkien critics to pick up the frequent and tantalizing clues for allegory and follow them through to their dead-end.

That is where allegory in *The Lord of the Rings* leads, and one job of work for the critic is to follow along—not merely to show the futility of allegorizing but to trace the patterns by which Tolkien deliberately delineates the futility of allegory. Similarly the symbolic capacity of both texture and structure of *The Lord of the Rings* must be probed. Every hint of symbolism picked up by the reader must be pursued by the critic until he sees where the symbolism (sometimes built up with an elaborate accretion of details) breaks down. Tolkien's imagination has thus produced a game of symbol-tease, and surely there are lessons for the players and the spectators to learn about their own games, their own sports, practices, and delights. But perhaps the most significant conclusion to be derived from these suggested critical approaches is the general negative (and obvious) one that Tolkien's world is, after all and most of all, *not* our world, and that our patterns, the ways in which we impose formal order or a semblance of meaning upon the chaotic experience which is life, do not quite work for Middle-earth.

Yet Reilly in "Tolkien and the Fairy Story" provides a neat defense of the trilogy precisely in the very terms in which it has been attacked as bearing no relation to the real world. Providing a sketch of a history-of-ideas approach and employing Tolkien's own definitions and distinctions as well as those of his critics, Reilly discusses "Tolkien's Christianized romantic imagination." Thus, finally, Reilly's ex-

5

terior approaches, applying material of the known world to the Third Age of Middle-earth, end up relating Tolkien's created world to ours—both ultimately are seen as reflections of divine creation.

Along similar lines I would like to see an analysis of folk-elements in Tolkien, an actual accounting of motifs according to the Aarne-Thompson index. An interesting aspect of this study would be Tolkien's habitual doubling or echoing of motifs, after the manner of late medieval romances. On a larger scale, I would like to see a thorough accounting of the mythic materials in *The Lord of the Rings.* A study of the many biblical parallels might be in order here; and a mythographer might well show how Tolkien has used existing myths, reshaped (abused?) others, and forged new ones. Gasque's "Tolkien: the Monsters and the Critters" marks the beginning of such an approach and attempts to evaluate the effectiveness of borrowings as opposed to inventions, the relative degree of fear inspired by the known and the unknown. Inevitably there will be an analysis of archetypes in Tolkien; Auden's treatment of the trilogy as a Quest paradigm and Moorman's thematic analysis of the complex image of the City make substantial contributions to such study.

Certain particular and special aspects of Tolkien's created world require particular and special attention. The names, for example, are an onomatologist's delight, and John Tinkler has begun the investigations in this area. The allusiveness of many of the names in what Reilly calls "philological *jeux d'esprit*" suggests that a study of the naming would primarily require an exterior approach, yet several systems of forming names may be discovered. An interior approach might well analyze the appropriateness of naming practices by the various races. Of course onomastic investigation would form just one aspect of the large area of linguistic material which should be examined. Here, too, exterior relationships need to be explored, established, and explained; but again I think the most rewarding part of a study of linguistics in Middle-earth would show the significance of language to Middle-earth and the various creatures who people it. Here again there are philosophical, even moral, overtones which extend beyond the Secondary World to the primary one. Tolkien's own off-hand remarks about the importance of philology to the creative conception of the trilogy need not be taken too seriously, but they cannot be ignored in the light of the philological emphases of the books.

A separate study might well be devoted to visions, dreams, and prophecies. Their frequency and importance in and for Middle-earth requires explanation in the light of the special way they seem to operate. I mean that in two senses: the way they operate on and for the characters and the way they operate as part of the artistic structure of the book. I see little need, however, for indulging in psychoanalytical speculation here, except perhaps to show that the familiar psychological postulates of our world, of whatever school, do not seem quite to hold for Middle-earth. Yet Hugh Keenan in "The Appeal of *The Lord of the Rings:* A Struggle for Life," has made a good case for the position that the trilogy embodies and dramatizes the historico-psychoanalytical principle of Norman O. Brown.

In the textural detail of the trilogy may be discerned many patterns of imagery. Off-hand I think of colors and weathers, suns and moons, stars and landscapes, and the light and dark as the outstanding patterns. Repeated patterns and clusters of details are present and they seem to act as leitmotivs. I must, however, reassert the cautions concerning symbolism and allegory in Tolkien. The meanings carried in these image-patterns, these leitmotivs, are limited. Eventually the simplicity of an analytical insight will break down

7

in complexities, ambiguities, and deliberate ironies. Perhaps the recognition of the presence of the patterns would be sufficient accomplishment for such a critical approach, though an understanding of their workings would contribute substantially to an appreciation of the artistry of the whole.

Observations of imagery of course are ancient and honored staples, almost clichés, of formalist criticism, but no less valuable for all that. Another staple of formalist procedure, the study of point of view, could with great benefit be followed with regard to *The Lord of the Rings*, as Sale has demonstrated in part. Tolkien's shifting of "centres," to use Jamesian terminology, is artfully patterned and subtly meaningful. In fact, the limits imposed upon the vision of the centres, those characters through whom the action is viewed, and the gradual (though not at all steady) development of that vision form a central and unifying embodiment of at least one major theme of the trilogy. The shifts, the limits, and the overall development (growth-cum-setbacks) in the point of view should all be charted in detail.

Still another staple of objectivist criticism, though of more recent vintage, is analysis of time in a work of literature. For purposes of application to *The Lord of the Rings*, this approach should be expanded to include the dimensions of space. The time-space configurations of Middle-earth in the Third Age (and before and beyond) provide fascinating material for study, evaluation, and conjecture. And for this kind of approach especially, the appendices and maps may be looked upon as integrally and intrinsically vital parts of the work.

One of the important special aspects of Tolkien's narrative is the inclusion of a great deal of poetry. It is this element which has received the most frequent adverse criticism, though there has been no attempt on the part of the detractors to analyze the verse either for itself or for the way it operates in context. Mary Quella Kelly's essay serves as a thorough, convincing defense of the poetry, treating both of these major issues of interior criticism analytically rather than impressionistically.

So far I have suggested interior approaches for critical study of various special elements to be found in the world of Middle-earth. But I think attention should also be focused on the missing elements. The frequently noted absence of women (and of sex) is deliberate rather than incidental. The problems raised by this exclusion, touched on in part by Marion Zimmer Bradley in "Men, Halflings, and Hero-Worship," need thorough-going treatment. And so do the problems raised by the more complete exclusion of any organized religion or even mention of deity (with two exceptions in one Appendix).

Up to this point I have studiously avoided listing examples for the various categories of critical approaches I have been suggesting. In the first place, I do not want to limit or channel investigations with any pedantic strictures. In the second place, Tolkien's readers, admirers, and potential critics will probably be struck immediately by any obvious examples I might list and will very likely prefer supplying their own illustrations to acknowledging mine. In one hitherto neglected area of Tolkien criticism, however, I cannot resist noting a few specifics while urging thorough investigation. This is the area of humor, in which Tolkien may be amusing, droll, witty, or even ribald. At least part of the charm of the Secondary World of Middle-earth is produced by the devices for humor. Occasionally, Tolkien employs comedy of action, comedy of situation, and comedy of character, but the primary source of humor is comedy of language. Oblique references, sardonic suggestions, philological puns, and off-color incongruities are all part of the repertoire of Tolkien as humorist; but it is important to realize that no joke is present just for its own sake. Anything for a laugh is not one of Tolkien's mottoes; invariably there will be some overriding tonal or thematic significance to the humor, and this I think is why most of the comedy appears in the early part of *The Fellowship of the Ring*, in the Shire that is, and before the Quest proper begins.

My list includes the apparently innocent references to Gorhendad Oldbuck (I, 108, a phonological joke), to the Town Hole at Michel Delving (I, 168, a double philological pun), to the Battle of Greenfields (I, 15, with its wealth of suggestions of ludicrous critical controversy and perhaps even of Falstaff himself), to colonists (I, 18, where the irony cuts two ways), to the S.-B.'s (I, 272, the inevitable reduction of this family branch to an essentially-characterizing abbreviation), to 1417 as "a good year" (II, 180), to "posts and pillars" (II, 181), to the punning verb in Treebeard's speech—"There'll be the Lord of the Fields of Rohan, mark you!" (II, 179), and to the deceptively naive puns in Goldberry's "I see you are an elf-friend; the light in your eyes and the ring in your voice tells it" (I, 135). My favorite (with which I close, lest I go on and on) is a linguistic double-take which is set up with masterful timing. At *The Green Dragon* in Bywater, Sam's cousin is referred to as "Hal" three times (I, 53, 54—Hal has apparently seen an Ent who was probably seeking signs of the entwives on a rare excursion to the Northfarthing of the Shire). Since hobbit names are anglicized we have no reason to think that Hal is anything but short for Harold or Henry. But when Sam calls him Halfast, we recognize Hal-fast by analogy with his cousin Sam-wise, or rather with his uncle Ham, Sam's father, whom Bilbo addresses formally as Hamfast (I, 30; Sam's full name is not revealed until later). Look again: Halfast, who has a reputation for "saying that he's seen things," is not "Hal-fast" to Ted Sandyman and company, but "Half-ast."

A series of wholly distinct and separate problems are raised by the appendices. They are pertinent to and substantially integral parts of the created world of Middle-earth, the Secondary World; but the question remains whether they are parts of the artifact called *The Lord of the Rings.* Conceptions of art and definitions of genre need to be called in question here; the presence of the appendices makes for rather large problems of aesthetics. A structural analyst of the trilogy would be hard put to justify any one appendix, I think, in terms of whatever patterns of structure he may discover in the six Books. Still, under the pervasive influence of Kenneth Burke, one might take a larger view of *form* and account for the appendices in terms of fulfillment of expectations aroused in the course of the Books proper.

Clearly, in contemplating the artistry of Tolkien, one must broaden not only one's horizons but also one's definitions. Prose fiction has taken new turns or even jumps with Tolkien, and the critics must try to keep up. Thus Raffel's argument in "*The Lord of the Rings* as Literature" is both a failure and a triumph: his (sentimentally) narrow definition of literature excludes Tolkien; and the very fact of such valid (according to the limits of his definition) exclusion demands a revision, a growing up, of ideas about prose fiction. One day I hope to tackle the problem of form in *The Lord of the Rings* myself, in an attempt to account for what C. S. Lewis in "The Dethronement of Power" has called "a structural invention of the highest order."

THE DETHRONEMENT OF POWER

C. S. Lewis

WHEN I REVIEWED THE FIRST VOLUME OF THIS WORK, I hardly dared to hope it would have the success which I was sure it deserved. Happily I am proved wrong. There is, however, one piece of false criticism which had better be answered: the complaint that the characters are all either black or white. Since the climax of Volume I was mainly concerned with the struggle between good and evil in the mind of Boromir, it is not easy to see how anyone could have said this. I will hazard a guess. "How shall a man judge what to do in such times?" asks someone in Volume II. "As he has ever judged," comes the reply. "Good and ill have not changed . . . nor are they one thing among Elves and Dwarves and another among Men" (II, 40-41).

This is the basis of the whole Tolkinian world. I think some readers, seeing (and disliking) this rigid demarcation of black and white, imagine they have seen a rigid demarcation between black and white people. Looking at the squares, they assume (in defiance of the facts) that all the pieces must be making bishops' moves which confine them to one color. But even such readers will hardly brazen it out through the two last volumes. Motives, even on the right side, are mixed. Those who are now traitors usually began with comparatively innocent intentions. Heroic Rohan and imperial Gondor are partly diseased. Even the wretched Sméagol, till quite late in the story, has good impulses; and, by a tragic paradox, what finally pushes him over the brink is an unpremeditated speech by the most selfless character of all.

There are two Books in each volume and now that all six are before us the very high architectural quality of the romance is revealed. Book I builds up the main theme. In Book II that theme, enriched with much retrospective material, continues. Then comes the change. In III and V the fate of the company, now divided, becomes entangled with a huge complex of forces which are grouping and regrouping themselves in relation to Mordor. The main theme, isolated from this, occupies IV and the early part of VI (the latter part of course giving all the resolutions). But we are never allowed to forget the intimate connection between it and the rest. On the one hand, the whole world is going to the war; the story rings with galloping hoofs, trumpets, steel on steel. On the other, very far away, two tiny, miserable figures creep (like mice on a slag heap) through the twilight of Mordor. And all the time we know that the fate of the world depends far more on the small movement than on the great. This is a structural invention of the highest order: it adds immensely to the pathos, irony, and grandeur of the tale.

This main theme is not to be treated in those jocular, whimsical tones now generally used by reviewers of "juveniles." It is entirely serious: the growing anguish, the drag of the Ring on the neck, the ineluctable conversion of hobbit into hero in conditions which exclude all hope of fame or fear of infamy. Without the relief offered by the more crowded and bustling Books it would be hardly tolerable.

Yet those Books are not in the least inferior. Of picking out great moments, such as the cock-crow at the Siege of

Gondor, there would be no end; I will mention two general, and totally different, excellences. One, surprisingly, is realism. This war has the very quality of the war my generation knew. It is all here: the endless, unintelligible movement, the sinister quiet of the front when "everything is now ready," the flying civilians, the lively, vivid friendships, the background of something like despair and the merry foreground, and such heavensent windfalls as a *cache* of choice tobacco "salvaged" from a ruin. The author has told us elsewhere that his taste for fairy-tale was wakened into maturity by active service; that, no doubt, is why we can say of his war scenes (quoting Gimli the Dwarf), " 'There is good rock here. This country has tough bones' " (II, 137). The other excellence is that no individual, and no species, seems to exist only for the sake of the plot. All exist in their own right and would have been worth creating for their mere flavor even if they had been irrelevant. Treebeard would have served any other author (if any other could have conceived him) for a whole book. His eyes are "filled up with ages of memory and long, slow, steady thinking" (II, 66). Through those ages his name has grown with him, so that he cannot now tell it; it would, by now, take too long to pronounce. When he learns that the thing they are standing on is a hill, he complains that this is but "a hasty word" (II, 69) for that which has so much history in it.

How far Treebeard can be regarded as a "portrait of the artist" must remain doubtful; but when he hears that some people want to identify the Ring with the hydrogen bomb, and Mordor with Russia, I think he might call it a "hasty" word. How long do people think a world like his takes to grow? Do they think it can be done as quickly as a modern nation changes its Public Enemy Number One or as modern scientists invent new weapons? When Tolkien began there was probably no nuclear fission and the contemporary incarnation of Mordor was a good deal nearer our shores. But the text itself teaches us that Sauron is eternal; the war of the Ring is only one of a thousand wars against him. Everytime we shall be wise to fear his ultimate victory, after which there will be "no more songs." Again and again we shall have good evidence that "the wind is setting East, and the withering of all woods may be drawing near" (II, 76). Every time we win we shall know that our victory is impermanent. If we insist on asking for the moral of the story, that is its moral: a recall from facile optimism and wailing pessimism alike, to that hard, yet not quite desperate, insight into Man's unchanging predicament by which heroic ages have lived. It is here that the Norse affinity is strongest: hammerstrokes, but with compassion.

"But why," some ask, "why, if you have a serious comment to make on the real life of men, must you do it by talking about a phantasmagoric never-never-land of your own?" Because, I take it, one of the main things the author wants to say is that the real life of men is of that mythical and heroic quality. One can see the principle at work in his characterization. Much that in a realistic work would be done by "character delineation" is here done simply by making the character an elf, a dwarf, or a hobbit. The imagined beings have their insides on the outside; they are visible souls. And Man as a whole, Man pitted against the universe, have we seen him at all till we see that he is like a hero in a fairytale? In the book Éomer rashly contrasts "the green earth" with "legends." Aragorn replies that the green earth itself is "a mighty matter of legend" (II, 37).

The value of the myth is that it takes all the things we know and restores to them the rich significance which has been hidden by "the veil of familiarity." The child enjoys his cold meat, otherwise dull to him, by pretending it is buffalo, just killed with his own bow and arrow. And the child is wise. The real meat comes back to him more savory for having been dipped in a story; you might say that only then is it real meat. If you are tired of the real landscape, look at it in a mirror. By putting bread, gold, horse, apple, or the very roads into a myth, we do not retreat from reality: we rediscover it. As long as the story lingers in our mind, the real things are more themselves. This book applies the treatment not only to bread or apple but to good and evil, to our endless perils, our anguish, and our joys. By dipping them in myth we see them more clearly. I do not think he could have done it in any other way.

The book is too original and too opulent for any final judgment on a first reading. But we know at once that it has done things to us. We are not quite the same men. And though we must ration ourselves in our rereadings, I have little doubt that the book will soon take its place among the indispensables.

3

THE LORD OF THE HOBBITS:
J. R. R. TOLKIEN

Edmund Fuller

J. R. R. TOLKIEN HAS DEFINED FANTASY AS "THE MAKING OR glimpsing of Other-worlds." As such a maker, his own accomplishment is extraordinary. It is embodied in a four-part work introduced by *The Hobbit* and developed through the trilogy called *The Lord of the Rings.*

The other world which he has invented carries us back into untold depths of prehistory to what he calls the Third Age of Middle-earth. It is a time when men have already long existed, have experienced heights and depths of being, and still share the world with other rational creatures of several different orders, with some of whom, in fact, they have interbred.

For this world he has created a self-contained geography, with maps, a mythology and balladry, a history in great depth and completeness of organization, stretching back far behind the time-span of his story. He has created several languages and runic alphabets, and within them traced elaborate linguistic interrelationships and pursued many etymologies. The historical frame of his world is filled out with genealogies and what might be called ethnic treatises on his other-than-human species. There are extensive flora and fauna in addition to those already known to us. All these elements are woven through the tale, but so deep is Tolkien's immersion in this world that at the end of the trilogy there are six appendices, totaling 103 pages, elaborately footnoted, dealing with the subjects remarked above. Though the appendices contribute to the persuasive verisimilitude of the tale, they are not necessary for such a purpose. They reflect Tolkien's own intensity of inner experience and total absorption in his act of subcreation. It is this that makes his spell so great and in turn draws readers with him into these further compilations of data about an imaginary world they are loath to leave.

The four-part structure of the work is analogous to Wagner's Ring cycle of operas. A shorter, relatively childlike wonder tale (*Das Rheingold* and *The Hobbit* respectively) in each case introduces a massive trilogy. It is odd and interesting that a ring of power is central to both stories and lends its name to their titles, and that dragons and a broken sword to be mended by a warrior hero occur in each. But noting these coincidences between the *Ring of the Nibelungs* and *The Lord of the Rings* is as far as comparison should be carried in a discussion which is not concerned with tracing the incidence of familiar mythic motifs. Tolkien's great work is astonishingly underivative in terms of any specific sources or borrowings. To whatever he has drawn, as all must do, from the common cultural heritage of the human race, he has brought something uniquely his own.

Hobbits are Tolkien's authentic contribution to the lore of imaginary species. They are a small folk, manlike in shape and manner, somewhat furred, seldom attaining more than three feet in stature, but well formed. He tells us they are

> an unobtrusive but very ancient people, more numerous formerly than they are today, for they love peace and quiet and good tilled earth. . . . They do not and did not understand or like machines much more complicated than a forge-bellows,

a water mill, or a hand-loom, though they were skilled with tools. Even in ancient days they were, as a rule, shy of "the Big Folk," as they call us, and now they avoid us with dismay and are becoming hard to find. (I, 10)

Although hobbits belong to the large and mysterious genre of little people, they are a distinct and fresh invention, richly elaborated in all their histories, habits, and generic idiosyncrasies. Sometimes they are called "halflings" by the men of the story, and are already legendary within its frame so that many are astonished to learn that they really exist. They inhabit a gentle region of Tolkien's geography called The Shire, which has much the character of the Cotswold country.

The sheer creative feat of bringing a new creature into the realm of fairy story is almost too much for some to accept. Sir Stanley Unwin, Tolkien's publisher, told me that the first negotiations for German publication of *The Hobbit* were broken off abruptly when the publishers wrote that they had searched through all the encyclopedias and found that there was no such thing as a hobbit.

Yet it is part of the meaning of these books that this simple, obscure people should play a central role in a great contest involving the welfare of all earth. And it is not that people as a group, but a few individuals from among them, who play the determining role, thrust irresistibly from their wonted quiet into the heart of a vast struggle.

In *The Hobbit*, Bilbo Baggins is inveigled into an expedition by some dwarfs who seek stratagems to destroy a dragon who has long usurped their halls and treasures. The small size and ability for unobtrusive movement of the hobbit is deemed valuable for reconnaissance. In a memorable episode of the journey, Bilbo acquires a ring which he keeps secret for a long time. It has the power of conferring invisibility, which is all that Bilbo knows about it.

The Hobbit is a story which young children love. It can be read to, or by, them from seven years up. To this extent it may be called a children's book. But like any fine story that may lie within a child's range, it is not limited to children and, indeed, can scarcely be relished with ultimate appreciation by them. The more mature the reader, the more added qualities he can discern in it. Stories written not for their own sake, but "for children," seldom are of enduring merit for children or anyone else.

On the other hand, *The Lord of the Rings* cannot be approached by children as young as those who can cope with *The Hobbit*. It is more difficult in language and concept, and prospective child readers must wait a few years. Yet I know from experience that it can be read aloud to an intelligent nine-year-old with immense involvement and response. But the trilogy is an adult book, on any terms.

Its three parts are: *The Fellowship of the Ring*, *The Two Towers*, and *The Return of the King*. In the trilogy, the nature and significance of Bilbo's ring has been discovered by one of the major figures, Gandalf the Gray, a benevolent wizard. The aged Bilbo has turned over the ring to his nephew, Frodo. It proves to be a long-lost and portentous artifact.

A runic rhyme tells of:

Three Rings for the Elven-kings under the sky,
   Seven for the Dwarf-lords in their halls of stone,
Nine for Mortal Men doomed to die,
   One for the Dark Lord on his dark throne
In the Land of Mordor where the Shadows lie.
   One Ring to rule them all, One Ring to find them,
   One Ring to bring them all and in the darkness bind
      them
In the Land of Mordor where the Shadows lie.

Bilbo's Ring proves to be the "One Ring to rule them all." It had been wrought in an earlier age, in the land of Mordor, by Sauron the Great, a malevolent being of immense powers, now devoted to absolute evil. In the past history of the world, he has had times of ascendancy and decline. His earlier loss of the Ring forced him into a long withdrawal, during which he has planned a new campaign. He knows that the Ring has been found. Already he has launched his dark, terrible, and corrupt forces to recover it. If he succeeds, all earth and its creatures will be brought under his total sway.

It devolves upon Frodo to attempt to dispose of the powerful Ring in the only way by which it can be destroyed. This is to fling it into the Cracks of Doom, into the heart of the volcanic fire of Orodruin, Mount Doom, in the land of Mordor itself, near the tower which is the seat of Sauron's rule. This heroic attempt and its terrible hazards comprise the story of the trilogy.

The tale is spun out in a masterly way. It is plotted with an astonishing prodigality of invention that never fails in the approximate 600,000 words of the whole. Tolkien can evoke hideousness, terror, horror and dreadful suspense, as well as beauty, laughter, nobility and joy. The style is always graceful, often highly eloquent, occasionally lyrical with descriptive passages of much loveliness and color. Tolkien is an adept painter of scenes and evoker of images, who can orchestrate his narrative and descriptive effects with flexibility and variety, from pianissimo to forte, while keeping his themes or motifs tightly interwoven and steadily developing. Also he is a poet of much skill in the special veins appropriate to the work. He creates runic rhymes and bardic songs in a wide range of moods and meters, from comic to heroic to elegiac, in the modes of those that characterize Anglo-Saxon and Scandinavian literature.

The Lord of the Rings is a fairy tale in the highest aspect of its kind—which requires some discussion. *Fairy* is prominent in the long lexicon of words ruined by the nasty vulgarism of our time—at least in the American culture. It is probably irrecoverable for several generations because it has been made a sniggering, derisive synonym for homosexual. This unhappy association with effeminacy clearly came out of a saccharine sentimentality that previously had vulgarized an ancient and noble conception into a sickly-sweet, flutter-winged miniature image that flourished in Victorian times. To be fair, this corruption had earlier roots, and it has since reached its peak of nauseousness in the excruciating cutenesses of Walt Disney. What, then, was a fairy before this despoiling, and how is he to be restored to his lost stature and quality?

Here Tolkien has done a great rehabilitation, not only in the hobbit books, but in a long essay, "On Fairy-Stories," originally delivered as a lecture at St. Andrews University, in Scotland, and printed in the memorial volume, *Essays Presented to Charles Williams*. Professor Tolkien deprecates his expertness, but it is the most profound and illuminating discussion of the subject I have ever seen.

"Faërie," in its essence, means "enchantment." As a *place name*, perhaps its best usage, Faërie is the realm or world of enchantment, whether viewed as remote and separate in time and place or superimposed upon our own, for Faërie is wherever and whenever the enchantment is operable, when men have entered or fallen under it. A "fairy" is one of the denizens of that realm, the people of Faërie, the agents of its natural spells, the masters of its enchantments. A better name than fairy for such a being is Elf, and it is so used by Tolkien as it was by Spenser.

In Tolkien's story the Elven peoples are of major importance. It is before the separation of the ways of men and

Elves, before the withdrawal (not the end) of the latter. The Elves are of an antiquity greater than man; are uncorrupted, of tall stature and handsome visage, bear themselves with dignity and joy, preserve their ancient tongue and songs, have rich arts and crafts, which men call enchantments. It is the character of their workmanship to "put the thoughts of all that we love into all that we make." They use their powers benevolently, are immortal but not unconquerable. In a few instances they have wedded with men, producing a race of the Half-elven, still a noble kind though their powers are less and in them immortality is diminished to long living. All this is in Tolkien's canon. Fairy-tale at large has a tradition of bad fairies along with good, but I suspect that in primal origin the relationship is not unlike that of the fallen angels to the good.

It is important to remember that this realm of Faërie encompasses all the natural phenomena and creatures known to us, augmented by much else in plants, animals, and intelligent beings. In Tolkien's world there are not only Elves and men, but hobbits, dwarfs, and some unique creatures, such as Ents, his oldest living species, a kind of walking, talking tree. There are beornings—a sort of were-bear. We also meet an individual figure, unclassifiable other than as some primal nature spirit, Tom Bombadil. The passage about him is one of the most joyously lyrical and contains, too, one of the finest of the work's many poems.

There are wizards, also. The greatest of these, Gandalf, has profound aspects for further discussion. A wizard, as here drawn, is partly an enigma but seems to be in essence a man, but possessed of long life and magical powers. Following the lead of Tolkien, I have avoided the word "magic" in relation to Elves. Not that it may not be used, but that it may confuse a fine distinction. Enchantment is not a technique that Elves use, rather it is the total natural mode of their being and action. The wizard commands magic as an acquired technique and lore, consciously employed for specific effects, good or bad. From ancient times the lore of magic has known both the black magician and the white magician. Merlin was one of the latter, and even the poet Virgil was sometimes considered so.

Tolkien's world also has a variety of malevolent creatures. At the center are demonic powers, greatest of whom is Sauron, who is unmistakably a satanic figure, who might be nothing less than one of the fallen angelic host, and whose very name suggests the serpent. Orcs form the largest category of his mortal servants—goblin creatures of a debased order—but other mysterious powers, demonic or wraithlike, also are deployed under his command.

Here, then, is summarized the basic frame and cast. It seems wise not to attempt anything in the line of detailed synopsis. On this much we can attempt some examination of the story's meaning. In the first place, it is itself, at its face value, rich with inherent meaning, inescapably bonded with the events and characters. This is meaning of a sort that the reader translates into appropriate analogies for his own life, if he is so minded: as in the fact that courage and integrity, seen in any context, are enhancements and encouragements of those qualities wherever we have need of them. Beyond the inherent meaning lies the possibility of allegorical elements, in which there are many implications, subject to argument and disagreement among interpreters.

As to the inherent meaning, we are confronted basically by a raw struggle between good and evil. This contest offers challenge and demands decisions of several kinds. The power of evil is formidable and ruthless. The initial decision, in which many of the characters participate, is whether or not to attempt to resist it at all. So great and discouraging are the odds involved in resistance that the possibility of surrender, terrible as it may be, seems only in degrees more terrible than the fight—unless the deciding element is the moral choice of rejecting evil regardless of consequences.

Before some of the great ones is dangled the old temptation, "If you can't lick 'em, jine 'em." A corrupted wizard seeks to persuade Gandalf:

> " 'A new Power is rising. Against it the old allies and policies will not avail us at all. . . . This then is one choice before you, before us. We may join with that Power. . . . Its victory is at hand; and there will be rich reward for those that aided it . . . the Wise, such as you and I, may with patience come at last to direct its courses, to control it. We can bide our time . . . deploring maybe evils done by the way, but approving the high and ultimate purpose: Knowledge, Rule, Order . . . . There need not be . . . any real change in our designs, only in our means.' " (i, 272-273)

Tolkien pursues still further that most ancient and insidious moral dilemma, the problem of ends and means. If Sauron recovers his Ring, his power will be irresistible. The only means of assuring that he can never recover it is the awful one of carrying it right to the heart of his own realm and casting it into the volcanic fire in which it was first forged and that alone can destroy it. Yet an alternative constantly confronts the Fellowship in its resistance to Sauron. The Ring could be used to overthrow him by any one of several persons with advanced mastery of great powers. It is the nature of the Ring to give power according to the stature of its user—petty powers to the unknowing or inconsequential, vast ones to the strong and adept.

But the Ring and its potencies are evil, conditioned by its maker and his motives. It participates in the essence of its maker. At several crucial times the appeal arises: "Let the Ring be your weapon . . . . Take it and go forth to victory!" Each time that counsel is rejected, as here in the words of Elrond Half-Elven:

'We cannot use the Ruling Ring . . . . Its strength . . . is too great for anyone to wield at will, save only those who have already a great power of their own. But for them it holds an even deadlier peril. The very desire of it corrupts the heart. . . . If any of the Wise should with this Ring overthrow the Lord of Mordor, using his own arts, he would then set himself on Sauron's throne, and yet another Dark Lord would appear. And that is another reason why the Ring should be destroyed: as long as it is in the world it will be a danger even to the Wise. For nothing is evil in the beginning. Even Sauron was not so. I fear to take the Ring to hide it. I will not take the Ring to wield it.' (I, 281)

Here we are brought to the classic corrupting quality of power in direct proportion to its approach to the absolute. Yet, of course, it is not simply the power, in itself, that corrupts, but the pride which power may engender, which in turn produces the swift corruption of the power. The primal nature of the sin of Pride, bringing the fall of angels before the seduction and fall of Man, is the wish to usurp the Primal and One source of Power, incorruptible in His nature because He *is* Power and Source and has nothing to usurp, in being All.

The Ring had found its way into the hands of the hobbit Bilbo, who, in his old age, at the advice of the wizard Gandalf, reluctantly entrusts it to Frodo. Upon the back of the younger hobbit descends this monstrous burden. None of the great dare lift it from him. Frodo's first response is that of anyone caught abruptly in a responsibility too great to contemplate. "I wish it need not have happened in my time."

'So do I,' said Gandalf, 'and so do all who live to see such times. But that is not for them to decide. All we have to decide is what to do with the time that is given us.' (I, 60)

Then, further, Frodo protests:

'. . . I wish I had never seen the Ring! Why did it come to me? Why was I chosen?'

'Such questions cannot be answered,' said Gandalf. 'You may be sure that it was not for any merit that others do not possess: not for power or wisdom, at any rate. But you have been chosen and you must therefore use such strength and heart and wits as you have.' (I, 70)

The merit of Frodo, then, is not any built-in endowment, but the painfully, gradually ripening fruit of his response to the challenge set before him.

How Frodo fails or succeeds is the burden of the story—and it is not simple. Comparable tests are placed before other characters and are passed or failed in varying degrees, so that, in all, there are few aspects of challenge and response in the area of inexorable moral responsibility that Tolkien does not exemplify for us in this tale.

The next significant aspect involves the ability of the hobbits to cope with the actively malevolent Ring, so dreaded by greater and wiser than they. It is not to be assumed that the Ring does not work upon them, yet some circumstances help to shield them from its powers, at least at the outset. In the episode in *The Hobbit* when Bilbo acquired the Ring, he began his ownership with an act of pity which had an insulating effect. At the beginning of the trilogy he voluntarily gives it up—something which only he has ever done—though not without a wrench. In turn, Frodo, though subject to corruption like any creature, begins his guardianship of the Ring unwillingly and without ambition, accepting it as an obligation thrust upon him.

With so heavy odds, against so formidable an adversary, a significant factor provides one hopeful element in the grim web of Sauron's network of agents, tracking down the Ring. In Sauron's very nature, he is incapable of anticipating the policy adopted by his enemies. He cannot conceive that they would voluntarily relinquish the Ring and destroy it, for it would be incompatible with his nature to do so. Thus, the one move that he does not expect is that they would themselves convey it to his very threshold in an ultimate renunciation and destruction of its power.

Yet counterbalancing this small advantage is a demonstration of the fact that creaturely life does not always offer us clear choices of good or evil. Often we must choose between degrees of evil, and we are fortunate when we know that is what we are doing. Frodo, at times, is compelled to use the Ring for its power of invisibility as the immediate alternative to losing all. Yet every time he does so, two bad results are involved: the always baleful influence of the Ring gains perceptibly over Frodo, and Sauron is instantly aware of its use and his mind is able to grope, in a general way, toward its location, like a radio direction-fix. The expedient of employing it thus is doubly harmful each time momentary necessity forces it. In addition, the nearer Frodo gets to his destination, the heavier becomes the physical burden and the greater the influence of the Ring—consequences of its approach to its source. The question of endurance therefore is progressively acute.

At the outset, the Fellowship of the Ring comprises the wizard Gandalf; an Elf, Legolas; a Dwarf, Gimli; two men, Aragorn and Boromir, and four hobbits: Frodo, his servant Sam, and two others called Merry and Pippin. All the non-malevolent rational species thus have a hand, as well as a stake, in the enterprise. The Fellowship is dispersed early.

Frodo must make his grim attempt with the aid only of his loyal servant, Sam. In shuttling narrative patterns of the most prolific story-spinning, the others play a variety of necessary roles in the widely dispersed secondary campaign against Sauron's far-ranging forces.

Now we shall shift to another level of meaning. In this story there is no overt theology or religion. There is no mention of God. No one is worshipped. There are no prayers (though there are invocations of great names of virtue). Yet implicit in the conflict between good and evil is a limited eschatology for the Third Age of Middle-earth. A theology contains the narrative rather than being contained by it. Grace is at work abundantly in the story.

In the Judeo-Christian scriptures, God is seen at work in history, taking an initiative, intervening in the affairs of His creatures. Even in the pagan Homeric literature (and in all other primitive literatures) the heroes are seen operating, as in the *Iliad* and the *Odyssey*, with the constant intervention and support of the gods, without which their enterprises and achievements would be impossible.

In Tolkien's Third Age an Ultimate Power is implicit. There is the possibility of Sauron gaining total sway over Middle-earth, but it is clear that there are other realms where his machinations are inoperable. The "Blessed Realm" lies in the mystery of the West, beyond Sea, and certain characters sail toward it in an image akin to the passing of Arthur to Avalon.

It is a premise of Christian theology that man must cope with certain of his problems with all his own resources. There are things in which it is up to him to succeed or fail. Yet the Will of God, if not completed through one option, will complete itself through another, and in all contingencies there are helps of which a man may avail himself. The

Christian rejects utterly the notion that God is dead, or will be mocked, or even that He has withdrawn Himself from human affairs.

In Tolkien's Third Age, the powers that Gandalf and the High Elves can bring to bear against Sauron clearly are derived from the Prime Source, Who is in some way identified with the Blessed Realm. The great ancient names of men and Elves often invoked are on His side. Running through the story is a thread of prophecy being fulfilled, and Frodo is regarded as "chosen" for his heavy task.

Bilbo's acquiring of the Ring was not just a combination of chance and the power of the Ring itself to work its way back toward its master. Gandalf says to Frodo:

'Behind that there was something else at work, beyond any design of the Ring-maker. I can put it no plainer than by saying that Bilbo was *meant* to find the Ring, and *not* by its maker. In which case you also were meant to have it.' (I, 65)

A mysterious, over-arching purpose is manifested, too, in the enigmas of the odd, repulsive, but fascinating creature called Gollum, who had treasured the Ring for a long time before Bilbo came upon him. He haunts the Ring through the whole chronicle. There are moments when he is spared only in remembrance of Gandalf's early words:

'. . . he is bound up with the fate of the Ring. My heart tells me that he has some part to play yet, for good or ill, before the end; and when that comes, the pity of Bilbo may rule the fate of many—yours not least.' (I, 69)

The intricacy of Tolkien's web of cause and effect, of the interactions of motives and wills, natural and supernatural, is extraordinary and—notwithstanding the frame of fantasy —profoundly realistic.

30

As for the choosing of Frodo, it is said:

> 'This quest may be attempted by the weak with as much
> hope as the strong. Yet such is oft the course of deeds that
> move the wheels of the world: small hands do them because
> they must while the eyes of the great are elsewhere.' (I, 283)

There is no evading the problem of the Ring:

> '. . . they who dwell beyond the Sea would not receive it: for
> good or ill it belongs to Middle-earth; it is for us who still
> dwell here to deal with it.' (I, 279)

And so it is that the hobbit, Frodo, quietly, reluctantly, in
a sustained action surely as brave as any recorded in imaginative literature, assents:

> 'I will take the Ring,' he said, 'though I do not know the way.'
> (I, 284)

Thus, at its core, still leaving unreckoned all the wealth
of its detailed unfolding, this wonder tale is rich with teaching for life as *we* lead it. This places it among the true elite
of books that can claim to offer such rewards.

Yet so far we have dealt only with inescapable inherent
meanings. Possible allegorical elements can be discerned in
it, whether or not they were a part of Tolkien's conscious
purpose. It is true that things can be got out of a work of art
that its creator did not knowingly put in. Yet rather than
say it *is* an allegory, which is too rigid for so large, free, and
flexible a story, I will say that it has allegorical possibilities
and suggestions underlying the face value of the narrative.
It is some of these which suggest themselves to me that I put
forward, rather than any complete and systematic scheme.

Tolkien vigorously rejects any formal allegorical or other
elaborately schematized "interpretations" of his stories.
These tend to proliferate even more in the wake of the im-

31

mense surge in the popularity of the books since this essay was first published in 1962. Reluctantly he concedes the right of readers to find certain "correspondences" to the modern world, if they insist. The intent of this essay is no more than that. He really wishes we would read his work at its face value and keep quiet about it. One cannot blame him, or help feeling slightly guilty about such a discussion as this.

It has for me an allegorical relation to the struggle of Western Christendom against the forces embodied, successively but overlappingly, in Nazism and Communism. The work was conceived and carried forward when the darkest shadow of modern history was cast over the West and, for a crucial part of that time, over England in particular.

Although the notion of the Blessed Realm in the true West is an ancient motif, it is no simple association that also makes the Westernesse of Middle-earth—Númenor as he calls it (which suggests land of spirit)—and its men, the hope for justice, peace, and order. In the story, men are the inheritors of earth and theirs is the new age coming. The other creatures are withdrawing, having completed their destinies, but a man is king again in the West and the future lies with his kind.

For those to whom Christianity—not any political or economic or military system—is the one possible counterpoise to the Communist doctrine of man, Tolkien's image of the West is a meaningful parable. He shows us a challenge that must be met, or to which surrender is the only other alternative. All the seductions and rationalizations are there, including that of accepting a "wave of the future," or of using power in such ways as to supplant the enemy with nothing better than ourselves corrupted into his own image. Though Tolkien could not have foreseen it, a natural analogy arises between the hydrogen bomb and the Ring of power which by its nature could not be used to achieve anything that could be called good.

In both the Third Age and our world, evil is never defeated once for all. Even men who fight evil devotedly are not themselves free of its taint:

> Always after a defeat and a respite, the Shadow takes another shape and grows again . . . . The evil of Sauron cannot be wholly cured, nor made as if it had not been . . . . Other evils there are that may come; for Sauron is himself but a servant or emissary. Yet it is not our part to master all the tides of the world, but to do what is in us for the succor of those years wherein we are set, uprooting the evil in the fields that we know, so that those who live after may have clean earth to till. (I, 60; II, 154; III, 155)

If we survive the hydrogen crisis, we will find new technologically pressing moral dilemmas, from genetics to space-colonization. There is never a hiding place, or a time when the perennial but Protean moral dilemma has been solved forever. Though we feel with Frodo, "I wish it need not have happened in my time" (I, 60), we must accept the fact that "The wide world is all about you: you can fence yourselves in, but you cannot for ever fence it out" (I, 92). We are faced with what Aragorn, foremost of the men in the story, sternly calls "The doom of choice . . . . There are some things that it is better to begin than to refuse, even though the end may be dark" (II, 36, 43).

> 'How shall a man judge what to do in such times?'
> 'As he ever has judged,' said Aragorn. 'Good and ill have not changed since yesteryear; nor are they one thing among Elves and Dwarves and another among Men.' (II, 40-41)

So, likewise, one faces with Frodo the necessity that he expresses: " 'It must often be so, Sam, when things are in danger: some one has to give them up, lose them, so that others may keep them' "

The parallels for our world continue:

'. . . in nothing is the power of the Dark Lord more clearly shown than in the estrangement that divides all those who still oppose him.' (I, 362)

Part of this divisive power is the force with which everyone sometimes nurses the thought

that he was offered a choice between a shadow full of fear that lay ahead, and something that he greatly desired: clear before his mind it lay, and to get it he had only to turn aside from the road and leave the Quest and the war against Sauron to others. (I, 373)

We have seen enough to show that it is impossible not to be haunted by parallels between Tolkien's Middle-earth and our here and now. Greater than the samples that are offered is the cumulative effect of the whole tale. It is a moral fable on a scale commensurate with its narrative scope.

Other things remain unremarked. The blight of Mordor, and the damage sustained as far away as The Shire, are images of the blight which the first half-century of the industrial revolution laid upon fair lands, especially England. The sins of the Christian West in that era are directly visited upon the heads of the generations since, in the warped and fragmentary version of the neglected Christian ethic which, since Marx, has been the ideological appeal of the adversary.

We have noted already the general harmony of the elements in this story with Christian theology. It is clear from the nature and powers of Sauron—not always evil, but become so, and not himself the greatest of his kind—that he is a type of the fallen Angels. In the era of the making of the twenty Rings of the runic rhyme, even certain of the sub-angelic High Elves were for a time deceived by him and, with biblical and Faustian parallels, ensnared by "their eagerness for knowledge" (I, 255). We learn that "It is perilous to study too deeply the arts of the Enemy, for good or for ill" (I, 276).

I shun a too-eager search for supposed Christ-figures in literature, and excessively elaborate constructions in pursuit of them. But it is possible to say that both Gandalf and Frodo, each in his way, appear not as Christ equivalents, but as partial anticipations of the Christ. With Frodo, quite simply and movingly, it lies in his vain wish that the cup might be taken from him, and since it may not, he goes his long, dolorous way as Ring-bearer—a type of the Cross-bearer to come. More mystically with Gandalf, indicative of the operation of an unexpressed Power behind the events, the wizard undergoes a harrowing prefiguring of the death, descent into Hell, and rising again from the dead. Also he experiences something of the temptation in the wilderness in his refusal of the Ring which he has power enough to wield.

In a conversation in June of 1962, too late for inclusion in the original printing of this essay, Professor Tolkien was explicit about the nature of Gandalf. In response to my question he said, unhesitatingly, "Gandalf is an angel." He went on to explain that Gandalf had voluntarily accepted incarnation to wage the battle against Sauron. Gandalf the Gray does indeed die in the mortal flesh in the encounter with the Balrog in the Mines of Moria. Gandalf the White, who returns, is the angel in the incorruptible body of resurrection.

Professor Tolkien worked on the whole enterprise for more than fourteen years. He brought to it, apart from his great inventive gifts as what he nicely insists on calling a Subcreator, a background as an authority on Anglo-Saxon language and literature. He is richly steeped in an enormous lore—but it is not that he has pillaged it for his story. Rather he has so profoundly penetrated the spirit of a genre that he has created a modern work in its mode.

Internal evidence indicates that *The Hobbit* was begun as a complete and self-sufficient tale. Somewhere in the stages of its growth, I believe the vision of the larger projection in the trilogy came upon him, and that the gathering darkness and gloom over the remnants of the West in the Third Age of Middle-earth grew from the darkness and threats looming over Western Christendom in the 1930's when *The Hobbit* was written. The trilogy was produced during and after the years of World War II, a circumstance which seems to support much of what I read into it.

The volumes of the trilogy appeared in 1954 and 1955, and were received with a critical acclaim so great as to carry in it the danger of faddism and an inevitable counterreaction —a natural hazard of any work unique in its time that kindles a joy by its very freshness. The names of Spenser, Malory, and Ariosto were immediately invoked in the search for comparisons.

Tolkien is not admired by all. Naturally some eight or nine years later, in our succession of glutted publishing seasons, the books are no longer on everyone's tongue. This, together with an apparent total temperamental antipathy, led Philip Toynbee, in an article in the London *Observer* in the late summer of 1961, to make a rashly sweeping assumption.

> There was a time when the Hobbit fantasies of Professor Tolkien were being taken very seriously indeed by a great many distinguished literary figures. Mr. Auden is even reported to have claimed that these books were as good as "War and Peace"; Edwin Muir and many others were almost equally enthusiastic. I had a sense that one side or other must

be mad, for it seemed to me that these books were dull, ill-written, whimsical and childish. And for me this had a reassuring outcome, for most of his more ardent supporters were soon beginning to sell out their shares in Professor Tolkien, and today those books have passed into a merciful oblivion.

As a small shareholder, I challenge Mr. Toynbee. His case against the book rests on four adjectives. It is clear that the hobbits are not his cup of tea, and he may rest on the unassailable privilege of personal taste. Still—"dull"? This is a judgment only possible for someone allergic to the basic genre. If you cannot or will not enter its realm then you could not truly encounter its proliferating invention and narrative pace. "Ill-written" is a more strange indictment. I am puzzled as to how he can look upon the writing of our time and say this, unless his basic resistance to the story's content has made him impervious to its expression. "Whimsical" is a more difficult and complex idea. Philip Toynbee gives the word a pejorative tone. But whimsical means so many things, and is in some respects so fitting to this tale that a more concrete bill of particulars needs to be offered. What kind of whimsy? How much of it in the proportions of the work? And what is bad about it? There are occasional touches of whimsicality that might not reach one reader, or might irritate another, but they are swallowed up in the scale and scope of the story. Mr. Toynbee seems to have equated "whimsical" with his final accusing word, "childish." Here he has elected the unfavorable suffix, where I would say "child*like*." The kingdom of wonder, like that of Heaven, is one scarcely to be entered except ye be as a little child. I am afraid that the critic here is too anxious to preserve his adult standing because the work lies within the reach of children and contains elements altogether mistakenly thought by some to be reserved exclusively for them.

Philip Toynbee blinds himself totally to the substance and weight of the profound elements in the story which I have demonstrated here. He might wish to challenge their worth, rejecting the conceptual structure of the work, but he either does not know it is there, or simply chooses to disregard it. Challenge would be a legitimate critical posture—lack of perception is not. His conclusion is, "today those books have passed into a merciful oblivion."

What Toynbee mistakes for oblivion is, instead, a constantly growing following. To continue his own metaphor, those of us who have held on to our shares feel them to be gilt-edged securities. The audience is certain to go on expanding, for it consists of enthusiasts, upon whom the work has made a lasting impression, who reread it, lend it, present it, and always publicize it by word of mouth—that greatest of all media for the dissemination of a book. Because this is not happening in Toynbee's own circle, he is unaware of it.

The English edition of Tolkien has been reprinting steadily from 1954 to 1959. The sale of *The Hobbit* is extremely large. *The Lord of the Rings* has sold over 35,000 sets in England alone. It is an expensive set of books, which means that an unusually high percentage of its readership is through libraries. The double advantage it has of being the kind of book that its enthusiasts want their children to know, and that children in general love, gives it a prospect enviable for any book. If it were to go out of print forthwith, it would be certain of a long-continuing audience. Sir Stanley Unwin expressed to me the opinion that the hobbit books were more likely to outlast his own time and his son's than anything else he had ever published, in a career that would include many of the foremost literary figures of our day. Tolkien, retired from Oxford, is at work on another saga creation of comparable scale, to be called *The Silmarillion*.

Actually begun before *The Lord of the Rings*, it is a vast myth of the Creation and the Fall. It portrays the earlier ages and some of the history out of which *The Lord of the Rings* arises. There are many of us awaiting it eagerly.

I think it safe to say that whatever anyone might hold to be the flaws, idiosyncrasies, or excesses of the hobbit story, this extraordinary imaginative feat in the making of an Other-world, meaningfully related to our own, is likely to be one of the most tenacious works of fiction in this present age of Middle-earth. It gives joy, excitement, a lift of spirits, and it contains the kind of wisdom and insight which, if applied to the world we inhabit, might help our sore-beset race to hang on through the present shadows of modern Mordor into yet another age.

4

THE QUEST HERO

W. H. Auden

I.   GENERAL OBSERVATIONS

TO LOOK FOR A LOST COLLAR BUTTON IS NOT A TRUE QUEST: to go in quest means to look for something of which one has, as yet, no experience; one can imagine what it will be like but whether one's picture is true or false will be known only when one has found it.

Animals, therefore, do not go on quests. They hunt for food or drink or a mate, but the object of their search is determined by what they already are and its purpose is to restore a disturbed equilibrium; they have no choice in the matter.

But man is a history-making creature for whom the future is always open; human "nature" is a nature continually in quest of itself, obliged at every moment to transcend what it was a moment before. For man the present is not real but valuable. He can neither repeat the past exactly—every moment is unique—nor leave it behind—at every moment he adds to and thereby modifies all that has previously happened to him.

Hence the impossibility of expressing his kind of existence in a single image. If one concentrates upon his ever open future, the natural image is of a road stretching ahead into unexplored country, but if one concentrates upon his unforgettable past, then the natural image is of a city, which is built in every style of architecture and in which the physically dead are as active citizens as the living. The only characteristic common to both images is a sense of purpose; a road, even if its destination is invisible, runs in a certain direction; a city is built to endure and be a home.

The animals who really live in the present have neither roads nor cities and do not miss them. They are at home in the wilderness and, at most, if they are social, set up camps for a generation. But man requires both. The image of a city with no roads leading from it suggests a prison; the image of a road that starts from nowhere in particular suggests, not a true road, but an animal spoor.

A similar difficulty arises if one tries to describe simultaneously our experience of our own lives and our experience of the lives of others. Subjectively, I am a unique ego set over against a self; my body, desires, feelings, and thoughts seem distinct from the *I* that is aware of them. But I cannot know the Ego of another person directly, only his self, which is not unique but comparable with the selves of others, including my own. Thus, if I am a good observer and a good mimic, it is conceivable that I could imitate another so accurately as to deceive his best friends, but it would still be I imitating him; I can never know what it would feel like to be someone else. The social relation of my Ego to my Self is of a fundamentally different kind from all my other social relations to persons or things.

Again, I am conscious of myself as becoming, of every moment being new, whether or not I show any outward sign of change, but in others I can only perceive the passage of time when it manifests itself objectively; So-and-so looks older or fatter or behaves differently from the way he used to behave. Further, though we all know that all men must die, dying is not an experience that we can share; I cannot take part in the deaths of others nor they in mine.

Lastly, my subjective experience of living is one of having continually to make a choice between given alternatives, and it is this experience of doubt and temptation that seems more important and memorable to me than the actions I take when I have made my choice. But when I observe others, I cannot see them making choices; I can only see their actions; compared with myself, others seem at once less free and more stable in character, good or bad.

The Quest is one of the oldest, hardiest, and most popular of all literary genres. In some instances it may be founded on historical fact—the Quest of the Golden Fleece may have its origin in the search of seafaring traders for amber—and certain themes, like the theme of the enchanted cruel Princess whose heart can be melted only by the predestined lover, may be distorted recollections of religious rites, but the persistent appeal of the Quest as a literary form is due, I believe, to its validity as a symbolic description of our subjective personal experience of existence as historical.

As a typical example of the traditional Quest, let us look at the tale in the Grimm collection called *The Waters of Life*. A King has fallen sick. Each of his three sons sets out in turn to find and bring back the water of life which will restore him to health. The motive of the two elder sons is not love of their father but the hope of reward; only the youngest really cares about his father as a person. All three encounter a dwarf who asks them where they are going. The first two rudely refuse to answer and are punished by the dwarf, who imprisons them in a ravine. The youngest answers courteously and truthfully, and the dwarf not only directs him to the castle where the Fountain of the Waters of Life is situated but also gives him a magic wand to open the castle gate and two loaves of bread to appease the lions who guard the Fountain. Furthermore, the dwarf warns him that he must leave before the clock strikes twelve or he will find himself imprisoned. Following these instructions and using the magic gifts, the youngest brother obtains the Water of Life, meets a beautiful Princess who promises to marry him if he will return in a year, and carries away with him a magic sword which can slay whole armies and a magic loaf of bread which will never come to an end. However, he almost fails because, forgetting the dwarf's advice, he lies down on a bed and falls asleep, awakening only just in time as the clock is striking twelve; the closing door takes a piece off his heel.

On his way home he meets the dwarf again and learns what has happened to his brothers; at his entreaty the dwarf reluctantly releases them, warning him that they have evil hearts.

The three brothers continue their homeward journey and, thanks to the sword and the loaf, the youngest is able to deliver three kingdoms from war and famine. The last stretch is by sea. While the hero is asleep, his older brothers steal the Water of Life from his bottle and substitute sea water. When they arrive home, their sick father tries the water offered by the youngest and, naturally, is made worse; then the elder brothers offer him the water they have stolen and cure him.

In consequence the King believes their allegation that the youngest was trying to poison him and orders his huntsman to take the hero into the forest and shoot him in secret. When it comes to the point, however, the huntsman cannot bring himself to do this, and the hero remains in hiding in the forest.

Presently wagons of gold and jewels begin arriving at the palace for the hero, gifts from the grateful kings whose lands he had delivered from war and famine, and his father becomes convinced of his innocence. Meanwhile the Princess, in preparation for her wedding, has built a golden road to her castle and given orders that only he who comes riding straight along it shall be admitted.

Again the two elder brothers attempt to cheat the hero by going to woo her themselves, but, when they come to the golden road, they are afraid of spoiling it; one rides to the left of it, one to the right, and both are refused admission to the castle. When the hero comes to the road he is so pre-occupied with thinking about the Princess that he does not notice that it is made of gold and rides straight up it. He is admitted, weds the Princess, returns home with her, and is reconciled to his father. The two wicked brothers put to sea, never to be heard of again, and all ends happily.

The essential elements in this typical Quest story are six.

1) A precious Object and/or Person to be found and possessed or married.

2) A long journey to find it, for its whereabouts are not originally known to the seekers.

3) A hero. The precious Object cannot be found by anybody, but only by the one person who possesses the right qualities of breeding or character.

4) A Test or series of Tests by which the unworthy are screened out, and the hero revealed.

5) The Guardians of the Object who must be overcome before it can be won. They may be simply a further test of the hero's *arete*, or they may be malignant in themselves.

6) The Helpers who with their knowledge and magical powers assist the hero and but for whom he would never succeed. They may appear in human or in animal form.

Does not each of these elements correspond to an aspect of our subjective experience of life?

1) Many of my actions are purposive; the *telos* toward which they are directed may be a short-term one, like trying to write a sentence which shall express my present thoughts accurately, or a lifelong one, the search to find true happiness or authenticity of being, to become what I wish or God intends me to become. What more natural image for such a *telos* than a beautiful Princess or the Waters of Life?

2) I am conscious of time as a continuous irreversible process of change. Translated into spatial terms, this process becomes, naturally enough, a journey.

3) I am conscious of myself as unique—my goal is for me only—and as confronting an unknown future—I cannot be certain in advance whether I shall succeed or fail in achieving my goal. The sense of uniqueness produces the image of the unique hero; the sense of uncertainty, the images of the unsuccessful rivals.

4) I am conscious of contradictory forces in myself, some of which I judge to be good and others evil, which are continually trying to sway my will this way or that. The existence of these forces is given. I can choose to yield to a desire or to resist it, but I cannot by choice desire or not desire.

Any image of this experience must be dualistic, a contest between two sides, friends and enemies.

On the other hand, the Quest provides no image of our objective experience of social life. If I exclude my own feelings and try to look at the world as if I were the lens of a camera, I observe that the vast majority of people have to earn their living in a fixed place, and that journeys are confined to people on holiday or with independent means. I observe that, though there may be some wars which can be called just, there are none in which one side is absolutely good and the other absolutely evil, though it is all too common for both sides to persuade themselves that this is so.

As for struggles between man and the forces of nature or wild beasts, I can see that nature is unaware of being destructive and that, though there are animals which attack men out of hunger or fear, no animal does so out of malice.

In many versions of the Quest, both ancient and modern, the winning or recovery of the Precious Object is for the common good of the society to which the hero belongs. Even when the goal of his quest is marriage, it is not any girl he is after but a Princess. Their personal happiness is incidental to the happiness of the City; now the Kingdom will be well governed, and there will soon be an heir.

But there are other versions in which success is of importance only to the individual who achieves it. The Holy Grail, for example, will never again become visible to all men; only the exceptionally noble and chaste can be allowed to see it.

Again, there are two types of Quest Hero. One resembles the hero of Epic; his superior *arete* is manifest to all. Jason, for example, is instantly recognizable as the kind of man who can win the Golden Fleece if anybody can. The other type, so common in fairy tales, is the hero whose *arete* is concealed. The youngest son, the weakest, the least clever, the one whom everybody would judge as least likely to succeed, turns out to be the hero when his manifest betters have failed. He owes his success, not to his own powers, but to the fairies, magicians, and animals who help him, and he is able to enlist their help because, unlike his betters, he is humble enough to take advice, and kind enough to give assistance to strangers who, like himself, appear to be nobody in particular.

Though the subject of this essay is the Quest in its traditional form, it is worth while, perhaps, to mention, very briefly, some variants.

46

A. THE DETECTIVE STORY

Here the goal is not an object or a person but the answer to a question—Who committed the murder? Consequently, not only is there no journey, but also the more closed the society, the more restricted the locale, the better. There are two sides, but one side has only one member, the murderer, for the division is not between the Evil and the Good but between the Guilty and the Innocent. The hero, the Detective, is a third party who belongs to neither side.

B. THE ADVENTURE STORY

Here the journey and the goal are identical, for the Quest is for more and more adventures. A classic example is Poe's *Gordon Pym*. More sophisticated and subtler examples are Goethe's *Faust* and the *Don Juan* legend.

The condition laid down in his pact with Mephisto is that Faust shall never ask that the flow of time be arrested at an ideal moment, that he shall never say, "Now, I have reached the goal of my quest." Don Juan's Quest can never come to an end because there will always remain girls whom he has not yet seduced. His is also one of the rare cases of an Evil Quest which ought not to be undertaken and in which, therefore, the hero is the villain.

C. MOBY DICK

Here the Precious Object and the Malevolent Guardian are combined and the object of the Quest is not possession but destruction. Another example of a Quest which should not have been undertaken, but it is tragic rather than evil. Captain Ahab belongs in the company of Othello, not of Iago.

D. The Kafka Novels

In these the hero fails to achieve his goal, in *The Trial* either to prove himself innocent or learn of what he is guilty, in *The Castle* to obtain official recognition as a land surveyor; and he fails, not because he is unworthy, but because success is humanly impossible. The Guardians are too strong and, though Kafka avoids saying so I think one can add, too malevolent. What makes K a hero is that, despite the evidence that Evil is more powerful than Good in the world, he never gives up the struggle to worship the Prince of this world. By all the rules he ought to despair; yet he does not.

Any literary mimesis of the subjective experience of becoming is confronted by problems of form and limitations of subject matter. Like a man's life which has a beginning, birth, and an end, death, the Quest story has two fixed points, the starting out and the final achievement, but the number of adventures in the interval cannot but be arbitrary; for, since the flow of time is continuous, it can be infinitely divided and subdivided into moments. One solution is the imposition of a numerical pattern, analogous to the use of meter in poetry. Thus, in *The Waters of Life* there are three brothers, three kingdoms to be delivered from war and famine, and three ways of approaching the Princess' castle. There are two tests, the dwarf and the golden road, but the right and wrong behavior are symmetrically opposed; it is right to take notice of the dwarf but wrong to take notice of the road.

The hero twice nearly comes to disaster by falling asleep, on the first occasion in direct disobedience of the dwarf's instructions, on the second in neglect of the warning that his brothers are evil men.

To take a man on a journey is to cut him off from his everyday social relations to women, neighbors, and fellow-workers. The only sustained relation which the Quest Hero can enjoy is with those who accompany him on his journey, that is to say, either the democratic relation between equal comrades-in-arms, or the feudal relation between Knight and Squire. Aside from these, his social life is limited to chance and brief encounters. Even when his motive for understanding the Quest is erotic, the lady has to remain in wait for him either at the start or the end of the road. Partly for this reason and partly because it deals with adventures, that is, situations of crisis in which a man behaves either well or badly, the Quest tale is ill adapted to subtle portrayals of character; its personages are almost bound to be archetypes rather than idiosyncratic individuals.

So much for general observations. I shall devote the rest of this essay to an examination of a single work, J. R. R. Tolkien's trilogy, *The Lord of the Rings*.

II.   THE SETTING

Many Quest tales are set in a dreamland, that is to say, in no definite place or time. This has the advantage of allowing the use of all the wealth of dream imagery, monsters, magical transformations and translations, which are absent from our waking life, but at the cost of aggravating the tendency of the genre to divorce itself from social and historical reality. A dream is at most capable of allegorical interpretation, but such interpretations are apt to be mechanical and shallow. There are other Quest tales, a thriller like *The Thirty-Nine Steps*, for example, which are set in places which we can find in the atlas and in times we can read of in history books. This gives the Quest a social significance, but the moral ambiguities of real history clash with the presupposition which is essential to the genre, that one side is good and the other bad.

Even in wartime, the sensitive reader cannot quite believe this of the two sides which the writer of thrillers takes from real life. He cannot help knowing that, at the same time that John Buchan is making the heroes English and American and the enemies German, some German author may be writing an equally convincing thriller in which the roles are reversed.

Tolkien sets his story neither in a dream world nor in the actual world but in an imaginary world. An imaginary world can be so constructed as to make credible any landscape, inhabitants, and events which its maker wishes to introduce, and since he himself has invented its history, there can be only one correct interpretation of events, his own. What takes place and why is, necessarily, what he says it is.

But the construction of a convincing imaginary world makes formidable demands upon the imagination of its creator. There must be no question which, according to our interests, we ask about the real world to which he cannot give a convincing answer, and any writer who, like Tolkien, sets out to create an imaginary world in the twentieth century has to meet a higher standard of concreteness than, say, his medieval predecessor, for he has to reckon with readers who have been exposed to the realistic novel and scientific historical research.

A dream world may be full of inexplicable gaps and logical inconsistencies; an imaginary world may not, for it is a world of law, not of wish. Its laws may be different from those which govern our own, but they must be as intelligible and inviolable. Its history may be unusual but it must not contradict our notion of what history is, an interplay of Fate, Choice, and Chance. Lastly, it must not violate our moral experience. If, as the Quest generally requires, Good and Evil are to be incarnated in individuals and societies, we must be convinced that the Evil side is what every sane man, irrespective of his nationality or culture, would acknowledge as evil. The triumph of Good over Evil which the successful achievement of the Quest implies must appear historically possible, not a daydream. Physical and, to a considerable extent, intellectual power must be shown as what we know them to be, morally neutral and effectively real: battles are won by the stronger side, be it good or evil.

To indicate the magnitude of the task Tolkien set himself, let me give a few figures. The area of his world measures some thirteen hundred miles from east (the Gulf of Lune) to west (the Iron Hills) and twelve hundred miles from north (the Bay of Forochel) to south (the mouth of the River Anduin). In our world there is only one species, man, who is capable of speech and has a real history; in Tolkien's there are at least seven. The actual events of the story cover the last twenty years of the Third Historical Epoch of this world. The First Age is treated as legendary so that its duration is unknown, and its history is only vaguely recalled, but for the 3441 years of the Second Age and the 3021 years of the Third, he has to provide a continuous and credible history.

The first task of the maker of an imaginary world is the same as that of Adam in Eden: he has to find names for everyone and everything in it and if, as in Tolkien's world, there is more than one language, he has to invent as many series of names as there are tongues.

In the nominative gift, Tolkien surpasses any writer, living or dead, whom I have ever read; to find the "right" names is hard enough in a comic world; in a serious one success seems almost magical. Moreover, he shows himself capable of inventing not only names but whole languages which reflect the nature of those who speak them. The Ents, for example, are trees which have acquired movement, consciousness, and speech, but continue to live at the tempo of trees. In consequence their language is "slow, sonorous, agglomerated, repetitive, indeed long-winded." Here is only a part of the Entish word for *hill:*

a-lalla-lalla-rumba-kamanda-lind-or-burúmë.

The extremes of good and evil in the story are represented by the Elves and Sauron, respectively. Here is a verse from a poem in Elvish:

A Elbereth Gilthoniel,
silivren penna míriel
o menel alglar elenath!
Na-chaered palan díriel.
o galadhremmin ennorath,
      Fanuilos, le linnathon
      nef aer, sí nef aearon.

And here is an evil spell in the Black Speech invented by Sauron:

Ash nazg durbatulûk, ash nazg gimbatul, ash nazg thrakatalûk, agh burzum-ishi-krimpatul.

An imaginary world must be as real to the senses of the reader as the actual world. For him to find an imaginary journey convincing, he must feel that he is seeing the landscape through which it passes as, given his mode of locomotion and the circumstances of his errand, the fictional traveler himself saw it. Fortunately, Mr. Tolkien's gift for topographical description is equal to his gift for naming and his fertility in inventing incidents. His hero, Frodo Baggins, is on the road, excluding rests, for eighty days and covers over 1800 miles, much of it on foot, and with his senses kept perpetually sharp by fear, watching every inch of the way for signs of his pursuers, yet Tolkien succeeds in convincing us that there is nothing Frodo noticed which he has forgotten to describe.

Technologically, his world is preindustrial. The arts of mining, metallurgy, architecture, road and bridge building, are highly developed, but there are no firearms and no mechanical means of transport. It is, however, a world that has seen better days. Lands that were once cultivated and fertile have gone back to the wilderness, roads have become impassable, once famous cities are now ruins. (There is one puzzling discrepancy. Both Sauron and Saruman seem to have installed heavy machinery in their fortresses. Why, in that case, are they limited to waging untechnological warfare?) Though without machines, some people in this world possess powers which our civilization would call magical because it lacks them; telepathic communication and vision are possible, verbal spells are effective, weather can be controlled, rings confer invisibility, etc.

Politically, the commonest form of society is a benevolent monarchy, but the Shire of the hobbits is a kind of smalltown democracy and Sauron's kingdom of Mordor is, of course, a totalitarian and slave-owning dictatorship.

Though the unstated presuppositions of the whole work are Christian, we are not told that any of the inhabitants practice a religious cult.

The Elves, the Wizards, and Sauron, certainly, and perhaps some others, believe in the existence of the One and the Valar, to whom He has entrusted the guardianship of Middle-earth, and a Land in the Uttermost West which I take to be an image of Paradise.

III. THE QUEST HERO

In our subjective experience, of which the Quest is, I have suggested, a literary mimesis, what we ought to become is usually dependent upon what we are; it is idle and cowardly of me if I fail to make the fullest use of any talent with which I have been endowed, but it is presumptuous of me to attempt a task for which I lack the talent it requires. That is why, in the traditional Quest story, the hero desires to undertake the quest and, even when to others he appears lacking in power, he is confident of success. This problem of vocation is specifically dealt with in one Quest tale, *The Magic Flute*. Prince Tamino is the typical hero, who must dare the trials by Fire and Water to attain wisdom and win the hand of the Princess Pamina.

But beside him stands Papageno, who is, in his own way, a hero too. He is asked whether he is prepared to endure the trials like his master and he answers, no, such dangers are not for the likes of him. "But," says the priest, "if you don't, you will never win a girl." "In that case," he replies, "I'll remain single." This answer reveals his humility, and he is rewarded with his mirror image, Papagena. In contrast to him stands the villain Monostatos. Like Papageno, he is incapable of enduring the trials but, unlike him, he lacks the humility to forego the rewards of heroism; he is even unwilling to accept an equivalent of Papagena and demands nothing less than the Princess.

But there is another kind of vocation which may be called religious. Not everybody experiences it, and even for those who do, it may concern only moments of their life. What characterizes the religious vocation is that it comes from outside the self and, generally to the self's terror and dismay, as when God calls Abraham out of the land of Ur, or when a man, by nature physically timid, is called to enter a burn-

54

ing building to rescue a child because there is no one else around to do it.

Some of the characters in *The Lord of the Rings*, Gandalf and Aragorn, for instance, are expressions of the natural vocation of talent. It is for Gandalf to plan the strategy of the War against Sauron because he is a very wise man; it is for Aragorn to lead the armies of Gondor because he is a great warrior and the rightful heir to the throne. Whatever they may have to risk and suffer, they are, in a sense, doing what they want to do. But the situation of the real hero, Frodo Baggins, is quite different. When the decision has been taken to send the Ring to the Fire, his *feelings* are those of Papageno: "such dangerous exploits are not for a little hobbit like me. I would much rather stay at home than risk my life on the very slight chance of winning glory." But his conscience tells him: "You may be nobody in partic- ular in your self, yet, for some inexplicable reasons, through no choice of your own, the Ring has come into your keep- ing, so that it is on you and not on Gandalf or Aragorn that the task falls of destroying it."

Because the decision has nothing to do with his talents, nobody else can or should try to help him make up his mind. When he stands up at the Council of Elrond and says: " 'I will take the Ring though I know not the Way,' " Elrond replies: " 'It is a heavy burden. So heavy that none could lay it on another. I do not lay it on you. But if you take it freely, I will say that your choice is right' " (I, 284).

Once he has chosen, Frodo is absolutely committed; the others who set out with him are not.

> 'The Ring-bearer is setting out on the Quest of Mount Doom: on him alone is any charge laid—neither to cast away the Ring nor to deliver it to any servant of the Enemy, nor indeed to let any handle it, save members of the Company and the Council, and only then in gravest need. The others go

with him as free companions to help him on his way. You may tarry, or come back, or turn aside to other paths as chance allows. The further you go, the less easy it will be to withdraw; yet no oath or bond is laid upon you to go further than you will. For you do not yet know the strength of your hearts and you cannot foresee what each may meet on the road.'

'Faithless is he who says farewell when the road darkens,' said Gimli.

'Maybe,' said Elrond, 'but let him not vow to walk in the dark who has not seen the nightfall.'

'Yet sworn vow may strengthen quaking heart,' said Gimli.

'Or break it,' said Elrond. 'Look not too far ahead. But go now with good hearts.' (I, 294)

IV.   THE CONFLICT OF GOOD AND EVIL

If it is a defect in the usual Quest tale that Good triumphs over Evil simply because Good is more powerful, this is not a defect that can be avoided by giving Good no power at all. Quite rightly, Tolkien makes the elves, dwarfs, wizards, and men who are Sauron's opponents a formidable lot indeed, but in sheer strength, Sauron is, even without his Ring, the stronger. Yet their power has its part to play, as Gandalf points out.

'Victory cannot be achieved by arms. . . . I still hope for victory but not by arms. For into the midst of all these policies comes the Ring of Power, the foundation of Barad-dûr and the hope of Sauron. . . . If he regains it, your valour is vain, and his victory will be swift and complete; so complete that none can foresee the end of it while this world lasts. If it is destroyed, then he will fall; and his fall will be so low that none can foresee his arising ever again. . . . This, then, is my counsel. We have not the Ring. In wisdom or great folly, it has been sent away to be destroyed lest it destroy us. Without it we cannot by force defeat his force. But we must at all costs keep his Eye from his true peril. We cannot achieve victory by arms, but by arms we can give the Ring-bearer his only chance, frail though it be.' (III, 154-156)

The Quest is successful and Sauron is overthrown. One of Tolkien's most impressive achievements is that he convinces the reader that the mistakes which Sauron makes to his undoing are the kind of mistakes which Evil, however powerful, cannot help making just because it is Evil. His primary weakness is a lack of imagination, for, while Good can imagine what it would be like to be Evil, Evil cannot imagine what it would be like to be Good. Elrond, Gandalf, Galadriel, Aragorn are able to imagine themselves as Sauron and therefore can resist the temptation to use the Ring themselves, but Sauron cannot imagine that anyone who knows what the Ring can accomplish, his own destruction among other things, will not use it, let alone try to destroy it. Had he been capable of imagining this, he had only to sit waiting and watching in Mordor for the Ring-bearer to arrive, and he was bound to catch him and recover the Ring. Instead, he assumes that the Ring has been taken to Gondor where the strongest of his enemies are gathered, which is what he would have done had he been in their place, and launches an attack on that city, neglecting the watch on his own borders.

Secondly, the kind of Evil which Sauron embodies, the lust for domination, will always be irrationally cruel since it is not satisfied if another does what it wants; he must be made to do it against his will. When Pippin looked into the Palantír of Orthanc and so revealed himself to Sauron, the latter had only to question him in order to learn who had the Ring and what he intended to do with it. But, as Gandalf says: " 'He was too eager. He did not want information only: he wanted *you*, quickly, so that he could deal with you in the Dark Tower, slowly' " (II, 199).

Thirdly, all alliances of Evil with Evil are necessarily unstable and untrustworthy since, by definition, Evil loves only itself and its alliances are based on fear or hope of profit, not on affection. Sauron's greatest triumph has been his seduction of the great wizard Saruman but, though he has succeeded in making him a traitor to the cause of Good, he has not yet completely enslaved him, so that Saruman tries to seize the Ring for himself.

Lastly, unforeseeable by either side, is the role played by Sméagol-Gollum. When Frodo first hears about him from Gandalf, he exclaims:

> 'What a pity Bilbo did not stab that vile creature, when he had the chance!'
>
> 'Pity? It was Pity that stayed his hand. Pity, and Mercy: not to strike without need. And he has been well rewarded, Frodo. Be sure that he took so little hurt from the evil, and escaped in the end, because he began his ownership of the Ring so. With Pity. . . .'
>
> 'I cannot understand you. Do you mean to say that you, and the Elves, have let him live on after all those horrible deeds? . . . He deserves death.'
>
> 'Deserves it? I daresay he does. [But] do not be too eager to deal out death in judgment. For even the very wise cannot see all ends. I have not much hope that Gollum can be cured before he dies, but there is a chance of it. And he is bound up with the fate of the Ring. My heart tells me that he has some part to play yet, for good or ill, before the end; and when that comes, the pity of Bilbo may rule the fate of many—yours not least.' (I, 68-69)

Gollum picks up Frodo's trail in the Mines of Moria and follows him. When Frodo manages to catch him, he remembers Gandalf's words and spares his life. This turns out to his immediate advantage for, without Gollum's help, Frodo and Sam would never have found their way through the Dead Marshes or to the pass of Cirith Ungol. Gollum's motives in guiding them are not wholly evil; one part of him, of course, is waiting for an opportunity to steal the Ring, but another part feels gratitude and genuine affection for Frodo.

Gandalf was right, however, in fearing that there was little hope of his being cured; in the end his evil side triumphs. He leads Frodo and Sam into Shelob's lair and, after their escape, pursues them to Mount Doom and attacks them. Once again they spare his life. And then the unexpected happens.

. . . there on the brink of the chasm, at the very Crack of Doom, stood Frodo, black against the glare, tense, erect, but still as if he had been turned to stone.

'Master!' cried Sam.

Then Frodo stirred and spoke with a clear voice . . . it rose above the throb and turmoil of Mount Doom, ringing in the roofs and walls.

'I have come,' he said. 'But I do not choose now to do what I came to do. I will not do this deed. The Ring is mine!' And suddenly, as he set it on his finger, he vanished from Sam's sight. . . . Something struck Sam violently in the back, his legs were knocked from under him and he was flung aside, striking his head against the stony floor, as a dark shape sprang over him. . . .

Sam got up. He was dazed, and blood streaming from his head dripped in his eyes. He groped forward, and then he saw a strange and terrible thing. Gollum on the edge of the abyss was fighting like a mad thing with an unseen foe. . . . The fires below awoke in anger, the red light blazed, and all the cavern was filled with a great glare and heat. Suddenly Sam saw Gollum's long hands draw upwards to his mouth; his white fangs gleamed, and then snapped as they bit. Frodo gave a cry, and there he was, fallen upon his knees at the chasm's edge. But Gollum, dancing like a mad thing, held aloft the Ring, a finger still thrust within its circle. . . .

'Precious, precious, precious!' Gollum cried. 'My Precious! O my Precious!' And with that, even as his eyes were lifted up to gloat on his prize, he stepped too far, toppled, wavered for a moment on the brink, and then with a shriek he fell. . . .

'Well, this is the end, Sam Gamgee,' said a voice by his side. And there was Frodo, pale and worn, and yet himself again; and in his eyes there was peace now, neither strain of will, nor madness, nor any fear. His burden was taken away. . . .

'Yes,' said Frodo. 'Do you remember Gandalf's words: *Even Gollum may have something yet to do?* But for him, Sam, I could not have destroyed the Ring. The Quest would have been in vain, even at the bitter end.' (III, 223-225)

V. THE FRUITS OF VICTORY

"And so they lived happily ever after" is a conventional formula for concluding a fairy tale. Alas, it is false and we know it, for it suggests that, once Good has triumphed over Evil, man is translated out of his historical existence into eternity. Tolkien is much too honest to end with such a pious fiction. Good has triumphed over Evil so far as the Third Age of Middle-earth is concerned, but there is no certainty that this triumph is final. There was Morgoth before Sauron and, before the Fourth Age ends, who can be sure that no successor to Sauron will appear? Victory does not mean the restoration of the Earthly Paradise or the advent of the New Jerusalem. In our historical existence even the best solution involves loss as well as gain. With the destruction of the Ruling Ring, the three Elven Rings lose their power, as Galadriel foresaw.

'Do you not see now wherefore your coming is to us as the footsteps of Doom? For if you fail, we are laid bare to the Enemy. Yet if you succeed, then our power is diminished, and Lothlórien will fade, and the tides of Time will sweep it away. We must depart into the West, or dwindle to a rustic folk of dell and cave, slowly to forget and to be forgotten.' (I, 380)

Even Frodo, the Quest Hero, has to pay for his success.

'But,' said Sam, and tears started from his eyes, 'I thought you were going to enjoy the Shire . . . for years and years, after all you have done.'

'So I thought too, once. But I have been too deeply hurt, Sam. I tried to save the Shire, and it has been saved, but not for me. It must often be so, Sam, when things are in danger: some one has to give them up, lose them, so that others may keep them.' (III, 309)

If there is any Quest Tale which, while primarily concerned with the subjective life of the individual person as all such stories must be, manages to do more justice to our experience of social-historical realities than *The Lord of the Rings*, I should be glad to hear of it.

5

THE APPEAL OF
THE LORD OF THE RINGS:
A STRUGGLE FOR LIFE

Hugh T. Keenan

LONG BEFORE THE LORD OF THE RINGS BECAME POPULAR
with children, educated readers began taking it enthusiastically and seriously. But how could mature readers take to
the melodramatic incidents, the superficial brotherhood
theme, and the one-dimensional characters of the trilogy?
Most only hint at the reason, and few reveal themselves as
did W. H. Auden, who says, "by the time one has finished
his [Tolkien's] book, one knows the histories of Hobbits,
Elves, Dwarves, and the landscape they inhabit as well as
one knows one's own childhood."[1] This hint from Auden
marks the elemental nature of the book, I think. The major
appeal of *The Lord of the Rings* grows from its underlying
and pervasive presentation of the basic struggle of Life
against Death. Tolkien's thematic presentation explores in
its course the psychological meaning of childhood, another
strong appeal for the mature reader.

But it is not often realized that psychology rather than
philosophy or literary merit is responsible for a large portion
of this growing esteem. Sober critics have read the novel as

[1] "The Hero is a Hobbit," *New York Times Book Review* (Oct. 31,
1954), 37.

a basic conflict of good and evil in moral or Christian lights. They have debated the novel's determinism or free will. They have made the obvious comparisons between Tolkien's trilogy and the novels of C. S. Lewis and Charles Williams.[2] One critic has even compared Tolkien's theories about the fairy-tale genre to his practice in this story.[3] All of their efforts have been somewhat disappointing, for they have to conclude that *The Lord of the Rings* differs from more than it resembles any of these philosophies, novels, or theories.

Despite their basic differences, three of the critics—Reilly, Sale, and Spacks—agree that the world depicted by Tolkien is amazingly alive.[4] His world includes hobbits, elves, dwarfs, orcs, monsters, and ghosts. The abstracts of Death and Life are personified by the Nazgûls and the tree-like Ents. The creatures of this world interact and communicate to a surprising degree. The Rangers, as Miss Spacks points out, "understand the language of beasts and birds," whereas Tom Bombadil "is in the most intimate communion with natural forces; he has the power of 'the earth itself.' "[5] Hobbits, men, and even orcs can talk through a universal

[2] W. R. Irwin, "There and Back Again: The Romances of Williams, Lewis, and Tolkien," *Sewanee Review*, LXIX (1961), 566-578, Douglass Parker, "Hwaet We Holbytla. . . ," *Hudson Review*, IX (Winter, 1956-57), 598-609. Roger Sale, "England's Parnassus: C. S. Lewis, Charles Williams, and J. R. R. Tolkien," *HR*, XVII (1964), 203-225, Patricia Meyer Spacks, "Power and Meaning in *The Lord of the Rings*," below pp. 81-99. Douglass Parker gives lesser emphasis to the conflict of good and evil. He says the novel is "the story of the *end of an age*, an age which the author has gone to a fantastic amount of effort to make specific, to make real. And it is from the varied reactions of races and individuals to this end and to other ends of other ages, past and future, that the meaning of the work arises" (603).

[3] Robert J. Reilly, "Tolkien and the Fairy Story," below pp. 128-150. Mark Roberts, "Adventure in English," *Essays in Criticism*, VI (1956), 450-459, examines the same question briefly and gives Tolkien high marks.

[4] "Tolkien and the Fairy Story," 139, 149; "England's Parnassus," 216-221; "Power and Meaning in *The Lord of the Rings*," p. 95.

[5] "Power and Meaning," p. 84.

language, the Common Speech. Some living creatures do not speak the Common Speech, and others which we ordinarily consider as inanimate in the real world are sentient in the world of the novel. These include the Balrog, the other spirits of Moria (I, 428), the Eldar beyond the Sea, and the mountain Caradhras (I, 302-307). Even stone statues cry out a warning in this gothic land (III, 179), while stones, trees, and blades of grass listen for the advance of an enemy army (III, 160).

In view of the reiterated fertility-sterility conflict in this world[6] and the absence of a clearly defined deity or religion,[7] the forcing of a vague moral pattern (good vs. evil) on the book's contents is an unpromising endeavor. Something is more important than good vs. evil. This something is life vs. death. Questions of life and death dominate the minds and actions of the inhabitants. As Sale observes in passing, "The world is alive, and the story is the story of the ways in which it is called on to *be* alive when the shadows threaten and darkness grows powerful" (217).

The peculiar achievement of the author is to have created a world which is at once completely (or to a superlative degree) sentient and yet dying, to have presented vividly, objectively, and emotionally the eternal conflict between life and death. The reader of this essay may rightly catch an allusion to Norman O. Brown's *Life Against Death: the Psychoanalytical Meaning of History*, to which this line of argument is greatly indebted. In applying Freudian analysis

[6] The wasted land or decline theme occurs prominently. See I, 257-258, 271-272, 329-330, 363, 380, 388-389, 392, 393, 396; II, 45, 71, 287, 311; III, 22, 36, 151, 155-156.

[7] Faramir does observe a kind of grace before meals (II, 284-285); there is mention of a god or God, called the One (III, Appendix A, 317, 344). Spacks uses these slight references to the One in arguing that the world of the novel is guided by a purpose (p. 89 f.).

to mankind rather than to individual man, Brown concludes that

> mankind, in all its restless striving and progress, has no idea of what it really wants. Freud was right—our real desires are unconscious. It also begins to be apparent that mankind, unconscious of its real desires and therefore unable to obtain satisfaction, is hostile to life and ready to destroy itself.[8]

This statement seems equally valid for the fictional world of *Lord of the Rings*.

In Tolkien's trilogy as in the science fiction trilogy of C. S. Lewis (especially the final volume *That Hideous Strength*), man is bent on destroying himself through sociological, technological, and psychological means. Man's technology is the enemy of his humanity. But whereas Lewis' world is heavily Christian and he traces the source of man's perversity to the influence of the Devil, Tolkien's world is almost nonreligious. He traces the perversity of his creatures —in the Shire and outside it—to their own twisted natures. The greed of the dwarfs for *mithril* causes them to destroy their home in Moria by disturbing the Balrog (i, 331). Consequently they lose much of their skill in metalworking (i, 241-242). The exiled Númenor have become practicers of the black arts in their vain search for immortality and so have fallen into sloth. Faramir confesses that even " 'Gondor . . . brought about its own decay, falling by degrees into dotage, and thinking that the Enemy was asleep, who was only banished not destroyed' " (ii, 286). The pride of Théoden and his people makes them isolate themselves and ally with Saruman, the tool of the Dark Lord.

In *Beowulf,* Grendel and his mother can be seen as the objectifications (in part) of the flaws of the king Hrothgar

[8] (New York, 1959), xii.

and of the faults of his court. In *The Lord of the Rings*, Sauron can be similarly viewed as the objectification of the fears and self-destruction (death instinct) of the inhabitants of Middle-earth.

Frodo, the hero of the trilogy, and his three fellow hobbits overbalance the nine-man fellowship. The question is why are so many representatives chosen from the Shire. To know the answer, we must find out what hobbits are. Then we may be able to understand too why Frodo is made the hero of the novel. Neither he nor his fellow hobbits are daring, handsome, or even clever as heroes typically are.

Exactly what are hobbits? Edmund Wilson, despite what else he says, seems to have a fair answer:

> The hobbits are a not quite human race who inhabit an imaginary country called the Shire and who combine the characteristics of certain English animals—they live in burrows like rabbits and badgers—with the traits of English country-dwellers, ranging from rustic to tweedy. (The name seems a telescoping of rabbit and Hobbs.)[9]

Like rabbits or country folk, the hobbits emphasize family and fertility as manifested by their love for genealogical facts and by their well-populated, clan-size burrows. Their love of domestic comforts is in line with their dual nature. Like children they enjoy birthday parties as frequent as those in *Alice in Wonderland*, the receiving of presents, and the eating of snacks plus full meals, while they do little work and mostly play. Yet furry and fat like rabbits (or country squires) though they be, they prove to be the human-like creatures most interested in preserving life. The hobbits combine the strongest traditional symbols of life: the rabbit for fertility and the child for generation. They represent the

[9] "Oo, Those Awful Orcs!" *Nation*, CLXXXII (April 14, 1956), 312.

earthly as opposed to the mechanic or scientific forces. Therefore they are eminently suitable heroes in the struggle of life against death.

In the journey to Mordor, these hobbits link the Men of Gondor to the Ents, Gollum, the Rohirrim, the Dwarfs, the Elves, the Barrow-wights, the Orcs, and all the rest of the creatures (except the birds)—even Shelob. Gandalf, whose sole purpose is to preserve the life of the world (III, 30-31), acts in a similar capacity, but the hobbits become more personally involved. Gandalf interests himself in the fate of future living creatures. The hobbits Merry and Pippin act for the present. Merry becomes the retainer of Théoden (III, 50-51) and Pippin becomes the retainer of Denethor, the Steward of Gondor (III, 28).

What justifies Frodo's being the hero? Here one comes to a paradox. Frodo has the usual rabbit-like and child-like nature of a country hobbit. He enjoys smoking, birthday parties, presents, good food, and good company. But as he journeys toward Mordor, he loses some of this vitality. He becomes isolated, less humorous, more rational, and even mystical, in contrast to his old emotional, animal self. In other words Frodo grows up; he becomes adult in a human sense. He becomes conscious of his sacrificial duty. He becomes humble as he learns more about the world outside the Shire and as he perceives the pathos of mortality through the passing of the fair and the beautiful.

The sacrificial nature of Frodo brings us to two interesting points. Since the ensuing age is to be that of Men and since hobbits resemble markedly the Men who live isolated lives, prefer war and comfort to learning and beauty, and pride themselves on their sense of duty and honor, there is a strong suggestion that Frodo and his kind represent psychologically the eternal child who must be sacrificed so that the man may live. The national languages of the hobbits and the Men are very close (III, Appendix F, 414). Douglass Parker puts it in other terms:

> Their [hobbits'] real name, translated as 'halfling' is very significant. Half-fairy, half-man, yet neither, they are a transition-stage from the Third Age to the Fourth, and, in the destruction of the Ring by Frodo, Sam, and the erstwhile hobbit Gollum, they are the efficient causes of the transition itself.[10]

At a more universal level, Frodo is the Child who fathers the Age of Men.

The second point may prove clearer to see. When Frodo reaches the Crack of Doom, he suddenly puts on the Ring and vows to keep it, thus defeating the purpose of the arduous Quest (III, 223). Why does he do it? Because of the Ring's powers. These include strengthening of hearing, while diminishing sight (III, 174), preservation of youth if the Ring is kept but not worn (see the cases of Bilbo and Frodo, I, 29, 52), and invisibility when the Ring is worn, plus permanent vanishing if the Ring is worn too long (I, 56). But primarily, it grants one the power to rule and to achieve his chief desire. For instance, when Sam puts on the Ring, he has a vision of controlling the world and making it one large garden (III, 177). As gardening is the *idée fixe* of Sam, for him the promise the Ring gives is the world cultivated as a magnificent garden. Gandalf and Galadriel also experience the power of the Ring; it offers them the chance to achieve their most cherished desires. Fortunately all three individuals refuse this unlimited power. Exactly what the Ring promises Frodo at this moment at the Crack of Doom we do not learn. But we may be assured that this includes the power to rule and to dominate in achieving the desire.

[10] "Hwaet We Holbytla," 607.

Norman O. Brown interprets such aggressiveness as an extroversion of the Freudian death instinct; in this way people repress the recognition of the existence of death.[11] Sale comes to a similar conclusion about Frodo's mental conflict at this moment. In speaking of Frodo's blindness to the powers and the results of keeping the Ring, Sale observes

> Tolkien does not enforce this irony but he does make clear that the struggle is not so much one of good against evil as of life against itself in its effort to stay alive. (223)

Additionally, since the Ring is a female symbol, the possession—not the use—of it makes Frodo a type of the perfect hermaphrodite, the perfect androgynous Adam, or simply a child. Norman Brown says that for the unconscious or for the child,

> the sexual differentiation of the adult libido, as presupposed in genital organization and the human family—masculine aggressiveness and feminine passivity—is a loss of sexual completeness; hence the fact of sexual differentiation is regarded with horror. In each sex, says Freud, it is the attitude belonging to the opposite sex which succumbs to repression. In each sex the unconscious does not accept the repression but wants to recover the *bisexuality of childhood*. (p. 132; italics mine)

Frodo's conscious assumption of the Ring is a symbolic assumption of sexuality, a symbolic coitus and acceptance of death. Gollum rushes forward and bites off the finger of the invisible and therefore symbolically dead Frodo. This symbolic castration returns Frodo to life temporarily. But as castration is not unconsciousness of sexual role (the

---

[11] *Life Against Death*, p. 101. Brown acknowledges that this opinion opposes that of Freud who viewed aggressiveness as "a fusion of the life instinct with the death instinct, a fusion which saves the organism from the innate self-destructive tendency of the death instinct by extroverting it, a desire to kill replacing the desire to die."

child's state) but loss of sexuality, the act represents a death of the body. On his return to the Shire, Frodo's conduct is marked by passivity as compared to the masculine aggressiveness of Sam, Merry, and Pippin. He becomes a retired, Messianic figure; in a short time, he is almost forgotten by the hobbits whom he leaves for the Grey Havens.

One should notice that this decline in aggressiveness and this change in Frodo's protagonist role are compensated for by an increased focus on the developing strength of Sam (III, 218). Sam becomes the vital, the interesting hero in the latter pages of the novel. He fights the orcs at Cirith Ungol and becomes increasingly protective toward the rapidly weakening Frodo, who in Mordor loses his zest for life (III, 215).

This life strength of Sam's comes from his gardening, his relation to the soil. He is the good country person *par excellence*. Only two characters wear the Ring without ill effects: Tom Bombadil and Sam, who becomes Samwise. As the more primitive, the more vital, and the more mysterious, Tom Bombadil has the greater strength. When he puts on the Ring, he does not vanish. Tom can laugh and then return the Ring to Frodo without hesitation (I, 144). Because Sam is weaker than Tom, Sam vanishes when he wears it. But his vitality and his love for Frodo are so strong that he can return the Ring easily to Frodo (III, 188).

One may notice that the last volume closes with Sam happily married, a fulfilled adult, the father of his first child. It is he to whom Galadriel entrusts the magic dust which makes the seedlings sprout into saplings in one season, thus replacing the Shire trees destroyed by the Enemy's minions. Since Sam is the agent for this reforestation, he becomes closely akin to Tom Bombadil, who has been called "a kind of archetypal 'vegetation god.' "[12]

[12] Reilly, below, p. 131.

The marked absence of women in the novel calls attention to its fertility theme, an important part of the continuing struggle of life against death. It might be argued that women are naturally excluded from a battle story. But here the story is more that of a journey than that of a battle or wars. The women are missed. The Ents tell of the disappearance of the Entwives long ago in explaining why there are no young Ents; the dwarfs have few women and fewer children (II, 78-80; III, 360). In Gondor, too, there are not enough young people (III, 24, 36).

In considering the women who are present, we need not be as unchivalrous as Edmund Wilson, who says that "the fair ladies would not stir a heartbeat; the horrors would not hurt a fly."[13] Though the ladies are scarce, they do capture hearts. Though a dwarf and an enemy, Gimli becomes enraptured of the elven queen Galadriel, so much so that he offers to fight Faramir. The hobbits—Frodo, Merry, Pippin, and Sam—are charmed by Goldberry, Tom Bombadil's consort. There is the inset story of Tinúviel, the elf queen, and her tragic love for Beren, a mortal man (I, 204-205). This story of Elrond's ancestors foreshadows the love of Elrond's daughter Arwen for Aragorn (I, 239; III, 252-253). There is Éowyn's unrequited love for Aragorn and her happy marriage with Faramir. There is nurse Ioreth, who is the garrulous domestic. Although her type characterization has charm, it is underdeveloped.

What the trilogy lacks is a mother with children. The women, even if married, are not shown as mothers. They have charm but not earthiness. Or they are cold, though they may not be as cold as the Lady Éowyn. She becomes a Britomartis figure. Disguised as a young man, she rides to the war alongside her uncle Théoden, without his knowledge or consent. After the defeat of Mordor, she abandons

13 "Oo, Those Awful Orcs," 314.

71

significantly her desire to be a soldier or a queen; she elects instead to be " 'a healer, and love all things that grow and are not barren' " (III, 243).

Not until the end of the book do women as child-bearers appear. Then their role is prominent. When Sauron is defeated, the Ring destroyed, and the lands cleansed, there comes a succession of marriages: Faramir marries Éowyn; Aragorn marries Arwen; Sam marries Rose Cotton. The marriage of Aragorn and Arwen has been foreshadowed. That of Sam and Rose is more of a surprise. Like the end of a Shakespearean comedy, the trilogy concludes with a series of engagements and marriages.

One famous female—Shelob—has been passed over. This horror, this travesty of love and generation, refutes Edmund Wilson's pronouncement that the horrors would not hurt a fly. True, if her appearance and function are judged by standards of realism, the giant spider is a flaw. She reminds us of the insect villains of too many poor science-fiction movies. But in the story, Shelob is symbolically appropriate.

She is the feminine counterpart to Sauron. As he represents Death, the opposite of Life, she represents destruction and physical corruption, the opposites of generation and birth. This mistress of Sauron greets the visitors to Mordor with death. Nor does she spare even her own brood, she "who only desired death for all others, mind and body, and for herself a glut of life, alone, swollen till the mountains could no longer hold her up and the darkness could not contain her" (II, 333).

When one considers the structure of the trilogy in which these characters play their parts, the struggle of life against death is very important. To a reader of Jessie L. Weston's *From Ritual to Romance*, Tolkien's use of the Wasted-Land-and-the-Wounded-King theme is obvious. As Tolkien uses these traditional elements in the fertility theme, Gandalf comes to Théoden's court, rouses the old king from illness, drives out Wormtongue, and thus restores the leader to his people and the land to its former vigor. (There is a parallel to Beowulf and Hrothgar too in all of this.) Traditional elements appear also in Aragorn's restoration of the kingdom of Gondor: the reforging of the broken sword, the return of the kingdom to its rightful owner, and the consequent revitalization of the city and its inhabitants.

Older than these motifs is the seasonal significance of the time span of the novel. The Quest begins in winter, a traditionally dead period. Frodo and his friends leave the Shire on September 22, for Rivendell; they depart from Rivendell on the last of December. The Quest is achieved in the spring, March 25, to be exact. And at the end of a year, Frodo and Sam are home again in the Shire. The traditional associations of the seasons underscore the theme of a change from death to life.

The change in landscape is symbolic. As Miss Spacks observes,

> The progress toward the heart of evil, toward the Crack of Doom into which, in the trilogy's central fable, the Ring-bearer must throw his Ring of Power, is a progress from natural fertility to the desolation of nature. (p. 84 below)

To this observation, one need add only two comments. First, the desolation of nature at Isengard and at Mordor is due to the technological devices of the Enemy.[14] Second, the journey does not stop at the Crack of Doom; Frodo and Sam return to the Shire and restore the land to its former fertility. So the complete pattern circles from natural fertility in the Shire to technological desolation of nature at Mordor and

---

[14] Spacks notes (p. 85 below) that the Enemy tends to use "machinery rather than natural forces."

afterwards ends at the Shire and fertility again. Or as Bilbo might say, " 'there and back again.' "

Tolkien regards advanced tools and mechanics with suspicion. He praises the hobbits and dwarfs for using only simple hand tools and such necessary, simple machinery as water mills (I, 10). Fangorn characterizes Saruman as having " 'a mind of metal and wheels' " and possessing no concern " 'for growing things, except as far as they serve him for the moment' " (II, 76). The land of Mordor itself is a place of "mines and forges" (III, 201). On the other hand, the Elves have as their concerns, not "strength or domination or hoarded wealth, but understanding, making, and healing, to preserve all things unstained" (I, 282).

The numerous tunnels, the trees, and the bodies of water —especially the Sea—are important to the fertility theme, although Mark Roberts doubts that the numerous tunnels are so much Freudian symbols as they are ruts marking the author's lack of inventiveness.[15] Some are associated with death and corruption, such as the lair of Shelob, the Paths of the Dead, and the tunnels of Moria. But in the Shire and at Helm's Deep, tunnels are linked with health, happiness, and safety. While none are insignificant, context determines whether they are associated with death or with life. Although trees seem ambiguous at first, they stand for life. The malevolent trees in the Old Forest and in Fangorn are more than offset by the good influences of Tom Bombadil and the Ents. Trees, as a general symbol of naturalness and fertility, are more than commonly important to the hobbits returning to the Shire. The elves are almost druidic in their worship of and empathy with trees. Legolas is drawn to them as strongly as Gimli is to caves. And still better, elves understand the language of the trees. In Lothlórien the elves make their homes in giant trees and venerate especially the *mal-*

15 "Adventure in English," 459.

lorn tree. In Gondor one of the primary symbols of the life of Minas Tirith is the White Tree in the courtyard. Its dead trunk and branches betoken the dying of the city. Likewise the discovery of a scion of this tree symbolizes the rebirth of Minas Tirith under the leadership of Aragorn (III, 250).

Finally there are the Ents—especially Fangorn or Tree-beard—and their tree herds. The life history of these living trees demonstrates the literal and symbolical import of their preservation. For as the forests have disappeared by being pushed back, burned, or cut down, the land and its peoples have suffered. The return of the forests to Isengard and to the Shire signals the return of life to the dead and dying lands.

In addition to symbols, we find patterns of contrast in character, incident, and place which define the theme of life against death. At the beginning of the journey, Frodo and the three hobbits meet Tom Bombadil and his consort Goldberry. At the end of the journey, Frodo and Sam encounter Gollum and his mistress-ruler Shelob. Besides the parallels and contrasts of character—Tom Bombadil (life) and Gollum (death), Goldberry (preserver) and Shelob (destroyer)—there are parallel actions. At the beginning of the story, Tom rescues the lost Frodo and company from the Old Forest and then saves them from the Barrow-wights. Later Gollum rescues the lost Frodo and his companion Sam in the wilderness of Emyn Muil and guides them through the treacherous Valley of the Dead. As one guide leads them to safety and life, the other one leads them to treachery and death. While Tom Bombadil cannot be moved by the Ring, Gollum can never be free of it.

The contrasts of Minas Tirith and Minas Morgul are equally clear. The Tower of the Sun, which is held by the Men of Gondor, rises up on the mountain. The Tower of the Moon, which is held by the Enemy, lies in the valley

(III, 160). Both are white-walled cities, but one has the white color of life (though it is dying) and the other has the white pallor of death. The decay of the Babylon-like, seven-tiered city of Minas Tirith is clear to Pippin:

> Pippin gazed in growing wonder at the great stone city, vaster and more splendid than anything that he had dreamed of; greater and stronger than Isengard, and far more beautiful. Yet it was in truth falling year by year into decay; and already it lacked half the men that could have dwelt at ease there. In every street they passed some great house or court over whose doors and arched gates were carved many fair letters of strange and ancient shapes: names Pippin guessed of great men and kindreds that had once dwelt there; and yet now they were silent, and no footstep rang on their wide pavements, nor voice was heard in their halls, nor any face looked out from door or empty window. (III, 24)

To Sam, Frodo, and Gollum, Minas Morgul (Ithil) appears even worse:

> Paler indeed than the moon ailing in some slow eclipse was the light of it now, wavering and blowing like a noisome exhalation of decay, a corpse-light, a light that illuminated nothing. In the walls and tower windows showed, like countless black holes looking inward into emptiness; but the topmost course of the tower revolved slowly, first one way and then another, a huge ghostly head leering into the night. (II, 312)

Unlike the eager travellers to Minas Tirith, Frodo and Sam pass this dead city with fear and reluctance. The river, the flowers, and even the statuary there are corruptions of life, bitter opposites to the fruitful land of Gondor and the healthful Anduin River:

> Wide flats lay on either bank, shadowy meads filled with pale white flowers. Luminous these were too, beautiful and yet

horrible of shape, like the demented forms in an uneasy dream; and they gave forth a faint sickening charnel-smell; an odour of rottenness filled the air. From mead to mead the bridge sprang. Figures stood there at its head, carven with cunning in forms human and bestial, but all corrupt and loathsome. The water flowing beneath was silent, and it steamed, but the vapour that rose from it, curling and twisting about the bridge, was deadly cold. (II, 313)

The implication left is that as Minas Morgul is, so Minas Tirith will be if the war goes against Gondor.

The decay theme of the trilogy is carried out in the contrasts of Edoras and Minas Tirith too. Of the cities, that of Rohan is the more healthful, the brighter, the stronger in spirit, the more natural. Legolas is first to see Edoras set on a green hill in a valley and close by a white stream. From afar, the elf sees the Meduseld, the hall of Théoden, shine like gold (II, 111). This land is spring-like, grassy, well-watered, and planted with budding willows and ever-blooming white flowers (II, 111). The gleam of the armor of the men, their bright golden hair, and their formal yet ceremonious courtesy (II, 112-116) are in contrast to the dark armor and the coldness of spirit found at Gondor.

The interior of the Meduseld is much brighter and livelier than that of the Hall of Minas Tirith:

The hall was long and wide and filled with shadows and half lights; mighty pillars upheld its lofty roof. But here and there bright sunbeams fell in glimmering shafts from the eastern windows, high under the deep eaves. Through the louver in the roof, above the thin wisps of issuing smoke, the sky showed pale and blue. As their eyes changed, the travellers perceived that the floor was paved with stones of many hues; branching runes and strange devices intertwined beneath their feet. They saw now that the pillars were richly carved, gleaming dully with gold and half-seen colours. Many woven cloths

were hung upon the walls, and over their wide spaces marched
figures of ancient legend, some dim with years, some darkling
in the shade. But upon one form the sunlight fell: a young
man upon a white horse. He was blowing a great horn, and
his yellow hair was flying in the wind. The horse's head was
lifted, and its nostrils were wide and red as it neighed, smell-
ing battle afar. Foaming water, green and white, rushed and
curled about its knees. (II, 116)

Théoden, their leader, retains some of the vigor of this
young heroic man. Though white-haired, the Lord of Rohan
leads his men against Sauron's forces and laughs to scorn
the wiles of Saruman at Isengard. Even Aragorn recognizes
the unfallen state of these Men in contrast to the lesser
vigor of those of Gondor (II, 33).

In Gondor, the Hall of Minas Tirith is much darker, less
lively, less human, more like a tomb; its Steward Denethor,
unlike Théoden, scorns help, despairs of victory, and com-
mits suicide. Here is the Hall as Pippin sees it:

It was lit by deep windows in the wide aisles at either side,
beyond the rows of tall pillars that upheld the roof. Monoliths
of black marble, they rose to great capitals carved in many
strange figures of beasts and leaves; and far above in shadow
the wide vaulting gleamed with dull gold, inset with flowing
traceries of many colours. No hangings nor storied webs, nor
any things of woven stuff or of wood, were to be seen in that
long solemn hall; but between the pillars there stood a silent
company of tall images graven in cold stone. (III, 26)

The two halls mirror the different natures of their leaders
and peoples.

This contrast of the quick and the dead is seen most simply in the cities of Caras Galadon and its enemy Dol Guldur.
From a platform in the ancient city of Cerin Amroth, Frodo
sees the green city of the Elves and the dark tower (Dol

Guldur) of the Enemy in Southern Mirkwood, the evil forest. Haldir tells him:

> 'In this high place you may see the two powers that are opposed one to another; and ever they strive now in thought, but whereas the light perceives the very heart of the darkness, its own secret has not been discovered. Not yet.' (I, 366)

Caras Galadon, which from a distance appears "a hill of many mighty trees, or a city of green towers," (I, 366) reveals itself to be a city built in great branches of the forest, a city gleaming with green, gold, and silver lamps (I, 368). This is the good place for Frodo, Gandalf, Legolas, Aragorn, Sam, and even Gimli the dwarf. But this natural paradise set in a tree is fated to perish and its Elves must depart to the West when the battle against Sauron is over.

Perhaps one more contrasting pair in the life and death theme may be added. In the central incident of the journey through the tunnels of Moria, whose name carries important suggestions,[16] we find two contrasting lakes. The one before the entrance is dark, loathsome, and artificial, a product of the evil within; and in it lurks an octopus-like monster (I, 322). Only two ancient holly trees remain there as evidence of benevolent influence and symbols of the former friendship between the Elves and the Dwarfs (I, 316). On the other side of Moria lies the beautiful, natural, life-giving lake of Mirrormere, which is worshipped by the dwarf Gimli as he looks into its depths with Frodo:

> At first they could see nothing. Then slowly they saw the forms of the encircling mountains mirrored in a profound blue, and the peaks were like plumes of white flame above them; beyond there was a space of sky. There like jewels sunk in the deep shone glinting stars, though sunlight was in

16 *Mor* is "mountain" in A.S.; but *Moria* suggests also *moira*, "fate" in Gr. and *mors*, "death" in Lat.

the sky above. Of their own stooping forms no shadow could be seen. (I, 348)

By looking deeply into *The Lord of the Rings*, we see our world and something beyond. The hero, the other characters, and the structure of the trilogy appeal to us not rationally but emotionally. Its characters are caught up in the decay theme of the novel, the eternal struggle of life against death, just as we are. We recognize that the hobbits are emblematic of naturalness, of childhood, and of a life which will yield to the Age of Men with its technology, its rational adulthood, and death. This recognition strikes a sympathetic chord in the human heart. The reiteration of the decay theme and the recognition of the temporary triumph of the forces of life over the forces of death as the Third Age ends —both of these give the book a bitter-sweet tone. This truth of vision makes the book appealing to readers who acknowledge that of them also, at the last, not a shadow of their stooping forms will be seen.[17]

[17] I wish to thank Professors Neil Isaacs and Rose Zimbardo for reading the Ms. of this article and offering suggestions for its improvement. Thanks are due also to my colleagues and friendly critics: Stephen Cox, Laura Keenan, and Helen Hollingsworth.

6

POWER AND MEANING IN
THE LORD OF THE RINGS

Patricia Meyer Spacks

AS A WRITER OF FICTION, J.R.R. TOLKIEN HAS OFTEN BEEN thought of in connection with the excursions of C. S. Lewis and Charles Williams into the "serious" supernatural. Both Williams and Lewis, formerly fellow members with Tolkien of an Oxford discussion group in which portions of their fiction were read aloud for criticism, have received recent critical attention in this country as Christian "myth-makers." Tolkien, however, has been neglected ever since Edmund Wilson, in a review in *The Nation*, informed us that he was not to be taken seriously.[1]

---

[1] "Oo Those Awful Orcs!" CLXXXII (April 14, 1956), 312-314. One notable reply to Wilson is Douglass Parker's "Hwaet We Holbytla . . . ," *Hudson Review*, IX (Winter, 1956-1957), 598-609, which brilliantly refutes Wilson's attack and makes a strong defense of the trilogy. Mr. Parker is largely, though not exclusively, concerned with the success of *The Lord of the Rings* as fantasy. He reads the trilogy as most essentially concerned not with the struggle of Good against Evil, but with an account of "the end of an age," an account which defines the human condition perceived in basically pagan terms. Although I agree with Mr. Parker on many counts, I must quarrel with his easy rejection of free will as a theme of Tolkien's. "Free will," he writes, "has not, as some critics think, been restored [as a result of the Ring's destruction]; it never existed in the first place, nor did determinism reside in the Ring" (604). Surely the situation, for Tolkien as for the *Beowulf*-poet, is more complicated: the universe paradoxically combines qualified determinism with qualified free will.

Yet in a fuller sense than Lewis or Williams, Tolkien is a modern myth-maker. In *The Lord of the Rings*, his epic trilogy, he virtually created a new genre: one possessing obvious affinities with folk epic and mythology, but with no true literary counterpart. The novels of Williams and Lewis gain from their Christian teleology an effect of cosmic scope and depth; the novels of Tolkien possess, in addition to enormous physical scope, a mythic structure of yet more subtle complexity.

In "Oo, Those Awful Orcs!" Wilson remarked of Tolkien's trilogy: "The hero has no serious temptations, is lured by no insidious enchantments, perplexed by few problems. What we get is a simple confrontation—in more or less the traditional terms of British melodrama—of the Forces of Evil with the Forces of Good" (313). But the confrontation of the Forces of Evil with the Forces of Good is the basic theme also of tragedy, epic, and myth. Tolkien's presentation of this theme is by no means so simple as Wilson suggests. Indeed, the force and complexity of its moral and theological scheme provides the fundamental power of *The Lord of the Rings*.

For this scheme, there are no explicit supernatural sanctions: *The Lord of the Rings* is by no means a Christian work. An anonymous early review in the *Times Literary Supplement*[2] remarked on the fact that throughout the trilogy no character, good or bad, performs an act of worship. Although supernatural powers abound, no deity is evident on the side of the good or of the evil. A clear ethos rules the virtuous, but its derivation is unclear.

The principles of that ethos are simple, embodied primarily in the hobbit-heroes, members of a Tolkien-created race essentially human in characteristics, gnome-like in appearance. The first important representative of the hob-

[2] (Nov. 25, 1955).

bits is Bilbo Baggins, eponymous hero of *The Hobbit*, a children's book which was an offshoot along the way of Tolkien's trilogy. Its events immediately antedate those of *The Lord of the Rings;* its hero closely resembles Frodo Baggins, Bilbo's nephew, who is the central character of the trilogy. Both hobbits possess the same morality, share the same virtues. They are unfailingly loyal, to companions and to principles. They are cheerful in the face of adversity, persistent to the point of stubbornness in pursuit of a goal, deeply honest, humble in their devotion to those they consider greater than they. And as their most vital attributes they possess "naked will and courage."

The quotation is from Tolkien in reference to quite different heroes, and its context is significant. In 1936, Tolkien published one of the most important pieces of *Beowulf*-criticism of the past several decades. Entitled "Beowulf: The Monsters and the Critics," it defends the Anglo-Saxon poem's structural dependence on encounters with nonhuman monsters, Grendel, his dam, and the dragon. The defense could stand equally well for Tolkien's own fiction, which, even in the comparatively slight children's book, *Farmer Giles of Ham*, centers characteristically on encounters between human beings—or such symbolic representatives of humanity as the hobbits—and inhuman monsters. In connection with *Beowulf*, Tolkien points out the difference between the Christian imagination and the northern mythological imagination. The archetypal Christian fable, he observes, centers on the battle between the soul and its adversaries. (This, of course, is the battle which preoccupies Williams and Lewis.) In this struggle, the Christian is finally triumphant, in the afterlife if not on earth. But northern mythology takes a darker view. Its characteristic struggle between man and monster must end ultimately, within Time, in man's defeat. Yet man continues to struggle;

his weapons are the hobbit-weapons: naked will and courage.

These are the basic virtues of most epic heroes. Their opposites are apparent in Tolkien's representatives of evil, who are characteristically disloyal, whose courage depends on numbers, whose wills are enslaved. The conflict between good and evil appears, in this trilogy, to be a contest between representatives of opposed ethical systems.

The opposed forces also differ in their relation to nature. Goodness is partly equated with understanding of nature, closeness to the natural world. The Rangers, important forces on the side of Good, understand the languages of beasts and birds. Tom Bombadil, who rescues the hobbits from evil in the forest, whose natural power for good is so great that he can see the wearer of the Ring which makes men invisible to all other eyes and he does not become invisible himself when wearing it, is in the most intimate communion with natural forces; he has the power of "the earth itself" (I, 279). The power of the noble Elves gives Frodo new awareness of trees: "it was the delight of the living tree itself" (I, 366). The most potent force in the destruction of the realm of Saruman, a corrupted sorcerer, is provided by the Ents, guardians of the forest so closely involved with its life that their form is that of giant trees. The progress toward the heart of evil, toward the Crack of Doom into which, in the trilogy's central fable, the Ring-bearer must throw his Ring of Power, is from natural fertility to the desolation of nature. The Enemy's territory, even its outskirts, is physically and morally a Wasteland; the implication is strong that the barrenness of nature here is a direct result of the operations of evil. "We see that Sauron can torture and destroy the very hills" (I, 279). And, later, "What pestilence or war or evil deed of the

Enemy had so blasted all that region even Aragorn could not tell" (I, 396).

It is characteristic of the Enemy to depend upon machinery rather than natural forces. Saruman's city has smithies, furnaces, iron wheels revolving endlessly, hammers thudding, steam rising; Treebeard, the great Ent, describes Saruman as having "a mind of metal and wheels" (II, 76). The Dark Tower, which looms above the Crack of Doom and is the very heart of Sauron's power, is described as "that vast fortress, armoury, prison, furnace of great power" (II, 161)—the reverse of the natural.

As a corollary of their different relations to nature, the representatives of Good tend to be vegetarian, to rely on the simplest of food—bread and honey, mushrooms, compressed grain cakes—whereas the evil powers eat corrupt flesh, drink intoxicating beverages compounded of dreadful, nameless ingredients.

On this level the difference between good and evil seems rather simple. The good possess the Boy Scout virtues; the evil are treacherous and cowardly. The good love nature, the evil destroy it. The good eat good food, the evil eat bad food. If this were all, one might agree with Wilson in his condemnation of Tolkien's trilogy for impotence of imagination, superficiality of conception.

But the simplicity of this ethical system is redeemed by the philosophic complexity of its context: simplicity does not equal shallowness. The pagan ethos which that of *The Lord of the Rings* most closely resembles is redeemed from superficiality by the magnitude of the opposition it faces. The Anglo-Saxon epic hero operates under the shadow of fate; his struggle is doomed to final failure—the dragon at last, in some encounter, will win. His courage and will alone oppose the dark forces of the universe; they represent his triumphant assertion of himself as man, his insistence on human importance despite human weakness. Even the classic hero, Achilles or Odysseus, operates always in the face of the possibility of motiveless malignance. His gods are arbitrary and unpredictable; they do not necessarily reward courage and loyalty. Chance and fate are almost equivalent—for the classic hero as for Beowulf.

Frodo's steadfast adherence to virtue, too, achieves importance first of all in being maintained in maximum adversity, unwaveringly upheld even against the most dreadful supernatural opposition—the pursuit, for example, of the faceless Black Riders, the Ringwraiths, who are faded into physical nothingness by their devotion to evil, possessed of enormous spiritual power for evil, the bringers of unearthly cold, the cold of the deepest reaches of Dante's Hell. But Frodo's virtue is more significant because it operates in a context of total free will: he is *not* the creature of chance and fate in the same way as Beowulf.

A theological scheme is implied though not directly stated in *The Lord of the Rings*, and it is of primary importance to the form and meaning of the work. The fact of freedom of the will implies a structured universe, a universe like the Christian one in that only through submission to the Good can true freedom be attained—willing acceptance of evil involves necessary loss of freedom; a universe like the Christian one, further, in that it includes the possibility of Grace.

The repeated emphasis on the importance of free will and on Fate which is not chance is one aspect in which *The Lord of the Rings* differs from its simpler predecessor, *The Hobbit*. In *The Hobbit*, freedom of the will is not an issue, and there is only one faint suggestion of pattern in the universe. That appears on the final page, after Bilbo is safely returned from his adventures, the dragon killed, although not by his hand. Gandalf, the good sorcerer, says to him then: " 'Surely you don't disbelieve the prophecies, because you have a hand in bringing them about yourself? You don't really suppose, do you, that all your adventures and escapes were managed by mere luck, just for your sole benefit? You are a very fine person, Mr. Baggins, and I am very fond of you; but you are only quite a little fellow in a wide world after all!' " (315).

In *The Lord of the Rings*, on the other hand, references to these two themes—freedom of will and order in the universe, in the operations of fate—are so strongly recurrent that it is remarkable that they have not been noted before in discussions of the work. Early in *The Fellowship of the Ring*, after Gandalf has told Frodo the dreadful nature of his Ring (it partakes of too much power and brings about the "fading" of its wearer into final submission to evil), the wizard comments that always after defeat the Shadow takes another shape and grows again. " 'I wish it need not have happened in my time,' " says Frodo. " 'So do I,' said Gandalf, 'and so do all who live to see such times. But that is not for them to decide. All we have to decide is what to do with the time that is given us' " (I, 60). The necessity for free decision is thus early affirmed: it is to become a central issue of the trilogy. In the same chapter, a few pages later, comes the first hint of plan in the universe. Gandalf has just finished the narrative of the Ring; he has been speaking of the Ring's attempt to get back to its master, an attempt foiled by Bilbo's picking it up. But there is no chance in Bilbo's apparently fortuitous discovery. As Gandalf explains, " 'there was something else at work, beyond any design of the Ring-maker. I can put it no plainer than by saying that Bilbo was *meant* to find the Ring, and *not* by its maker. In which case you also were *meant* to have it' " (I, 65). The italics are Tolkien's—and his point is worth emphasizing.

When Gandalf speaks of Gollum, the slinking creature from whom Bilbo first obtained the Ring, Frodo wonders why Bilbo did not kill him at once. Gandalf is even more emphatic in his reply: he praises Bilbo for his pity and explains that it is because he began his ownership of the Ring with an act of mercy that he was able to escape its power at last. Gollum, he says, " 'is bound up with the fate of the Ring. My heart tells me that he has some part to play yet, for good or ill, before the end; and when that comes, the pity of Bilbo may rule the fate of many—yours not least' " (I, 69). An act of virtue has become a part of Fate; by Fate—for lack of a better word—Frodo has been *chosen:* "I am not made for perilous quests," he cries, and Gandalf replies, " 'You have been chosen, and you must therefore use such strength and heart and wits as you have' " (I, 70).

The theme of responsibility, so closely linked with free will, is also reiterated—by the Elves, who know that their meeting with Frodo is more than chance; by Strider, who insists that even an innkeeper must do what little he can against the Shadow in the East, who feels strongly his own responsibility to protect the simple folk; by the Lady Galadriel, who offers Frodo the chance to look into a magic mirror and observes solemnly, " 'For the fate of Lothlórien you are not answerable, but only for the doing of your own task' " (I, 380). Frodo himself comes to realize that he must not refuse the burden that is laid on him; this realization is his weapon against the temptations of Boromir, the member of his company who would steal the Ring for his own purposes. This is also what sustains him in his dreadful journey across the Land of Mordor toward the

Crack of Doom, and what sustains his hobbit companion.
Sam, when he thinks Frodo killed and knows he must go
on. The responsibility involved here, and throughout the
epic, is not simply to one's individual integrity; it is cosmic
responsibility, justified by the existence of some vast, unnamed power for good. Gandalf's most sweeping statement
of the nature of responsibility, although it makes no reference to any such power, strongly implies the existence of an
ordering force in the universe: " 'Other evils there are that
may come; for Sauron is himself but a servant or emissary.
Yet it is not our part to master all the tides of the world, but
to do what is in us for the succour of those years wherein
we are set, uprooting the evil in the fields that we know,
so that those who live after may have clean earth to till.
What weather they shall have is not ours to rule' " (III,
155).

Both Gandalf and Aragorn, the great King, speak repeatedly of *purpose* in the operations of apparent chance;
the source of that purpose is never identified. The existence
of one ordering power in the universe, however, is explicitly
indicated in the appendices which recount the history of all
the races involved in the Quest for the Ring's destruction.
There we find repeated mentions of "the Valar, the Guardians of the World" (e.g., III, 314, 315, 316, 317). In a
moment of cosmic crisis, we are told, "the Valar laid down
their Guardianship and called upon the One, and the world
was changed" (III, 317). Again, death is referred to as "the
gift of the One to Men" (III, 343). This sort of reference
to "the One" is all we have as precise evidence that
Tolkien's universe has a Ruler, but it is sufficient, when
combined with the repeated mentions of cosmic purpose, of
beings "sent" for some particular mission. If the trilogy,
as has been said, deals with a "pre-religious" age, an age
in which worship was confined to adherence to a special

ethos, the fact remains that its author includes in it all the necessary materials for religion.

So it is that the Fate which governs all here is not arbitrary. Indeed, as has been hinted already in relation to Bilbo's act of mercy, it is to some extent determined by individual acts of will. " 'Now we have chosen,' " says the Lady Galadriel, " 'and the tides of fate are flowing' " (I, 381). In the Council of Elrond, in which the final decision that the Ring must be destroyed is taken, Elrond says, " 'That is the purpose for which you are called hither. Called, I say, though I have not called you to me, strangers from distant lands. You have come and are here met, by chance as it may seem. Yet it is not so. Believe rather it is so ordered that we, who sit here, and none others, must now find counsel for the peril of the world' " (I, 255). The theme is constant throughout the trilogy: over and over we find similar statements denying the existence of mere chance, insisting on some plan governing the activities of all. Tom Bombadil implies that his appearance for the rescue of the hobbits was no accident; Galadriel tells the company that their paths are laid out, although not apparent to them; Frodo feels that a way will be found for him to reach the Dark Tower because such is his "doom"; he speaks to Gollum of a fate moving them both. And, although all participants in the Quest realize that the Shadow repeatedly rises again, far more forceful is the affirmation made by Frodo—"in the end the Shadow was only a small and passing thing: there was light and high beauty for ever beyond its reach" (III, 199).

The universe of Tolkien, unlike that of the Anglo-Saxons, is ultimately affirmative. Within the vast affirmative context, however, there are enormous possibilities for immediate evil: the individual exists in a realm where choice is always necessary. The freedom of that choice, for the virtuous, is of paramount importance. " 'I count you blessed, Gimli son of Glóin,' " says Legolas the Elf to a Dwarf member of the Ring-bearer's company: " 'for your loss you suffer of your own free will, and you might have chosen otherwise' " (I, 395). When Aragorn meets the Riders of Rohan, their leader asks him what doom he brings out of the north. " 'The doom of choice,' " replies Aragorn (II, 36): all men must now choose good or evil. Sam, Frodo's closest companion, realizes how many opportunities they have had of turning back, and understands that heroism, in legend and in fact, consists of making repeatedly and freely the choice of good (II, 321). In his moment of crisis, he knows that destiny has put him in this dilemma, and that his most important responsibility is to make up his own mind (II, 341).

In this world as in the Christian one, the result of re-peated choices of good is the spiritual growth of the chooser. Frodo's stature increases markedly in the course of his ad-ventures, and the increase is in the specifically Christian virtues. When Gandalf first tells him of Gollum, he feels no pity and rejects the pity that Bilbo has felt. But by the time he has his own first encounter with the creature, he himself makes the choice of pity and mercy: he does not kill Gollum when he has him in his power. When they reach the depths of Mordor, Sam watches while Frodo sleeps. He notes in Frodo's face that a light seems to be shining within. "Now the light was even clearer and stronger [than when he first noticed it a few months earlier]. Frodo's face was peaceful, the marks of fear and care had left it; but it looked old, old and beautiful, as if the chiselling of the shaping years was now revealed in many fine lines that had before been hidden, though the identity of the face was not changed" (II, 269). Finally, Frodo has mercy even on Saruman who has been far more definitely than Gollum an active agent of evil, an agent who, indeed, has just tried to murder Frodo. Saruman looks at him with "mingled wonder and respect and hatred. 'You have grown, Halfling,' he said. 'Yes, you have grown very much. You are wise ...' " (III, 299). And, at the very end, it is Frodo who asserts the necessity and value of sacrifice. " 'When things are in danger,' " he says to Sam, " 'Some one has to give them up, lose them, so that others may keep them' " (III, 309). So he gives up his beloved Shire, and goes into the unknown West, to a land equivalent to Arthur's Avalon. He has become heroic in mind as well as in action; heroic in mind as a direct result of his action.

The course of the evil beings is equally well-defined. By using their freedom to choose evil, the wicked destroy freedom: emphasis is consistently upon the essential *slavery* of the servants of Sauron, who can no longer accept freedom when it is offered them. Pride and self-will, here as in so many great works, are often the sources of evil. Saruman has been corrupted through pride; even the trees of the forest which attempt to capture the hobbits are said to have become evil by the growth of pride in them. Denethor, the Steward of the King, kills himself as a direct result of pride and that other great Christian sin, despair. It is pride that leads Boromir to want the Ring—pride, indeed, that lures all toward the Ring: Sam is able to resist its pull solely because of his humility, the fact that he is content with his own garden (III, 177).

Saruman and Gollum provide the main case histories of the gradual destructive effect of willing submission to evil wills, but Gandalf makes it clear that the result of such submission must always be the same, even for one predominantly virtuous at the outset. Even Frodo began his ownership of the Ring with a lie intended to make his claim on it more secure. If a mortal often uses the Ring, says

Gandalf, he " '*fades:* he becomes in the end invisible permanently, and walks in the twilight under the eye of the dark power that rules the Rings. Yes, sooner or later—later, if he is strong or well-meaning to begin with, but neither strength nor good purpose will last—sooner or later the dark power will devour him' " (I, 56). The Ring represents power: and Frodo the hobbit is no more capable than Tamburlaine the Great of controlling unlimited power without himself being destructively controlled by it. Not even Gandalf can wield such force. Bilbo offers him the Ring because he is already "wise and powerful," but he rejects it vehemently. " 'Do not tempt me! For I do not wish to become like the Dark Lord himself. Yet the way of the Ring to my heart is by pity, pity for weakness and the desire of strength to do good. Do not tempt me! I dare not take it, not even to keep it safe, unused. The wish to wield it would be too great for my strength. . . . With that power I should have power too great and terrible. And over me the Ring would gain a power still greater and more deadly' " (I, 70-71).

Indeed, Saruman began from precisely the position of Gandalf, and even without possession of the Ring, pride and the lust for power destroy him. In one of the most dramatic scenes of the trilogy, Gandalf confronts Saruman in his ruined stronghold and offers him the choice of complete freedom—" 'free from bond, of chain or command: to go where you will, even, even to Mordor, Saruman, if you desire' " (II, 188)—or continued slavery to Sauron. But the sorcerer, too corrupted to choose, is forced by the decay of his own will to remain in a slavery resulting from free choice made long before.

So too with Gollum, a far more pitiable creature, essentially amoral, but degraded to the uses of evil: amorality is not really possible in Tolkien's scheme. Gandalf tells the story of his slow destruction through possession of the Ring: "All the 'great secrets' under the mountains had turned out to be just empty night: there was nothing more to find out, nothing worth doing, only nasty furtive eating and resentful remembering. He was altogether wretched. He hated the dark, and he hated light more: he hated everything, and the Ring most of all. . . . He hated it and loved it, as he hated and loved himself. He could not get rid of it. *He had no will left in the matter*" (I, 64; italics mine). As Frodo's Quest nears its end, Faramir advises him against trusting—as he is—to Gollum's leadership. Faramir is convinced that Gollum is wicked; Frodo maintains that the creature is not altogether wicked. " 'Not wholly, perhaps,' " agrees Faramir, " 'but malice eats it like a canker, and the evil is growing' " (II, 301). And this is apt: the progress of evil in an individual cannot be reversed without a specific, conscious act of will, an act that Gollum, like the other characters devoted to evil, is quite incapable of performing.

Yet this same Gollum, ever more corrupted by lust for the Ring, his "Precious," becomes finally the instrument of Grace for Frodo in one of the most perplexing episodes of *The Lord of the Rings.* At the very end of his Quest, having struggled against hideous adversity to reach the Cracks of Doom—at the very end, Frodo "changes his mind." " 'I have come,' he said. 'But I do not chose now to do what I came to do. I will not do this deed. The Ring is mine!' " (III, 223). He uses still the language of free will—"I do not choose"—but the speech and the act which accompanies it (he puts on the Ring) represent rather a crucial failure of will. For "he was come to the heart of the realm of Sauron and the forges of his ancient might, greatest in Middle-earth; *all other powers were here subdued*" (III, 222; italics mine). Strong as it is, Frodo's will here succumbs.

Yet still he is saved—not by an act of will, but by an act of Fate. Gollum, whose corruption is complete at this moment, leaps on Frodo, bites off the finger which wears the Ring, waves it aloft in triumph, and—falls into the Crack of Doom with it: the Quest is thus accomplished.

Dramatically, this final twist is quite unnecessary. It prolongs the suspense by barely a page; the dilemma raised by Frodo's failure is immediately resolved. Thematically it is essential. In the presentation of this event, the idea of free will intimately involved with fate receives its most forceful statement. The same idea has been suggested before; now it becomes inescapable. Free choice of good by the individual involves his participation in a broad pattern of Good; individual acts become a part of Fate. Frodo has repeatedly chosen to behave mercifully toward Gollum, even in the face of treachery on the other's part. His merciful acts determine his fate and, because he has by his acceptance of his mission come to hold a symbolic position, they determine also the fate of the world he inhabits. Gollum, on the other hand, though he is comparatively weak in evil, has become the symbolic representative of evil. His original acceptance of evil has made him will-less; it is appropriate that at the last he should be merely an instrument of that essentially benevolent fate through which, as Sam realizes, "his master had been saved; he was himself again, he was free" (III, 225)—free at the cost of physical maiming, the emblem of his human (or hobbit) weakness—like Lewis' hero, Ransom, who is in *Perelandra* successful in physical struggle with the Devil, but emerges from it with an unhealable wound in the heel.

So, although *The Lord of the Rings* is by no means allegorical, it gains much of its force from its symbolic concentration on the most basic human concerns: the problems of man's relation to his universe. The fact that Tolkien's cosmos seems at first totally alien to our own might mislead us into thinking that his trilogy has no more right than ordinary science fiction to be considered as serious literature, that it is really the "juvenile trash" that Wilson thinks it. Yet Tolkien removes his fiction from the realm of "real life" only to be enabled to talk more forcefully about reality. A serious reading of *The Lord of the Rings* must produce the realization that its issues are profoundly relevant to human problems. Tolkien's method of communicating that relevance differs markedly from that of Lewis and Williams, who write always with the clear and specific purpose of Christian apologetics. If they create weird and alien worlds, worlds of science fiction, of the ghost story, it is with the basic intent of demonstrating the engulfing power of Christianity. Their primary referents are Christian and (especially in Lewis) classic myth, and didacticism lurks always behind their tales: the ultimate success of *That Hideous Strength* or *All Hallows' Eve* would be the conversion of its readers.

Tolkien's apparent moral purpose is more subtle, less specific. The force of his trilogy comes from its mythic scope and imagination, its fusion of originality with timelessness. *The Lord of the Rings* is a more widely popular work than any adult fiction by Lewis or Williams; it has become, indeed, the center of a cult, inspiring rhapsodic articles in *Holiday* magazine and news reports in *McCall's*. The fact of the cult suggests the power of Tolkien's work; its manifestations offer an index to an important strength and weakness of the trilogy. Young people at Harvard and N.Y.U. band together in Tolkien societies to write letters in Elvish and discuss the nature of Middle-earth culture. They wear sweatshirts inscribed "Go Go Gandalf" and buttons saying "Frodo Lives." Their response is to the appeal of an imaginary world. One recalls C. S. Lewis' description of the development of "Animal-Land," the imaginary realm of his early youth: how he proceeded in his imaginings "from romancing to historiography," writing "a full history of Animal-Land," creating its legends, its traditions, its geography.[3] It is easy to assume that Tolkien's imagined world developed in much the same way and that it fulfills the same needs in its readers and perhaps in its author. One reason why *The Lord of the Rings* captivates readers so diverse as W. H. Auden and Edmund Wilson's eight-year-old daughter is that it creates a compellingly detailed and authentic imaginary universe which seems an appealing alternative to our own chaotic world. It is not the never-never land of science fiction or of James Bond, but a realm in which moral problems are taken seriously and in which it is possible—not easy, but possible—to make right decisions. Tolkien lavishes such loving detail on his world that he encourages the willing suspension of disbelief; the cultists try to maintain that suspension beyond the limits of the book.

But paradoxically the richness of detail which makes the world of Frodo and Gandalf convincing also weakens the literary effectiveness of the trilogy by detracting from its mythic authenticity. The fiction of Lewis and Williams occasionally suffers from its simplicity and constancy of didactic purpose. Tolkien tends rather to over-complicate—not in purpose, but in detail. His elaboration of the minutiae of his imagined world seems sometimes an end in itself; it diminishes the essential moral weight of his fable. The action of *The Lord of the Rings*, in the Aristotelian sense, is at times obscured by the decoration. Although that action is both powerful and significant, the reader can lose consciousness of it in a mass of detail which is itself vibrant with imaginative energy.

[3] C. S. Lewis, *Surprised By Joy: The Shape of My Early Life* (New York, 1956), p. 13.

Tolkien and the Critics

A second aspect of the trilogy which makes it difficult to take seriously in literary terms is its language, an important basis of Mr. Wilson's objections to it. Like the richly-imagined unreal world, the language appeals to the child-side of its readers; it evokes memories of fairy tales and of legends of chivalry. "The grey figure of the Man, Aragorn son of Arathorn, was tall, and stern as stone, his hand upon the hilt of his sword; he looked as if some king out of the mists of the sea had stepped upon the shores of lesser men. Before him stooped the old figure, white, shining now as if with some light kindled within, bent, laden with years, but holding a power beyond the strength of kings" (II, 104). The simple vocabulary recalls traditional material of romance: sword hilts, kingliness, the mists of the sea, shining light, the ancient man of mysterious power. But its rhetoric and its references seem automatic. Tolkien repeatedly employs the same imagery of mysterious inner light as an index of spiritual power; such imagery sometimes substitutes for demonstration of that power. All too often, Tolkien asserts rather than demonstrates character. By self-conscious alliteration and deliberately simple metaphor he may hope to recall the technique of primitive northern epic, but there is an inevitable and disastrous gap between the primitive and the pseudo-primitive. One is unavoidably conscious of Tolkien's artifice, and it does not seem sufficiently skillful to be self-justifying. A critic who demands verbal complexity, integrity, richness, subtlety, will find little to attract him in Tolkien's fiction. The language of the books is entirely an instrument of the story. When it demands attention in its own right, it is unlikely to justify the attention it receives. The depth and subtlety of imagination, both fictional and moral, which control the fable find no counterparts in the language of the trilogy, derivative and often impoverished or pretentious.

Yet the power of the fable remains, and remains important: other modes of criticism besides the verbal are relevant here. Although Tolkien's achievement is far outside the central modes of twentieth-century fiction, it is none the less significant. It demonstrates how even a framework of fantasy can provide a context for the exploration of serious concerns, how moral energy can animate far-fetched fiction, how a tale of other worlds than ours can incorporate and be enriched by a complex ethical structure. Its linguistic limitations may prevent its assuming a high position in recognized literary canons, but it will surely continue to exercise compelling power over its readers.

7

MORAL VISION IN
THE LORD OF THE RINGS

Rose A. Zimbardo

THE LORD OF THE RINGS EXPRESSES THE VISION OF RO-
mance: "theme rather than fable is the central structural
element."[1] The theme shaped in this structure centers on the
problem of the All versus the self in human consciousness.
To qualify further: tragedy concerns itself with the *division*
in human nature and describes the arc wherein man aspires
toward identification with the transcendent ideal and inevitably falls back down into the confines of the limited self.
Romance too is concerned with the self and the other, but
it envisions the other not as other but as All, a wholeness or
harmony to the operation of which man's unique nature
contributes. Moreover, while tragedy insists upon the *impossibility* of man's identification with the other, romance insists upon the absolute *necessity* of his identification with
the All, and while tragedy stresses the duality, the conflict
between the metaphysical and physical aspects of man's
nature, romance insists upon the harmony of human being.
The physical nourishes the metaphysical in man because in
human nature as in the cosmos, physical and metaphysical
are complementary parts of an embracing whole. In *The
Lord of the Rings*, for instance, the heroes in every coura-

[1] Cf. William Nelson, *The Poetry of Edmund Spenser* (New York,
1963), p. 116.

geous enterprise, those who against all expectation prove to be most durable in the face of evil, are hobbits, beings who operate best *within* physical nature, who prefer to live in snug dugouts and eat six meals a day.[2] Evil in the romance vision is not an aspect of human *nature*, but rather the perversion of human *will*. It results when a being directs his will inward to the service of the self rather than outward to the service of the All. The effects of such inversion is the perversion of nature, both man's nature and the greater nature of which it is a part.

The All in *The Lord of the Rings* is a chain of being, a scale of creatures, differing from one another in the degree to which substance combines with form in their natures, each degree necessary to the composition of the whole, and contributing to the formation of a *concors discordia*. Good is the cooperation of all levels of being, a harmony but not an interpenetration of kinds, for each kind of being has its particular excellence and consequently its peculiar contribution to make to the order of the whole.

The wizards are nearest to essence; they are sheer powers or colors: Radagast the Russet, Saruman the White, and Gandalf the Grey who becomes Gandalf the White by an act of sacrifice that he makes in the service of the All. In encountering the Balrog, he falls into the fiery center of the earth, where he undergoes a mighty contest of will and, triumphing, is resurrected. After his sacrifice he comes to embody the white or positive principle, the fellowship of beings.

The elves comprise the next level of being. They are associated with light, as Gandalf is, but theirs is a softer light, starlight. They are not powers, as the wizards are, but they

[2] Edmund Wilson, "Oo Those Awful Orcs!" *Nation*, CLXXXII (April 14, 1956), 312, suggests that their name is "a telescoping of rabbit and Hobbs."

are not groundlings either. Their nature is airy; they hover in trees and they are conceived as an aura, a halo that has surrounded the earth but that is fading from it. Their wisdom is neither the supernatural power of the wizards, nor the practical intelligence of natures below theirs on the scale. It is rather a mantic and bardic wisdom. Light of substance, fading in time, they transform experience into essence in poetry.

The creatures that follow the elves on the scale of being, as their age will follow the age of the elves in the cycle of time, are the Men. But these are the Men of Middle-earth, the giants that *were* in the earth. They are kings, and their peculiar virtue is heroic courage and statecraft. Theirs is the *bios politikos* that forges out of beautiful deeds and the materials of the earth the foundations of civilization.

After them come the hobbits, a linking kind, halflings between kingly nature and animal nature. Furry-footed, they are nearer to the earth than the Men and more animal the nearer they get. If the cycles of time have continued to revolve since the days of Middle-earth and if the Kings have faded as the elves before them were destined to fade, then we may assume that our age is the age of the hobbits. The hobbits are the common man, who does not seek out the opportunity for great deeds, who prefers his bounded life in the Shire. Yet the hobbits *are* the heroes. From Frodo the knightly Ring-bearer and Sam his faithful Squire to Merry, who dares battle with the Nazgûl, they unexpectedly transcend themselves in selfless action. Their peculiar excellence is not heroic honor but love. Frodo is finally saved because he has pitied Sméagol. Sam is moved to deeds of heroic exploit out of love for Frodo. Merry and Pippin are transformed into thanes out of love for the kings they serve. They comprise the core of the fellowship, and in the end, as in the beginning, it is love that binds them. It is significant that Tolkien makes them heroes in every enterprise because the virtue they embody is the idea of good that *The Lord of the Rings* shapes. *Caritas* is the virtue that sustains the fellowship of being, that makes a concordant whole of the discordant parts that comprise it.

But the hobbits are not the last beings on the scale. The harmony does not extend merely from the surface of the earth outward, for the physical is not damned in its physicality. Last on the scale are the beings under the earth, the dwarves. They are as heavy of substance as the elves are light. Their peculiar excellence is craft and as the elves forge substanceless language into beauty in poetry, the dwarves shape elemental metal into beautiful things. The potentiality for beauty exists even in the bowels of matter, but the creation of beauty depends upon the proper use of being. The operation of the harmony of being is expressed emblematically in the relation between Legolas and Gimli. The dwarves and elves are opposite in nature, that is, in the proportions of form and substance that each nature combines. When each holds the good of its own people above the good of the whole, they war, and warring, they endanger the whole. Yet they are drawn into harmony by love. Gimli's love for Galadriel prepares him to love Legolas and Legolas is in turn drawn into love for Gimli. Out of hostility grows loving competition and at last each is led to the desire to see the beautiful through the eyes of the other. But though Legolas may visit the caves and Gimli the forests in token of their fellowship, neither can become the other, for their fellowship depends on the maintenance of separate identity.

For each of the creatures on the chain there exists a perverse counterpart. Treebeard says that the creations of the Enemy are perversions or mockeries or counterfeits (II, 89). For Gandalf who sacrifices himself for the fellowship, there is Saruman who falls self-tempted and who tempts others to fall to the service of self. For the elves there are the orcs, made by the Enemy as imitation elves. Because of their maker's nature, they turn out to be the antithesis of elvishness. As the elves are refined almost to essence, the orcs are grotesquely gross. As the elves float above the earth, the orcs ferret under it. As the elves worship light, the orcs fear it. (The response of the Enemy, characteristic of *his* nature, is to breed a more efficient orc who will even withstand light in his urge to destroy.) As the elves glory in their elvish nature and tradition, the orcs fall upon each other in their spite.

The dark counterpart of Men are the Ringwraiths, the dark riders whose lust for the Ring's power has deprived them of that which is most characteristic of the Men, heroic identity. The Ringwraiths have lost any identity beyond the hollow malevolent force that drives them. At this level of being, as at the Wizards' level, the creature cooperates in the perversion of his own nature, so that there is no need for the Enemy to create an imitation of him. We are given some insight into the process by which the will of Men is misdirected in the contrasting fates of Théoden and Denethor. With the help of Gandalf, Théoden is able to shake off the paralysis of will that Wormtongue's temptations have brought him to. Exercising his will to the service of fellowship, he reasserts his natural excellence, kingly courage, and leadership. On the other hand, Denethor, having chosen to keep to his own use a power too great for him, a power beyond his stewardship, lusts for more. He mourns his son Boromir less than the loss of the power that Boromir would have brought him. Consequently, not only does the particular virtue of his kind, courage and loyalty, wither in him, but ultimately his nature itself is corrupted and, mad, he attempts to destroy Faramir.

Finally, the perverse counterpart of the heroic hobbits, more exactly the counterpart of Frodo, the Ring-bearer, is

Sméagol, who was himself a hobbit until desire for the Ring moved him to kill a fellow hobbit. Under the torment of his lust for the Ring, every aspect of his hobbit nature is distorted to parody. It is significant that the final destruction of the Ring occurs when Frodo and Sméagol are fighting for it. Frodo must conquer his own dark counterpart, the Ringbearer must prevail over his own image turned Ringwraith, before the destruction of that image, and with it the destruction of the Ring, can be accomplished.

As the fellowship of love is the ultimate positive power, the negation of fellowship, the rejection of the other and subjection of the All to the self, is the ultimate negative power. As in St. Augustine's, so in Tolkien's vision, nothing is created evil. Evil is good that has been perverted. Gandalf tells us that even Sauron had to fall from goodness. Moreover, the power of darkness cannot see into the heart of light. It must depend for its power upon a failure in the will to good. Yet the vulnerability of each creature to such a failure is built into his very nature. The singularity, the oneness of each creature leaves him open to the temptation of asserting the demands of self above those of the All, and finally of subjecting the All to the demands of self:

> *One* Ring to rule them all, *one* Ring to find them
> *One* Ring to bring them all and in the darkness bind them.
>   (Italics mine)

The Ring is all that we see of Sauron because Sauron has no other identity but that which the Ring stands for. He has only negative identity. He is a dark shadow, the negation of positive being itself. He has become the very principle of misdirected, self-directed will. His power, expressed in the power of the Ring, is the power to separate oneself from the community of positive being. The wearer of the Ring becomes invisible, and the more often he chooses to use the power, the more the power wears away his substance. Even after the Ring has been destroyed, the effects of having exercised its power remain. Frodo, who has endured the full temptation of the Ring's power and who has had to war with himself before it could be destroyed, has become, as Sam tells us, almost transparent. Even Bilbo has lost a great deal of his hobbit nature. Both have lost something of their substance and have moved off their own position in the scale of being toward a more elvish nature. It is significant that neither can live among hobbits, but Bilbo lives among the elves and at last they both must embrace the fate of the elves. In losing their hobbit nature they have changed their position in being as well as in time; they become part of the elvish aura that must fade from the earth.

This brings us to a second property of the Ring, the quality that makes it almost irresistible. It arrests time. Both Bilbo and Frodo are more youthful for having worn the Ring and Bilbo has lived beyond the time allotted to hobbit nature. Galadriel in refusing the Ring must resist not merely the demands of self but also the demands of kind, for she is aware that possession of the Ring would prevent the passing of the elves. The Ring, then, not only takes its wearer out of the community of positive being, but out of the cycle of time to which that being is subject. The permanence of the All consists in change. The harmony of being demands decay before regeneration begins. The age of the elves must end in order that the age of men can grow. And all that the elves can legitimately do to preserve their experience is to cast it into poetry. Their songs, full of the glory of their past and the sorrow of their decline, freeze into the permanence of art their having been. But it is because the individual, and even his age, must die that the urge to preserve one's own time at the cost of the cycle of time is so great. Individuation makes a creature vulnerable to the Ring. Only Tom Bombadil can wear it without disappearing because, as he says of himself,

'Eldest, that's what I am. . . . Tom was here before the river and the trees. . . . He knew the dark under the stars when it was fearless—before the Dark Lord came from Outside.' (I, 142)

When Frodo asks Gandalf why Tom cannot be one of the fellowship of the Ring, he is told that Tom would not remember the Ring nor be able to recognize its importance. He has neither history nor memory because change for him is only seasonal change. He is the permanence at the heart of change, the life-force itself that was present when "the dark was fearless," before the principle of self came. Tom Bombadil can restore the hobbits when they have been frozen by the Barrow-wight. He can reawaken life from death, but he cannot belong to the fellowship of love because his love is only to Goldberry, the substance he enlivens. The fellowship of love, the exercise of will in the service of an order that transcends the self, is moral action. It is possible only for those who are subject to individuation and time, that is, those who are conscious of the division between the self and the other.

However, the nearer the creature to nature, to the pattern that Tom Bombadil embodies, the greater his ability to resist the demands of self. Sam Gamgee is the only character in the book who is able to wear the Ring and yet to give it up without a struggle. He is not, like Tom, impervious to the Ring's power. Even Sam experiences the temptation to subject the All to self, but because he is a gardener, the very nature of his vision restores his balance. For the instant he wants the whole world as his garden, but because his particular excellence has been promoting and sustaining nature's life he sees at once the folly of a part of nature trying to consume the whole that embraces it. In Sam's dream of power we are given a flash of comic insight into man's moral dilemma. In Sam's response, love for and faithful service to another being that completely overcomes self, we are given the resolution of that dilemma that the vision of romance affects.

8

MEN, HALFLINGS, AND HERO WORSHIP

Marion Zimmer Bradley

LOVE IS THE DOMINANT EMOTION IN THE LORD OF THE *Rings*, and love in the form of hero worship is particularly evident in the relationship between Aragorn and the other characters and between Frodo and Sam. Other forms of love are also apparent; the most important of these is heroic love which includes love of honor and love of country; additionally there is Gandalf's paternal and Goldberry and Galadriel's maternal love. Relatively little romantic love is depicted and what is appears to follow the chivalric, although not courtly, love convention. Underlying all of these is the love of the fellowship—that of one man for another; this love extends beyond the initial fellowship as the original members extend their relationship to serve and battle with others.

It should be noted, briefly and in passing, that Tolkien's self-consistent world, along with an alien geography and ecology, has its own appropriate manners, in general those of the heroic ages; they are *not* the stiff-upper-lip unemotional ones of the modern English-speaking peoples. Affectionate and emotional displays are permitted not alone to women and children, but to men; thus Legolas trembles with terror and wails aloud before the Balrog without his courage or manliness (if this word may be used of an Elf) being suspect; Boromir weeps in passionate repentance after his attack on Frodo, and when he is slain, Aragorn kneels at his side so "bent with weeping" that Legolas and Gimli are dismayed, fearing he too has "taken deadly hurt." The men display affection freely, e.g., Faramir parts from Frodo with an embrace and kiss; this is simply a pattern of manners and does *not* in itself merit mention as ballast for the thesis that the major emotional threads of the story are drawn between men.

The prevalent emotion in general is the hero worship of a young man for one older, braver, and wiser. All the company treat Gandalf as an exalted Father-figure, but the major object of *hero* worship, as opposed to paternal veneration, is Aragorn himself. With the single exception of Boromir, the actual leadership is resigned to him by all; Frodo, a hero in his own right, immediately yields to him:

> '. . . yes, it was Strider that saved us. Yet I was afraid of him at first. Sam never quite trusted him, I think. . . .'
> Gandalf smiled. 'I have heard all about Sam,' he said. 'He has no more doubts now.'
> 'I am glad . . . for I have become very fond of Strider. Well, *fond* is not the right word. I mean he is dear to me; though he is strange, and grim at times . . . he reminds me often of you.' (I, 232)

Éomer and Faramir, too, quickly fall under Aragorn's spell. The only one who does not is Boromir, and one of the subtlest threads of the story is Boromir's competition for Aragorn's place. In many small episodes he attempts persistently to maneuver things his way, not Aragorn's—not in petty jealousy nor, at first, for any base motive. He is brave and valiant and well worthy of the admiration he gets from the young hobbits; he fights for them and defends them and at least in Pippin's case he partially succeeds (and this is very carefully, deftly studied, for Pippin is the persistent rebel against Gandalf). Slain in the first chapter of Volume II, Boromir is nevertheless a compelling force of emotional motivation throughout the book. He is emotionally present in Frodo's meeting with Faramir and Pippin's with Denethor; further it is Pippin's memory, his admiration for Boromir, that lies behind his service to Denethor which ultimately saves the life of Faramir.

If Gandalf plays the ideal Father, and Aragorn the heroically loved elder brother—and there is some hint of the sullen rivalry between Achilles and Agamemnon in Boromir's jealousy of Aragorn—then Peregrin Took, the hobbit Pippin, is most emphatically the spoiled youngest child. Here we reemphasize the peculiar chronology of fantasy, for Peregrin is twenty-nine years old, but four years short of his "coming of age," and thus equivalent to a boy in his teens. He is literally treated like a child. He falls asleep and is carried to bed while Frodo talks with the Elves. Elrond's "heart is against his going" on the dangerous Quest. Gandalf, who lets him come, nevertheless, in Pippin's words "thinks I need keeping in order," and singles him out, several times, for testy rebuke. He is in fact the childish mischiefmaker of the company, yet even Gandalf treats him indulgently when he is not squelching his bubbling spirits. This subtle study of Pippin as the "naughty rebel" against Gandalf's kind authority culminates in his logical resentment against being treated as a child, so that his theft of the Palantír—which is treachery in essence—is motivated and at last understood simply as an act of purely childish mischief and devilry. We should note that Gandalf fears and refuses the challenge of the Palantír, pointing out that Pippin's folly helped prevent him from daring to use it himself. He cautions Aragorn against looking into it (II, 200), but Aragorn later makes up his own mind. And the "moral" of this seems to be that the young, as they grow toward independence, sometimes have their own answers for what their elders fear. However, this father-son relationship remains; during the sequence of the Great Ride, when Gandalf flees on the wings of the wind of war, he bears Pippin with him on Shadowfax quite literally as a small child: "Aragorn lifted Pippin and set him in Gandalf's arms, wrapped in cloak and blanket" (II, 201). Volume III opens with the passage, "Pippin looked out from the shelter of Gandalf's cloak. He wondered if he were awake or still sleeping, still in the swift-moving dream in which he had been wrapped . . . since the great ride began." As Pippin slowly recovers, Gandalf first scolds, then lectures, and finally forgives him in true father-fashion. Their relationship in Minas Tirith continues to be that of loving, if stern father, and willful, but no longer rebellious child.

The character evolution of Meriadoc (Merry), the other of the young hobbits, is less obvious and takes place at a somewhat deeper level. Merry, older than Pippin, more sensible and quieter, seems less vital at first and, until Pippin draws attention to himself by the theft of the Palantír, seems to have remained in the background. Yet on second evaluation it becomes obvious that Merry, like a perfectly cast supporting actor, performs his quiet background activities in a perfectly consistent way. It comes slowly to the reader's notice that Merry has, in fact, played a very quiet part in all their adventures. It is Merry who provided ponies for their flight, who led them into the Old Forest, and after the attack on Weathertop it is consistently and logically Merry on whom Aragorn calls for help to bring them, quietly and without credit, through dangers—Frodo is wounded and too burdened, Sam too hostile and absorbed in Frodo, Pippin too irresponsible.

After Pippin's escapade, while the others show concern, Merry simply turns away; he shows all the earmarks of the

neglected "good" child resenting the kindness shown to the
naughty one who has drawn attention to himself; as Gandalf
rides away, his bitter comment to Aragorn is virtually his
clearest utterance:

A beautiful, restful night! Some people have wonderful luck.
He didn't want to sleep, and he wanted to ride with
Gandalf—and there he goes! Instead of being turned into
a stone himself to stand here forever as a warning. (II, 201)

And it seems significant that after the two are separated,
they follow paths similar on the surface but differing greatly
in emotional motivation. Both offer their sword and service
to a mighty King. "In payment of [his] debt" to Boromir,
slain defending him and Merry, Pippin impetuously enters
the service of Denethor; Gandalf is astonished saying:

'I do not know what put it into your head, or your heart,
to do that. . . . I did not hinder it, for generous deed should
not be checked by cold counsel. . . .' (III, 32)

But Merry's choice, though equally impulsive, is not motivated by pride:

Filled suddenly with love for this old man, he knelt on one
knee, and took his hand and kissed it. 'May I lay the sword
of Meriadoc of the Shire on your lap, Théoden King?' he
cried. 'Receive my service, if you will!'
'Gladly will I take it,' said the king; and laying his long old
hands upon the brown hair of the hobbit, he blessed him. . . .
'As a father you shall be to me,' said Merry. (III, 50-51)

When ordered later to remain behind, Merry reacts with
almost childish desperation. " 'I won't be left behind, to be
called for on return. I won't be left! I won't!' " (III, 73).
And he disobeys with the connivance of the other "disobedi-
ent son," Éowyn in her male disguise as Dernhelm.

Together Éowyn and Merry face and slay the Nazgûl, both striking an enemy far beyond their strength for the love of a father, Théoden. Later Faramir, Éowyn, and Merry all lie in the shadow of the Black Breath, and additionally Faramir lies in the shadow *of a father's displeasure.* Gandalf has had to counsel him when he goes in desperation on his last mission: " 'Do not throw your life away rashly or in bitterness . . . your father loves you, and will remember it ere the end' " (III, 90). When he is recalled by Aragorn, it is apparent that Merry has been through a profoundly maturing experience:

> '. . . I would like supper first, and after that a pipe.' 'No, not a pipe. I don't think I'll smoke again.' At this his face clouded.
> 'Why not?' said Pippin.
> 'Well,' answered Merry slowly, 'He is dead. It has brought it all back to me. He said he was sorry he had never had a chance of talking herb-lore with me. Almost the last thing he ever said. I shan't ever be able to smoke again without thinking of him, and that day, Pippin, when he rode up to Isengard and was so polite.'
> 'Smoke then, and think of him!' said Aragorn. 'For he was a gentle heart and a great king and kept his oaths. . . . Though your service to him was brief, it should be a memory glad and honourable to the end of your days.' Merry smiled. 'Well, then,' he said, 'if Strider will provide what is needed, I will smoke and think.' (III, 145-146)

This scene between Aragorn and Merry evidences not only warmth but also Aragorn's humanness; he consoles the grieving Merry, teases him, then confesses weariness, and for the first time Merry speaks in realization of Aragorn's real stature: " 'I am frightfully sorry . . . ever since that night at Bree, we have been a nuisance to you . . .' " (III, 146). And this change in Merry is made more emphatic when, left alone with Pippin, the irresponsible younger hobbit says: " 'Was there ever anyone like him? Except Gandalf, of course. I really think they must be related . . .' " and, of course spiritually, they are. Then he adds: " 'Dear me! We Tooks and Brandybucks, we can't live long on the heights!' " (III, 146). And here it is apparent that, if Pippin has changed from a rebellious child to a loving one, Merry has been far more deeply affected by his service to a beloved king; " 'No, I can't. Not yet, at any rate. But at least, Pippin, we can now see them, and honour them. It is best to love first what you are fitted to love, I suppose . . . still, there are things deeper and higher . . . I am glad that I know about them, a little' " (III, 146). Few clearer statements could be made of the way in which the young come to the simple but deeply affecting discovery of worlds far outside their own small selfish concerns and events greater than the small patterns of their lives. The experience is universal, even though Tolkien has cast it into heroic mold and scorned obvious moral or allegory.

Whatever hobbit chronology, neither Merry nor Pippin quite achieves full adult stature until they return to the Shire to set their own country in order; Gandalf resigns his authority, saying in effect, "you do not need me . . . you have grown up." Then Merry's firmness and Pippin's courage show echoes of Théoden, of Aragorn, even of Denethor and Gandalf. They have to some extent become what they admired. And it is Merry who perceives why Éowyn belongs to the story and Arwen does not. For Éowyn, too, achieves the passing of the "Heroic Age"—the age in which girls rebel against their sex and their limitations and dream of male deeds. Gandalf says with pity:

'She, born in the body of a maid, had a spirit and courage at least the match of yours . . . who knows what she spoke to the darkness, alone, . . . when all her life seemed shrinking,

> and the walls of her bower closing in about her, a hutch to
> trammel some wild thing in?' (III, 143)

She does indeed achieve great deeds in male disguise and
chafes at her "imprisonment" in the Houses of Healing.
When she meets Faramir she is abashed, after she complains
to him, thinking that he might see her as "merely wayward,
like a child" (III, 328) yet it is Faramir who sees Éowyn
most clearly. He describes her love for Aragorn in unmistakable terms—simple hero worship on a masculine level:
" 'And as a great captain may to a young soldier he seemed
to you admirable. For so he is. . . .' " And Éowyn, suddenly
understanding, accepts what she is, and is not: " 'I will be a
shieldmaiden no longer, nor vie with the great Riders. . . .
I will . . . love all things that grow and are not barren. . . .
No longer do I desire to be a queen' " (III, 242-243). In
other words, no longer does she desire to be a *king*, i.e., not
to identify with Aragorn, but to be a woman. This is not a
new theme—Wagner, at the end of *Siegfried*, puts such
words into the mouth of Brunhilde—but it is apt to the picture of the passing of the Heroic Age.

I have reserved for last, because most intense, the strong
love between Frodo and Samwise, and the curious part
played in it by the creature Gollum. Toward the end of the
third book Frodo and Sam reach classical "idealized friendship" equivalent in emotional strength to the ardor of
Achilles and Patrocles or David and Jonathan: "passing the
love of women." Wilson speaks with some contempt of the
"hardy little homespun hero" and the "devoted servant who
speaks lower-class and respectful and never deserts his
master"[1] thus displaying a truly cataclysmic ignorance of
the pattern of heroic literature. Both Frodo and Sam display, in full measure, the pattern of the Hero in Quest liter-

[1] Edmund Wilson, "Oo, Those Awful Orcs!" *The Nation*, CLXXXII
(April 14, 1956), 312-314.

tory." And they contain the Resurrection, which is "the eucatastrophe of the Incarnation."

The joy which the happy ending of the fairy story gives, says Tolkien, is of the same quality, though not the same degree, as the joy which we feel at the fact that the great fairy story of the Gospels is true in the Primary World, for the joy of the fairy tale "has the very taste of primary truth." This is the justification of the fairy story—and thus of the trilogy—that it gives us in small, in the beat of the heart and the catch of the breath, the joy of the infinite good news. For "Art has been verified. God is the Lord, of Angels, and of men—and of elves. Legend and history have met and fused."

It is not too much to say that Tolkien's view of the fairy story has made explicit Coleridge's claim for the worth of the creative imagination. The Secondary Imagination, which created literature, was for Coleridge an "echo" of the Primary Imagination, which is "the living Power and prime Agent of all human Perception, and . . . a repetition in the finite mind of the external act of creation in the infinite I AM."[14] For the fairy story—and the trilogy—are sheer creation, the making of a Secondary World out of, and by means of, the Imagination. That is the special activity of the fairy-story maker, and one by which he becomes, not a writer, but a subcreator of a kind of literature analogous— or more than analogous—to the universe created *ex nihilo* by the divine Creator. In his degree he creates Joy—or creates what gives Joy—as God, in the purposeful drama of creation, has created what also gives Joy, the world with the Christian happy ending. Speaking of Blake's definition of poetry, Northrop Frye has commented:

---

[14] *Biographia Literaria,* Ch. XIII.

> We live in a world of threefold external compulsion: of compulsion on action, or law; of compulsion on thinking, or fact; of compulsion on feeling, which is the characteristic of all pleasure whether it is produced by the *Paradiso* or by an ice cream soda. But in the world of imagination a fourth power, which contains morality, beauty, and truth but is never subordinated to them, rises free of all their compulsions. The work of imagination presents us with a vision, not of the personal greatness of the poet, but of something impersonal and far greater: the vision of a decisive act of spiritual freedom, the vision of the recreation of man.[15]

Tolkien's defense of Fantasy and, I would add, of the trilogy, in verse in which there is perhaps more truth than poetry, is also a defense and, it may be, the last defense, of the doctrine of the creative imagination, which brings the making of God and the making of man so close that they nearly touch:

> Although now long estranged,
> Man is not wholly lost nor wholly changed.
> Dis-graced he may be, yet is not de-throned,
> and keeps the rags of lordship once he owned:
> Man, Sub-creator, the refracted Light
> through whom is splintered from a single White
> to many hues, and endlessly combined
> in living shapes that move from mind to mind.
> Though all the crannies of the world we filled
> with Elves and Goblins, though we dared to build
> Gods and their houses out of dark and light,
> and sowed the seed of dragons—'twas our right
> (used or misused). That right has not decayed:
> we make still by the law in which we're made. (pp. 71-72)

---

[15] *Anatomy of Criticism*, p. 94.

10

TOLKIEN:
THE MONSTERS AND THE CRITTERS

Thomas J. Gasque

IN HIS 1936 GOLLANCZ MEMORIAL LECTURE, J. R. R. Tolkien makes this curious and not fully elaborated statement:

> It is the strength of the northern mythological imagination that . . . put the monsters in the centre, gave them victory but no honour, and found a potent but terrible solution in naked will and courage. . . . So potent is it, that while the older southern imagination has faded for ever into literary ornament, the northern has power, as it were, to revive its spirit even in our own times.[1]

What Tolkien may well have had in his mind when he spoke of the "power . . . to revive its spirit . . . in our own times" was his own use of the northern imagination in *The Hobbit*, which he had already written, and in *The Lord of the Rings,* which was probably well under way at that time (I, 5-6). Perhaps Tolkien was justifying his revival of the spirit in the same way that much of his essay "On Fairy-Stories" seems to be slanted toward a defense of his own work as well as of the genre. The defense is convincing,

[1] J. R. R. Tolkien, "Beowulf: The Monsters and the Critics," p. 77.

however, and one critic has used the essay to show how Tolkien has created, by his own definition, a successful fairy story.[2]

Although at times the landscape literally comes to life, in a geographical sense Middle-earth is hardly fantastic. Rather what really makes Tolkien's province a world of its own is the large population of sundry creatures, for Tolkien has put the monster—and the critters—at the center of his story, and it is they who provide the interest.

As a philologist and medieval scholar, Tolkien is steeped in traditional northern mythology; he has drawn on this lore in creating his characters and in refashioning a genre: ". . . he [Tolkien] has so profoundly penetrated the spirit of a genre that he has created a modern work in its mode."[3] Although Roger Sale disagrees,[4] I feel that, excepting the hobbits, Tolkien's fanciful elements are most successful when they are rooted in the traditional. In *The Hobbit* Tolkien's dragon was a dragon was a dragon, and the dragon as monster succeeds there in a way that whole shoals of Balrogs and Shelobs never would. It is not the fantastic monsters, fearful though they may be, but the dwarfs, elves, and even the orcs that give the greatest vitality to the work. And it is largely because of the traditional associations that they so succeed.

But the tradition can also be a hindrance, especially when it is inconsistent, as in the case of elves. Sometime around the sixteenth century the idea of an elf changed from a man-sized creature to one who could hide in a cowslip. The diminutive nature of elves, Tolkien suggests, is "largely a

[2] Robert J. Reilly, "Tolkien and the Fairy Story," above pp. 128-150.
[3] Edmund Fuller, "The Lord of the Hobbits: J. R. R. Tolkien," above p. 36.
[4] "England's Parnassus: C. S. Lewis, Charles Williams, and J. R. R. Tolkien," *Hudson Review*, XVII (1964), 219.

sophisticated product of literary fancy."[5] The word *"elf,"* he notes in the appendix, "has been diminshed, and to many it may now suggest fancies either pretty or silly. . . ." Elves "were tall, fair of skin and grey-eyed, though their looks were dark, save in the golden house of Finrod" (III, 415-416.) This garbled tradition perhaps makes it difficult for the reader—at least it did for me—to visualize these creatures, and even after the appearance of Glorfindel (I, 221), I had trouble disposing of the idea of tiny elves. The goblins of *The Hobbit* also evidence this hindrance. That Tolkien changed their names to orcs in the trilogy suggests that he saw in the word "goblin" overtones of harmless children on Halloween and chose a less familiar and hence less diminished name.

The tradition of a race of creatures beyond the human pale, then, is inconsistent. Although in traditional elf or dwarf lore there is general agreement, the stock is far from pure. When we attempt to arrange the folk of Faërie into a systematic structure, says Thomas Keightley, "we find the foundation crumbling under our feet."[6] In order to build a structure, Tolkien has selected those materials that make the system consistent. This is, of course, an artist's prerogative. Tolkien is not offering us *the* system of Faërie; he is offering us his own system—a new building made from the old lumber. But we must become aware of this structure gradually if we are to perceive its inner consistency and to accept what we see. Thus Tolkien must provide a bridge from the world of trees, birds, and ordinary people to the world of elves and dragons. In his fairy-story essay, he commented that the dream-frame is a trick, as bad as a time-machine, and one does better if he plunges his reader right

[5] "On Fairy-Stories," p. 40.
[6] *The Fairy Mythology* (London, 1850), p. 13.

153

into the middle of his imaginary world.[7] In the trilogy, he
does this for the hobbits by making no apologies for having
created them. But because hobbits are just a little different
from ordinary people and because these differences only
slowly make themselves felt, we tend to accept totally the
variants in their character delineation.

Hobbits, excepting Bilbo, are just as provincial in the
Shire as people are on the earth and have little awareness of
what the land beyond the Brandywine contains. The broad
scope of Middle-earth unfolds slowly and believably for us
as we cross the bridge from a known world to a fabulous
one. Early in the work, we hear the Shirefolk discuss the
land beyond the Brandywine, which in retrospect seems to
us so tame, as a mysterious place, "where folks are so
queer."

> 'And no wonder they're queer,' put in Daddy Two-
> foot . . . , 'if they live on the wrong side of the Brandywine
> River, and right agin the Old Forest. That's a dark bad
> place, if half the tales be true.' (I, 30)

Somewhat later, after we have accepted the existence not
only of hobbits but even of Gandalf the Wizard and of
dwarfs, Tolkien drops us in on another tavern conversation
at *The Green Dragon*:

> 'Queer things you do hear these days, to be sure,' said Sam
> 'Ah,' said Ted, 'you do, if you listen. But I can hear
> fireside-tales and children's stories at home, if I want to
> 'No doubt you can,' retorted Sam, 'and I daresay there's
> more truth in some of them than you reckon. Who invented
> the stories anyway? Take dragons now.'
> 'No thank 'ee,' said Ted, 'I won't. I heard tell of them
> when I was a youngster, but there's no call to believe i

[7] "On Fairy-Stories," p. 45.

them now. There's only one Dragon in Bywater, and that's
Green,' he said, getting a general laugh. (I, 53)

Then Sam brings up the matter of elves and recalls old
tales of elf-ships sailing west from the Grey Havens, leaving
the folk of Middle-earth. " 'Let them sail!' " says Ted.
" 'But I warrant you haven't seen them doing it.' " Sam
had not, but he "believed he had once seen an Elf in the
woods, and still hoped to see more one day" (I, 54).

Such is the mental state of the average hobbit-on-the-
street, who is almost, but not quite, ready to believe in
fabulous creatures. This previous scene and the credibility
of the hobbits are a preparation for the first meeting with
elves in the Green-Hill Country in the southern part of the
Shire (I, 88 ff.).

If elves are fantastic and unreal creatures, dwarfs are not;
they are merely "outlandish folk . . . with long beards and
deep hoods" (I, 33), who create a mild surprise at Bywater
when they drive in with a load of birthday presents. Tolkien
has asked us, then, to accept hobbits and dwarfs without
question, and with the help of Sam's qualified credulity, we
as readily accept the elves. The Black Riders are ambiguous
enough at first, so that we have believed in them as real
men before they are confirmed as Wraiths.

Not until we meet Tom Bambadil in the Old Forest do
we face our first problem of belief. The lack of preparation
for such a scene and its being followed by the episode at
Bree, back in the normal world, mark Tolkien's technical
failure, and hence it is a charming but slightly unconvincing
digression, much less effective than the organic and fascinating episode in Fangorn with the Ents. The failure of the
Bombadil episode happens, thinks Roger Sale, because it is
an "invention" rather than a "creation" and never really
comes alive. "As a result the unfriendly reader finds an easy

stopping place in Tom Bombadil; forty pages of such dull stuff so early in a long work is hard to get over" (221).

In addition to Tom Bombadil, there are in the trilogy two other important creatures—both of them monsters— who are different in conception and, we might say, in psychology from any of the others. They are the Balrog and Shelob. Most of the other creatures are more or less "human," with human-like motives and responses. The use of superficially nonhuman beings is Tolkien's method of characterization: "Much that in a realistic work would be done by 'character delineation' is here done simply by making the character an elf, a dwarf, or a hobbit. The imagined beings have their insides on the outside; they are visible souls."[8] But this is not true of Tom, of the Balrog, or of Shelob; they are entirely nonhuman and seem to represent natural rather than psychological forces. Bombadil is apparently some kind of nature god, or perhaps he is the embodiment of the life principle. His incantations alone can dispel the force of the Barrow-wight, who perhaps represents death; these incantations apparently revitalize nature and thus overcome death. The dark, grave-like abode of the Wight is in sharp contrast to the "clean grass" outside where Tom takes Frodo (I, 154). Regardless of what we think the meaning of Tom Bombadil is, he probably is not intended as a "character delineation," for he is even less human than the Ents.

Tom shares at least one characteristic with the two monsters: his indifference to the ring. For him, as for the Balrog and Shelob, it has no power to do either good or evil. He is interested only in sustaining life and fostering the enjoyment of it; they care only for destruction or, in Shelob's case, for satisfying the appetite. And none of the three

[8] C. S. Lewis, "The Dethronement of Power," above, p. 15.

willingly acknowledges any other creature as his master. All three possess an independence that places them outside the central moral concern of the story—the destruction of the Ring. Their amorality, like their nonhumanity, reveals them as allegorical principles: Tom of life or nature, Shelob of death or blind appetite, and the Balrog of a central disorder that no creature can withstand.[9]

We could object to Tolkien's inclusion of Bombadil and the two monsters because they are principles rather than personalities. But allegory in a work of this sort need not be an artistic failure. Tolkien does fail with these two, however, not because he chose to dehumanize them, but because he failed to make them convincing. Treebeard, for example, is much more interesting than Tom Bombadil, and the orcs more fearsome than the Balrog.

Although we could not call the adventures with the Balrog and with Shelob dull, they both seem to fail, not in execution but in conception. Tolkien has invented these monsters rather than created them from the raw material of folklore as he did his other creatures. We are unable to believe in the Balrog because we have no foundation either outside the work or in it. Dwarfs, orcs, and elves are familiar enough to most readers to stimulate a response. Other creatures, including hobbits, the Ringwraiths, and the Dark Lord himself are fully developed within the trilogy. Not so with the Balrog. There he is, all of a sudden, whiffling and burbling, a *Diabolus ex machina*, when the orcs were foe enough. He is not dull, but the excitement is on the surface, and we only half believe Gandalf when he cries, " 'Fly! This is a foe beyond any of you' " (I, 344).

Shelob is better executed than her counterpart, but both episodes are artistically weak. For sheer terror, they are on

[9] The ideas on the significance of these three creatures were suggested to me by Professor Rose Zimbardo.

a level with the invention of dozens of science-fiction writers, but terror is not enough. Nor is the argument that only such supernatural creatures could cause Gandalf's death or Frodo's paralysis, for there is still the feeling that these demons are not real. They are unreal because they are extraneous to the traditional framework of the story.

I think that Tolkien failed with his extra-fabulous monsters because he himself did not believe in them. On the other hand, he did, and still does, believe in elves, dwarfs, hobbits, orcs, and Ents, and it is these, along with the men, who really come alive. And a good portion of this vitality comes, I think, not just from the author's potent imagination, but from a combination of that with the centuries-old traditions in the northern mind which are capable of endless revitalization.

That Tolkien believes in elves, or in the idea of Faërie, the realm of fairies, is inferred from his fairy-story essay. And that he believes that there is a spirit which dwells in growing things is suggested by his Introductory Note to *Tree and Leaf*. A neighbor's poplar tree was cut down for the crime of being "large and alive. I do not think it had any friends, or any mourners, except myself and a pair of owls."[10] I do not of course mean that Tolkien is so naive as to believe in them in the same way that he would believe in, say, elephants or termites. Rather, it is a state of mind, a quality of kinship with a primal essence and with nature. Thus it is that his characters who are on the side of good are closely identified with and appreciate nature,[11] and those

[10] Tolkien, *Tree and Leaf* (London, 1964), p. 5.

[11] Patricia Meyer Spacks, "Power and Meaning in *The Lord of the Rings*," above, pp. 84 ff. Mrs. Spacks mentions that the good people are usually vegetarians. This seems true, except in one instance when Sam cooks rabbit stew for Frodo (II, 261 ff.). In view of the rabbit-like nature of hobbits—the name is likely a portmanteau of *hob* (a variant of Rob, as in Robin Goodfellow) and *rabbit*—this scene strikes me as a bit cannibalistic.

on the bad are associated with barrenness and are hostile
to growing things. This contrast is first developed in Tom
Bombadil and the Barrow-wight. Sam the gardener is opposed to Ted Sandyman the miller, whose new mill in the
Sharkey regime looms up "in all its frowning and dirty
ugliness: a great brick building straddling the stream, which
it fouled with a steaming and stinking outflow" (III, 296).
Among the wizards, Gandalf is friend to the forests and to
Bombadil, but Saruman, according to Treebeard, "has a
mind of metal and wheels; and he does not care for growing
things, except as far as they serve him for the moment" (II,
76). This rather oversimplified relationship between good
and evil seems to be without exception.

Since hobbits and Ents[12] are essentially Tolkien's creations, not inventions, I shall look more closely at elves,
dwarfs, and orcs. Though no broadly inclusive category
can be drawn for dwarfs and elves, some generalizations
can be made. In Norse folklore, where these creatures are
most fully developed, elves were generally thought of as
good and friendly to men. Dwarfs, on the other hand, were
less esteemed, for they frequently sought to do mischief to
men. Trolls were a larger manifestation of the dwarf family.
Elves, as in Tolkien, prefer forest-homes, while dwarfs live
in hills or in the ground and sometimes under water. They
are traditionally masters of metallurgy, and many of the
swords of mythology were forged by them.[13] There seems
to be little tradition for elves as craftsmen, although

[12] There is evidence, though hardly a tradition, for hobbit-like dwellings
in the British Isles. The Picts of the third and fourth centuries A.D.
are thought to have lived in underground homes, or *souterrains*. See
F. T. Wainwright, *The Problem of the Picts* (New York, 1955), pp.
90-91. On Ents, we might compare Robert Graves, *The White
Goddess: A Historical Grammar of Poetic Myth* (New York, 1948),
who gives his version of a Celtic poem called "Câd Goddeu: 'The
Battle of the Trees,'" pp. 16ff.

[13] Keightley, pp. 63, 67.

Tolkien's elves fashioned the Rings of power and Aragorn's sword.

Tolkien's dwarfs are, in the main, traditional. In addition to their diminutive size, their underground homes, and their craftsmanship, they have a monarchical social order, have great stores of wealth, and are gifted with great strength.[14] Tolkien makes use of all of these characteristics. There is an interesting divergence, however. Dwarfs in folklore are more often than not mounted on steeds, suited to their size,[15] but Gimli is afraid of horses and would rather walk. Perhaps he is simply wary of such a large one as that offered by the Rohirrim, for he clings to Legolas as nervously as "Sam Gamgee in a boat" (II, 42).

The enmity between elves and dwarfs does not seem to be traditional, but Tolkien has created a long-standing feud between the two races and has made effective use of it. Legolas the elf is a creature of the woods and Gimli of the ground. The friendship which they eventually develop is a significant fusion of two elements of nature, already largely fused in the hobbits, who live in the ground and cultivate plants. The friendship of the elf and the dwarf is sealed when they convince each other of the beauty of the realms they each love. They make a bargain that Legolas will visit the caverns and Gimli the Forest of Fangorn, each to enjoy the unaccustomed beauties (II, 153).

Of the significant creatures, the orcs remain. What they are is never really clear. Treebeard says they were made by "the Enemy in the Great Darkness, in mockery of . . . Elves," just as trolls are counterfeits of Ents (II, 89). There is ample tradition to support the existence of such beasts; certain variants in dwarf lore were known as Cornish mine

[14] Vernon J. Harward, Jr., *The Dwarfs of Arthurian Romance and Celtic Tradition* (Leiden, The Netherlands, 1958), p. 19.
[15] Ibid., p. 111.

goblins—" 'miserable, little, withered, dried up creatures' "
with " 'big, ugly heads with red or grey locks, squintan
[sic] eyes, hook noses, and mouths from ear to ear.' "[16]
Another, more flexible, tradition is the generally later medieval concept of the Wild Man, which abounds in medieval
art. He was "a hairy man curiously compounded of human
and animal traits, without, however, sinking to the level
of an ape."[17] He is that same wild man whose character
was ameliorated into the Noble Savage, but in the Middle
Ages, he was merely a savage, incapable of intelligent
speech, of upright posture, and of Grace.[18]

Medieval theologians had considerable difficulty in accounting for the wild man, since he did not seem to belong
on the Chain of Being as a separate species. Therefore, they
viewed his state as psychological rather than theological,
brought to his condition by loss of mind or extreme hard-
ship. He was thus not totally beyond Grace.[19] It is clear
that Gollum, perhaps Tolkien's most delightfully disgusting
creation, fits this pattern. The wild man, like Gollum,
usually lived alone, had no use for metallurgy, and ate
berries, acorns, and raw flesh.[20] Gollum also is in a depraved
condition as a result of having lost his humanity, and his
salvation, or rather the Middle-earth equivalent of it, is
not entirely impossible.

But wild men were not all bad. Unlike the creatures of
evil in the trilogy, they had a close identification with
nature, and a wild man's life was often bound up with

[16] Harward, pp. 31-32, quoting William Bottrell, *Traditions and Hearth-
side Stories of West Cornwall* (Penzance, 1873), p. 188.
[17] Richard Bernheimer, *Wild Men in the Middle Ages* (Cambridge, Mass.,
1952), p. 1.
[18] Ibid., pp. 4, 7-8. The most famous of these subhuman figures in literature is Caliban; and Nebuchadnezzar, in his sojourn in the wilderness,
was thought of as having temporarily become a wild man (pp. 11-13).
[19] Ibid., p. 8.
[20] Ibid., p. 9.

the life of a certain tree. Furthermore, they were good with animals and were often thought of as herdsmen. In some cases, especially when the state of wildness was intermittent—love sickness a cause more often than not—the wild man was a dispenser of wisdom, for he gleaned secrets from the forces of nature. Merlin, in some of the legends, was such a one.[21]

It is partially in the framework of this broad and flexible tradition that Tolkien created orcs. Even the name of that evil race is in tradition. It is from the Italic god of death and the underworld, Orcus, from whom the French got the word *ogre*;[22] and the word *orcus* occurs at least once in the Middle Ages referring specifically to the wild man.[23] But again Tolkien uses the elements he wants to use and makes a creature of his own. The normally hermit-like wild man becomes the gregarious orc, but each orc is savagely selfish and shows little spirit of cooperation. He is the dark counterpart to the elf and the dwarf, cutting down trees and desecrating caves, a symbolic embodiment of those people the author calls "orc-minded," whose speech is "dreary and repetitive with hatred and contempt, too long removed from good to retain even verbal vigour, save in the ears of those to whom only the squalid sounds strong" (III, 412).

Tolkien, then, makes effective use of two kinds of tradition: first, that which is the common heritage of the whole

---

[21] Ibid., pp. 13-14, 24-25. It is clear that Tolkien is in this tradition with the Woses, the Wild Men of Druadan Forest. They are of an ancient race and "have long ears and eyes; know all paths. . . . Wild men are wild, free," their headman says, "but not children. . . . I count many things: stars in sky, leaves on trees, men in the dark." They are bitter foes of orcs, whom they call *gorgûn*. The chief urges: ". . . you will kill *gorgûn* and drive away bad dark with bright iron, and Wild Men can go back to sleep in the wild woods." (III, 106-107). This manifestation of the wild man is in the better sense, almost the Noble Savage.

[22] Douglass Parker, "Hwaet We Holbytla . . . ," *Hudson Review*, IX (Winter, 1956-57), 605n.

[23] Bernheimer, p. 43.

culture, such as the elves and dwarfs, and his main adaptation of this is in his ordering of the tradition, his creation of a credible and organic system on which to structure his story. Second, he has adapted certain flexible traditions, like the wild man, to his own thematic pattern of good and evil, and to this extent he creates a tradition. Where his creations fail, they are outside the organic traditional pattern of Tolkien's world, not simply because they do not belong there but because they seem to be in another plane of existence, as out of place as a time machine. But when he succeeds, he does so beautifully, and his creatures are as real as a next-door neighbor. Hobbits, for all I know, may be still around, just "hard to find" (I, 10), dwarfs may be still in the hills, and the elves may only be waiting for another age, there where they sailed from the Grey Havens to the land beyond the sea.

OLD ENGLISH IN ROHAN

John Tinkler

WHEN THE HOBBITS, WHOSE SPEECH IS REPRESENTED IN *The Lord of the Rings* by modern English, encounter the Rohirrim, they recognize some words and feel that the language of Rohan is somehow related to their own.[1] That Tolkien intends the horsemen of Rohan to speak something very close to Old English becomes obvious when one analyzes the names he gives to people, to places, and to things and recognizes as Old English the occasional words of the language which appear in the text. An examination of some of the names and a few of the words of Rohan in light of the Old English words from which Tolkien has derived them can give the reader of *The Lord of the Rings* a deeper appreciation of the attention which Tolkien has given to the peopling of Middle-earth.

I. NAMES OF PEOPLE

The name of a character in a book often tells the reader something about him. The name may be a capsule characterization or it may be merely allusive to profession, parentage, or personality. Tolkien uses names in both ways.

[1] J. R. R. Tolkien, "On Translation," part II of Appendix F (III, 414).

A. NAMES WITH ÉO-

A number of names among the Rohirrim begin with Éo-. An Old English word for "horse" is *eoh;* and *éo-* appears as a combining form in *éored*, "cavalry."[2] Hence, *Éo-* in the names of men of Rohan alludes to their fondness for, association with, and dependence upon horses.

The earliest name for the people of Rohan which appears in the documents used by Tolkien is *Éothéod* (III, 344 ff.). Old English *þeod* means "nation, people." "Horse-people" is a fitting name for the men of Rohan. Individuals in Rohan also have names which allude to their horsemanship. The name of Éomer, the Third Marshal of Riddermark, seems to be particularly "horsey," since *mere* means "mare" in Old English and a related word *mearh* means "horse" or "steed." Éomer's father was Éomund, "a great lover of horses and hater of Orcs" (III, 351). *Mund* means "hand" and, by metaphorical extension, "protection, protector." Éomund, then, is a fitting name for a chief marshal.[3] Éomund's daughter, Éomer's sister, is named Éowyn, "delight in horses." *Wyn* means "joy, pleasure" in Old English. A member of Éomund's *éored* is called Éothain; OE *þegn* means "a follower of a great man."

B. OTHER OLD ENGLISH NAMES IN ROHAN

Théoden is Lord of the Mark who leads the Riders to victory at the Hornburg and is slain in the great battle on the fields of Pelennor. OE *þeoden* means "prince, king." Théoden's sister, wife of Éomund and mother of Éomer and Éowyn, was named Théodwyn, "joy of princes"; she was loved dearly by her brother and her father Thengel (OE *þengel*, "a prince.")

[2] Éored is the Rohirrim word for "a troop of horse" (II, 37, 39).
[3] *Marshal* is itself a word associated semantically and etymologically with horses.

Gandalf is called by several different names in *The Lord of the Rings*. Éomer calls him Gandalf Grayhame (II, 37). Grayhame is a modernization of the Old English *græghama*, literally "gray covering." He is referred to frequently as Gandalf the Grey. Wormtongue,[4] Théoden's evil counsellor, calls Gandalf *Láthspell* and then translates the epithet as "Ill-news." "Ill news" is a good translation of Old English *laðspell*, "a painful, grievous story."

Gandalf does not let Wormtongue badmouth him and get away with it. Gandalf, too, has names at his disposal. He refers to Wormtongue as Gríma, son of Gálmód, and says, "A witless worm have you become. Therefore be silent, and keep your forked tongue behind your teeth."[5] In Old English, *gríma* means "a spectre" and also "a mask." The epithet "mask" is as appropriate to the man as "Wormtongue" because he has indeed been wearing a mask before Théoden, pretending to serve him while serving Saruman. *Gálmód*, "licentious," appears twice in Old English poetry. Wormtongue's names and his lineage point up his villainy.

Several other personal names in Rohan obviously come from Old English words. Háma, the Door ward, is named from Old English *hám*, "home." Eorl, the first of the Kings of the Mark (III, 349), has a name which in Old English means "man of high rank." Gamling, an "old man" who guards the dike at Hornburg (II, 136), is aptly named: OE *gamol*, "old," cf. *geongling*, "young person." Baldor, who recklessly vowed to walk the Paths of the Dead, takes his name from OE *baldor*, "prince, ruler" (literally, "bolder"). Dernhelm, the *nom de guerre* of Éowyn, is from *derne*, "secret," and *helm*, "helmet." Each of the names of the

---

[4] This name is a modernization. See III, 414. The name, if it occurred in Old English, would be **wyrmtunge*.

[5] II, 118. Gríma seems, indeed, to be Wormtongue's real name. See II, 120.

Kings of the Mark (III, 349-352) can be analyzed as an Old
English word or compound. Clearly, in name-giving the men
of the Mark spoke Old English.

II. NAMES OF PLACES

Many of the place names in Rohan correspond to place
names which occur in Old English or are compounded of
Old English elements. The name the Rohirrim give their
own country, the *Riddermark*, seems to be related to Old
English *ridda*, "horseman," and *mearc*, "boundary." After
all, Rohan was given to the Éothéod by the kings of Gondor
so that the horsemen could protect Gondor, provide a
stronghold on the Northwest. Hornburg, the mountain fastness, can be analyzed as *horn*, "pinnacle," and *burg*, "fortified place." Edoras, the name of the courts of Théoden,
seems to come from Old English *edor*, "dwelling house."
Old English *edoras* would be plural, "houses." The great
golden hall of Théoden is called Meduseld, and *Meduseld*,
"mead-house, a house where feasting takes place," appears
in *Beowulf*.

Other place names in the language of Rohan refer to
places which have other names in other tongues. The name
in Rohan for Lórien, the Elvish woods, is Dwimordene,
aptly so, since *dwimor* means "delusion, allusion, appari-
tion" and *dene* means "valley, dale." Saruman's stronghold
is called Isengard, OE *isen*, "iron," and *geard*, "court, dwelling." The men of the Mark call Minas Tirith in Gondor,
Mundburg, "fortified place of protection." Several other
place names in Rohan have Old English words behind them;
the ones discussed are representative.[6]

---

[6] II, 160 gives a bit of Tolkien's own discussion of place names. Old
English *orþanc* means "skillful contrivance."

III. NAMES OF HORSES AND OF WEAPONS

Shadowfax, the name of the horse Gandalf rides, is a "modernization" (III, 414). His name in the language of the Rohirrim was probably Sceadufeax—Old English *sceadu*, "shadow," and *feax*, "hair of the head." The ancestor of Shadowfax and all the great horses of the Kings of the Mark was called Felaróf (III, 346). Old English *fela* means "very" and *róf* means "strong, valiant." At least two others of the horses of Rohan have names that are simply Old English words or compounds made from Old English. Hasufel, "a great dark-grey horse" (II, 42) lent to Aragorn is Greyhide —OE *hasu*, "grey, ash-colored," and *fel*, "hide." Legolas and Gimli (unwillingly) ride on Arod—OE *arod*, "quick, swift."

Two of the swords of Rohan which are given names are Herugrim and Gúthwinë. Herugrim is the ancient blade of Théoden. Old English *heorugrim* means "very fierce, cruel, sharp." Gúthwinë is Éomer's sword. Old English *guðwine* means "friend in battle." The great men of Rohan, like the heroes of Old English poetry, wield weapons with names and the names are Old English.

IV. WORDS AND PHRASES

A few pieces of Old English in Rohan are not associated altogether with names. The word *éored*, which the language of Rohan shares with Old English, has already been mentioned, and *mearas*, the name by which the royal descendants of Felaróf are called, is simply a plural form of OE *mearh*. The flowering grass, *Simbelmynë*, which Gandalf calls "Evermind" (II, 111) could well have been an Anglo-Saxon herb (though it was not) since *simbel*, "continual," and *myne*, "mind," are both good Old English words. When

Théoden shakes off some of the Wormtongue-induced languor and chants a war cry, Éomer cries, *"Westu Théoden hál!"* (II, 122). This part of Éomer's speech is italicized in the text, indicating that he is speaking the language of Rohan, which here, is simply Old English. Éomer has said, "Be thou healthy, Théoden!" When Éowyn passes the cup, offering it first to the king, as is proper,[7] she says, *"Ferthu Théoden hál!"* This is Old English for, "Go thou Théoden healthy!" The language of Rohan not only "resembles" Old English, it is Old English.

Clearly Tolkien has drawn upon Old English in giving speech to the people of Rohan. The common reader may not see in the *-wyn* of Éowyn's name any "joy" at all unless he knows what "winsome" means. Still, the common reader can sense a consistency in the names given to people, places, and things and can see that the men of Rohan speak a language of their own, even though they are also able to communicate in Westron. In a work such as *The Lord of the Rings*, in which peoples of many different languages are depicted, the differentiation is quite difficult. Tolkien has succeeded in depicting the men of Rohan as a separate people by using an archaic form of English. Moreover, he has provided for the reader who knows the Old English language and literature an added richness in connotation and allusion.

---

[7] See *Beowulf*, 11. 615 ff. for a similar feast. The whole of "The King of the Golden Hall" seems dependent for much of its action and a good bit of its language upon the Heorot passages in *Beowulf*.

THE POETRY OF FANTASY:
VERSE IN *THE LORD OF THE RINGS*

Mary Quella Kelly

THOSE WHO HAVE BEEN SPELLBOUND BY J. R. R. TOLKIEN'S narrative technique in *The Lord of the Rings* will probably acknowledge that one of the most distinctive and memorable characteristics of that technique is the inclusion of abundant poetry. Songs and verses of as many types as there are races in Tolkien's created world are used to expand, to emphasize, to rarefy the prose, and always the verse utterances of the various characters are natural and appropriate to the context. But the *Ring* poetry does much more; many of the verses are charming, imaginative, even evocative and deserve to be enjoyed in their own right. This study will attempt to show that the poetry in the *Ring* trilogy not only strengthens and enhances the work, but in its diversity and quality testifies to the poetic skill of the author-poet.

To appreciate the *Ring* poetry fully, one must keep in mind the nature of the work. *The Lord of the Rings* fulfills the definition of "fairy-story" worked out by Tolkien in his essay "On Fairy-Stories." Thus Tolkien states that the fairy story deals with *Fantasy* and the *fantastic:* "with images of things that are not only 'not actually present,' but which are indeed not to be found in our primary world at all, or are generally believed not to be found there (p. 66f.)." He also points out that anyone with the fantastic device of human language can say "the green sun" so that it can be imagined or pictured. But the true subcreator of Fantasy must do more: "To make a Secondary World inside which the green sun will be credible, commanding Secondary Belief, will probably require labour and thought, and will certainly demand a special skill, a kind of elvish craft. Few attempt such difficult tasks. But when they are attempted and in any degree accomplished then we have a rare achievement of Art: indeed narrative art, story-making in its primary and most potent mode" (p. 68). No attentive reader can deny Tolkien's skill and breadth of imagination in creating a Secondary World where Secondary Belief is possible, whether or not he sees in that world any relevance to the Primary one. If the reader is willing to seek or to erect a bridge between the two worlds, then the work gains in significance for him. Numerous ethical and moral implications are present in the *Ring* trilogy for those who look; Patricia Spacks, for example, believes the work illustrates the fundamental problem of man's relation to the universe.[1] Robert Reilly sees it as explicitly romantic and Christian.[2] Such considerations, however, have little to do with the success of the Fantasy as such. They are concerned not with the achievement of Secondary Belief but with the yielding of primary meaning.

The fantastic world of the *Ring* trilogy has several races of beings, different from those in the Primary World, which continually remind the reader that this is an unreal world, a removed world, an unlike world. Creatures look, act, and communicate differently from real-world men. The communication difference most noticeable to readers is the frequent use of poetry to represent the spontaneous versification of utterances as well as the recitation or singing of poems fa-

[1] Patricia Spacks, "Power and Meaning in *The Lord of the Rings*," pp. 81-99 above.
[2] Robert J. Reilly, "Tolkien and the Fairy Story," pp. 128-150 above.

miliar to the characters. Poetry, then, is a means Tolkien has utilized to reinforce the remoteness and unreality of his work. Once the reader is immersed in the fantastic *Ring* world (or once he achieves Secondary Belief), he accepts, even expects, the poems, for he realizes that the creatures have been so made that poetry is one of their natural modes of expression. The verse functions in other ways as well. In the tension-ridden passages of the story it helps create esthetic distance. Verse modifies emotion because it renders language unlike the language of every day (of every day both in the fantastic world and in the reader's world). Most importantly, meter gives pleasure, and certainly the giving of pleasure is one of the chief aims of *The Lord of the Rings*.

I. HOBBIT POETRY

Simple and occasional are the words which best describe the poetry of the hobbits. The meter, diction, and imagery of their poems reflect their instinctive love for peace, quiet, and order. Reciting or singing verse is for them the most natural way to express their emotions, the basic and primary emotions associated with the recurrent situations in the lives of all beings. Hobbits sing when they are happy and comfortable, when they are sad and troubled, when they are fearful and desperate, and when they are angry and vexed. Although their poetry is diverse in subject matter, the hobbits' inventiveness with language is limited. They reuse old poems from the Shire, altering a word or phrase to fit the occasion, and repeat verses from other kinds of folk for which a tradition exists in the Shire. Bilbo Baggins is the composer of most of the "original" hobbit poems.

Usually the songs of the hobbits function within the context to heighten or intensify the mood of the story while also indicating the emotional state of the speaker or speakers.

The indication of the manner in which a particular song is sung is thus almost as important as the song itself. For example, Bilbo's eight-line farewell to Gandalf (I, 44) before departing for Rivendell is sung softly in the dark "in a low voice, as if to himself." Frodo later repeats the verse when he, Sam, and Pippin are on their way out of the Shire (I, 82-83). The song comes to Frodo and suddenly he speaks, "aloud but as if to himself, . . . slowly." Although we see the travelers' reluctance to journey in both instances reflected in the hushed tones in which they repeat the poem, Frodo's hesitancy is more pronounced. Bilbo claims he is as happy as he has ever been as he goes off into retirement on "The Road [that] goes ever on and on." He will be "Pursuing it with eager feet" even though he is not sure of its ultimate end. Frodo, on the other hand, by varying a single word in the song reveals his insecurity about undertaking his quest. He is pursuing the road "with weary feet." The uncertainty of his destination is far more forbidding to him than to Bilbo, but despite his weariness Frodo has the same stoic acceptance of his lot as his uncle. Even though he senses the importance of his part, he is not yet aware of all the "paths and errands" which will be involved in the "larger way" that leads to his goal.

The hobbits' innate love of singing is repeatedly illustrated. Frodo, Sam, and Pippin begin to hum softly, as hobbits "have a way of doing . . . especially when they are drawing near to home at night" (I, 86). The song which they sing shortly after setting out on their quest, however, is a walking-song rather than the usual supper-song or bed-song. Appropriately, "Bilbo had made the words, to a tune that was as old as the hills, and taught it to Frodo as they walked in the lanes of the Water-valley and talked about Adventure" (I, 86). The three stanzas of the song each have ten lines of iambic tetrameter couplets, though the latter four lines of the first two stanzas omit the first unstressed syllable. The rhythm is thus suited to a marching song, and the effect of the omission is to add vigor and emphasis to the concluding lines of stanzas one and two. In the first stanza, the first six lines refer to the comforts of home which have been left behind and the beauties of nature which will be met; the last four lines urge that the hobbits "Let them pass!" In the second stanza there is a consolation:

> And though we pass them by today,
> Tomorrow we may come this way
> And take the hidden paths that run
> Towards the Moon or to the Sun.

But again the last four lines urge that for now these pleasures must be forsaken. The third stanza alludes to the quest ahead "through shadows to the edge of night," after which they can leave behind the world. There is a slight slackening of pace in the concluding four lines—only the first and third drop the initial unstressed syllable—as the hobbits sing of things most comforting to them.

> Fire and lamp, and meat and bread,
> And then to bed! And then to bed!

At the end of the trilogy, as Frodo, accompanied by Sam, is on his way to meet the Elven folk who are to take him on their voyage to the Grey Havens, he sings the old walking-song softly to himself with this significant variation of the second stanza (III, 308):

> And though I oft have passed them by,
> A day will come at last when I
> Shall take the hidden paths that run
> West of the Moon, East of the Sun.

Thus the vague "tomorrow" of the earlier version has finally arrived for Frodo; the quest complete, he is free to take the hidden path to everlasting peace. The walking-song serves to relate the beginning and the end of Frodo's journey more effectively than could a prose statement of his emotional state. The simple words eloquently express his innermost longing for rest and security, one of those primary desires common to all feeling creatures both inside and outside Tolkien's world. Verse in these instances gives poignancy to the expression of the feeling which otherwise might have seemed trite nostalgia.

Several of the hobbits' songs express the effusion of joy and good cheer. For them there is no better way to celebrate a happy moment than with a merry song. Thus they sing cheerfully before arriving at Farmer Maggot's when they find that the Elves have filled their bottles with a delicious honey brew (I, 99). The exuberant bath-song sung by Pippin after the hobbits' arrival at Crickhollow is another example (I, 111). The four ballad-like stanzas of the poem praise the hot water of the bath above all the uses of water:

> O! Water Cold we may pour at need
> down a thirsty throat and be glad indeed;
> but better is Beer, if drink we lack,
> and Water Hot poured down the back.

Sometimes the joyful hobbit songs are automatic responses to situations not examined intellectually by the singer. Thus Merry and Pippin compose a song of celebration, modeled on the dwarf song that started Bilbo on the adventures recorded in *The Hobbit*, when they receive permission from Frodo to accompany him and Sam to Rivendell and perhaps beyond. Although they sing enthusiastically of venturing into the unknown, it is evident that they have little concept of what lies ahead. They conclude:

> We must away: We must away!
> We ride before the break of day!

175

After praising the song, Frodo adds that there is much for them to do before going to bed. Pippin asks, already forgetting the last line of his song, " 'Do you really mean to start before the break of day?' " (I, 116).

Other hobbit states of mind are likewise indicated by the singing of songs, or sometimes by the attempt to sing a song, in the face of danger. Frodo tries to encourage his companions, oppressed by the force of the ill wood in the Old Forest (I, 123) but is unsuccessful. His voice begins as only a murmur, and by the time he reaches the seventh line, "For east or west all woods must fail . . . ," his voice fades into silence. The failure of his song signifies Frodo's inability to relieve the heavy gloom about him. Much later in the story, Sam, bearing the ring, despairs of ever again finding Frodo in the tower of Cirith Ungol. Weary and defeated, he sits down in the quiet darkness. "And then softly, to his own surprise, there at the vain end of his long journey and his grief, moved by what thought in his heart he could not tell, Sam began to sing" (III, 184). His singing, unconsciously undertaken, causes new strength to well up inside the exhausted hobbit until his voice rings out in a lyric statement of his indomitable courage. In the first eight-line stanza, the words depict the joys and beauties of the western lands. In the second stanza Sam reveals his despair in his surroundings which directly contrast with the previous ideal scence:

> Though here at journey's end I lie
>   in darkness buried deep,
> beyond all towers strong and high,
>   beyond all mountains steep,
> above all shadows rides the Sun
>   and Stars for ever dwell:
> I will not say the Day is done,
>   nor bid the Stars farewell.

Although despairing for himself, Sam yet affirms those things which he has learned to associate with good—the sun and stars of the western lands. Here, as before, the poem successfully reveals the state of mind of the character. At the same time it causes the reader's attention to linger in fuller appreciation of Sam's situation before proceeding with the narrative. The song has another function in the structure of of the story, for the orcs who overhear Sam's singing lead him to Frodo.

Another hobbit poem which depicts the state of mind of its speaker is Bilbo's at Rivendell. After instructing Frodo just before his departure to bring back all the news, old songs, and tables that he can, Bilbo turns to the window and sings (I, 291-292) a ballad-like song. In his advanced years he has become very sleepy; his song reveals his preoccupation with the stuff of dreams—with what he has seen, with what he has never seen, with people long ago, and with "people who will see a world/ that [he] shall never know." Despite his dreamy state, Bilbo's concluding stanza evidences his prior interest in the fateful quest:

> But all the while I sit and think
>   of times there were before,
> I listen for returning feet
>   and voices at the door.

Other kinds of hobbit poetry also have specific functions in the story. Bilbo's riddle about Aragorn, which he recites at the Council of Elrond to settle Boromir's doubts, is just as its speaker admits, "not very good perhaps, but to the point" (I, 261). The eight-line poem telescopes many important facts about the mysterious man—his wanderings, his age, his coming from the shadows, his broken sword, and his eventual coronation. The verse is sufficiently vague so that only those who have full knowledge about Aragorn's role in the forthcoming events completely understand it.

Frodo's only self-composed song in the trilogy is the six-stanza ballad he sings in Lothlórien lamenting the loss of Gandalf, his friend and guide. Having heard the Elves sing about the beloved wizard, "his thought took shape in a song that seemed fair to him; yet when he tried to repeat it to Sam only snatches remained, faded as a handful of withered leaves" (I, 374). The "snatches" reveal the hobbits' dependence on Gandalf. Frodo begins by referring to Gandalf's visits to the Shire, then to his far travels, his gift of tongues, his power, his wisdom and temperament, and finally, his brave death. Sam, Frodo's listener, in his usual child-like eagerness adds a stanza celebrating Gandalf's splendid fireworks displays. Sam, although as well-meaning as his master, is an incompetent poet; his phrasing is clumsy and he alters the simple rhyme scheme from abab to aabb.

The hobbits' innate love of poetry and song sometimes permits them to enjoy nonsense verse which some readers are likely to find insufferable. Two of Sam's verses are especially trying. The first is the Troll song (I, 219-220), which Sam correctly characterizes: " 'It ain't what I call proper poetry, if you understand me: just a bit of nonsense.' " His song has bad rhymes and crude nonsense words; the story about Tom's mistaking the stone troll for a live one, however, is amusing and consequently makes all the more ridiculous the hobbits' similar error. While Sam and Frodo are being led by Gollum to Mordor, the subject of Oliphaunts is brought up, giving Sam an opportunity to repeat the familiar Shire rhyme about the strange creatures (II, 254-255). Here the nonsense has the effect of helping Frodo to decide whether to follow Gollum further. "He had laughed in the midst of all his cares when Sam trotted out the old fireside rhyme of *Oliphaunt*, and the laugh had released him from hesitation" (II, 255). Within twenty pages of narrative Sam's loyalty to his master and the quest is rewarded with an actual encounter with an Oliphaunt (II, 269).

One of the hobbits' nonsense poems provides a treat for lovers of Fantasy. "The Man in the Moon" poem recited by Frodo at the Prancing Pony is certainly Tolkien's Mother Goose *tour de force*. One suspects the author shared Bilbo's feeling for it, for we learn the poem was one that "Bilbo had been rather fond of (and indeed rather proud of, for he had made up the words himself)" (I, 170). Unlike the other nonsense poems in the work, this one relates to a verse familiar to all readers of *The Lord of the Rings*, who thus gain increased pleasure from the clever inventiveness of Tolkien and at the same time identify themselves with the inn customers who appreciate Frodo's recitation. Something special is required for a hobbit to become the center of attention at the inn. The immense success of Frodo's verses results in an increase of boisterous good cheer so that all the more striking is the abrupt change in atmosphere occasioned by his leaping into the air and slipping on the ring. Frodo's disappearance, brought on by a foolish action suggested by the poem itself, arouses suspicions in some and confirms suspicions in others. The merry nonsense at both the inn in the poem and the inn at Bree is thus silenced.

II. TOM BOMBADIL'S SONGS

Gay, lighthearted nonsense with another dimension abounds in the songs of Tom Bombadil, a singular creature even within the singular world of *The Lord of the Rings*. Tom, the "Master of wood, water, and hill" (I, 135), is the voice of nature. He describes himself to the hobbits: " 'Eldest, that's what I am . . . . Tom was here before the river and the trees; Tom remembers the first raindrop and the first acorn' " (I, 142). Sound rather than sense is important in Tom's poetry because he, like nature, is nonrational. One cannot ask him what he means by "Hey dol! merry dol! ring a dong dillo!" (I, 130) any more than one can ask why a starfish has five points. Nonsensical words and syllables which are pleasing to the ear or which simply fill out the measure are a normal part of his discourse. Tom's communications do not require the ingenious compressiveness of metaphysical poetry; rather, his timelessness permits him to be as repetitious and diffuse as the luxuriant nature for which he speaks. But just as nature may be coherent and intelligible, so too Tom's speech and singing contain meaning for those with whom he wishes to communicate. When the hobbits first perceive his "deep glad voice," it seems to be singing nonsense only. As Tom approaches them, two of whom are trapped in the old willow, his nonsense-words are intermingled with the meaningful words of his song. He sings in couplets—sometimes poorly rhymed—about his Goldberry and all the beauties of nature associated with her, particularly sunlight, starlight, and flowers. After releasing the captives from the old willow, Tom encourages all the hobbits, who are "as if enchanted" (I, 130) by his singing, to follow him home. He bids them to watch for the light in the window after the sun sinks.

> Fear neither root nor bough! Tom goes on before you.
> Hey now! merry dol! We'll be waiting for you!

The irregular and nonrational rhythm of his song suggests Tom's motion as he hops and dances down the lane toward home.

Goldberry, Tom's complement, welcomes the weary travelers in her "clear voice, as young and as ancient as Spring,

like the song of a glad water flowing down into the night from a bright morning in the hills"—most fitting for the daughter of the river. She invites the hobbits to join with her in rejoicing for nature, whose spokesman has just saved them from peril:

> Now let the song begin! Let us sing together
> Of sun, stars, moon and mist, rain and cloudy weather,
> Light in the budding leaf, dew on the feather,
> Wind on the open hill, bells on the heather,
> Reeds by the shady pool, lilies on the water:
> Old Tom Bombadil and the River-daughter! (I, 133)

Aside from the end-rhyme, there are few artificial devices in this nature-song. It is as uncontrived and untainted as the aspects of nature which it catalogues.

Frodo, moved by the song and appearance of Goldberry and experiencing a joy he does not understand, bursts out in a short song of praise for the river-daughter, representing her in images of nature (I, 135). Later in a song that depicts symbolically the change of seasons (I, 137), Tom explains how he happened to find the hobbits. He gathers the last of the "green leaves and lilies white" before the winter snows for Goldberry to keep flowering at her feet and will not venture out again until the time for rebirth:

> not till the merry spring, when the River-daughter
> dances down the withy-path to bathe in the water.

Then when the snow has melted, the growing forces of nature are reactivated; Tom and Goldberry leave their house and pass among living things again.

The rhyme which Tom teaches the hobbits to sing if they should fall into danger after departing from him is an invocation to nature:

> Ho! Tom Bombabil, Tom Bombadillo!
> By water, wood and hill, by reed and willow,
> By fire, sun and moon, harken now and hear us!
> Come, Tom Bombadil, for our need is near us! (I, 145)

Tom promises to renew life—symbolized by water, wood, and hill—and to provide warmth and light—symbolized by fire, sun, and moon—when his aid is needed. The hobbits are soon forced into a situation which directly contrasts with Tom and his world when they are attacked by a representative of death, a Barrow-wight, on the cold, dark, foggy Barrow-downs. Frodo is chilled to the marrow when he hears the horrible dreary voice of the Wight rise from a murmur to the "grim, hard cold words, heartless and miserable," of his incantation. The verse is a negation of life and nature, a denial of Tom Bombadil and Goldberry:

> Cold be hand and heart of bone,
> and cold be sleep under stone:
> never more to wake on stony bed,
> never, till the Sun fails and the Moon is dead. . . . (I, 152)

After Frodo finds the strength to repeat the verse which summons his champion, Tom banishes the Wight with one of his "stronger songs" (I, 153) which commands the spirit of death and darkness to "Vanish in the sunlight!/ Shrivel like the cold mist" (I, 153). Bent on his important task, Tom utters no nonsense words and troubles not with rhyme. Again serious, Tom attends to Merry, Pippin, and Sam, who are "deadly" asleep, commanding them to awake and be warm (I, 154). When it is evident they will recover, Tom returns to the use of nonsense words in calling the horses: "Hey! now! Come hoy now! Whither do you wander? . . ." (I, 155).

Thus Tom Bombadil's poems, although they may be partly nonsense, have special functions in the structure of the story: they cheer the hobbits, encourage them in the pursuit of their quest, and even save them from danger. Early in the trilogy the forces of nature which they celebrate are allied with the forces of good.

III.   THE ELVISH POEMS

Of the dozens of poems in *The Lord of the Rings*, the most consistently musical are the elvish poems. In them Tolkien seems to have toyed with combinations of sound and sense; many of his results are a prosodist's delight. At the House of Elrond Bilbo explains to the four younger hobbits who have just arrived that it is difficult to stay awake there during the chanting of verses until one becomes accustomed to it. He adds, " 'Not that hobbits would ever acquire quite the elvish appetite for music and poetry and tales. They seem to like them as much as food, or more' " (i, 250). Because the elven folk enjoy hearing songs, and because the Elves and elvish lore share an important role in the trilogy, it is not surprising that the author has included so many examples of their songs. Many of them are repeated by other kinds of creatures who have inhabited Middle-earth for much shorter periods of time than have the Elves. Regardless of the singer or teller, the elvish poems always convey the feeling of remoteness, both from the Primary World of the reader and from the rest of the Secondary World of Tolkien's creation. The poems often celebrate persons and places of long ago when Middle-earth was very different from its state at the time of the Quest. The favorite images in elvish poetry are light and brightness, especially starlight; the favorite themes are romantic love and physical beauty. Although the Elves are fading toward their eventual extinction at the end of the story, their poetry reveals their attempts to cling to past achievements and to glorify the light which they yet bear and bring to other creatures of Middle-earth. Their songs most often function as contrasts to surrounding gloom and give the dejected, spiritually darkened listeners a new insight, a fresh glimpse of themselves and their roles in the great Quest. Elvish songs are a panacea for the kind of depression expressed by Sam on Weathertop: " 'I would dearly like to hear more about Elves; the dark seems to press so close' " (I, 203).

The first of the elvish songs in the trilogy is that sung by the exiled Elves who meet Frodo, Sam, and Pippin shortly after they begin their adventure (I, 88-89). The song expresses the Elves' homage to Elbereth, their ancient queen who has departed from Middle-earth. By first referring to her as "snow-white," Tolkien draws on his readers' associations of feminine brilliance and beauty with the traditional Snow White. The four ballad stanzas alternate between abab and aabb rhyme schemes. The first and third refer to Elbereth's effect on earth; she, the provider of the stars, is addressed as

> O Light to us that wander here
> Amid the world of woven trees!

The second and fourth stanzas invoke the queen by her elvish names, Gilthoniel and Elbereth, and assure her of the singers' devotion:

> We still remember, we who dwell
> In this far land beneath the trees,
> Thy starlight on the Western Seas.

The whiteness, brightness, and clarity associated both with Elbereth and the stars receive repeated emphasis. In this short poem there are four instances of alliteration[3]—one of the sound techniques Tolkien frequently employs in elvish songs.

On the journey from Bree to Rivendell, Sam surprises the company by singing part of Bilbo's translation of the elvish song, "The Fall of Gil-galad" (I, 197-198). The hobbit version retains the sad wistful mood of the Elves' own songs and has more deliberate sound effects than most hobbit poetry.[4]

During the dreary and fear-ridden night spent on Weathertop, Strider chants to his hobbit companions the charming story of Tinúviel, the foremother of Elrond. The subject is appropriate at this point because they are traveling to Elrond's house; even more relevant, however, is the similarity between the situation in the poem and that of the trilogy, for an elvish princess will forsake her immortality to become the wife of Strider, a mortal man. Strider characterizes the song: " 'It is a fair tale, though it is sad, as are all the tales of Middle-earth, and yet it may lift up your hearts' " (I, 203). The song is indeed one of the fairest in the entire work. The nine stanzas of eight iambic-tetrameter lines each have the complicated rhyme scheme of abacbabc. The poetic narrative, a compression of the prose story with which Strider explicates his song, begins with a description of the natural perfection of summer, the ideal setting of the elvish maid and her accompanying starlight.

> The leaves were long, the grass was green,
> The hemlock-umbels tall and fair,

---

[3] "World" and "women," 1. 4; "bright" and "breath," 1. 6; "hand" and "her," 1. 10; and "blossom" and "bloom," 1. 12.

[4] There are three instances of alliteration ("him" and "harpers," 1. 2; "fair" and "free," 1. 3; and "long" and "lance," 1. 5) and four of assonance ("him" and "sing," 1. 2; "between" and "Sea," 1. 4; "ago" and "rode," 1. 9; and "darkness" and "star," 1. 11).

> And in the glade a light was seen
>> Of stars in shadow shimmering.
> Tinuviel was dancing there
>> To music of a pipe unseen,
> And light of stars was in her hair,
>> And in her raiment glimmering.

But the picture of summery bliss is undercut in the next stanza by the arrival of Beren from the "mountains cold"; he wandered lost, "alone and sorrowing," until he saw Tinuviel. He was enchanted, as the third stanza relates, but he could not reach her in time:

> She lightly fled on dancing feet
> And left him lonely still to roam
> In the silent forest listening.

He searched for her during the fall (stanza 4) and the winter (stanza 5), and finally in spring she returned (stanza 6). Before she could part from him again, Beren, calling her by her elvish name, laid a spell on her which led to her doom (stanza 7), for the immortal Tinuviel fell in love with him, a mortal man (stanza 8). The two lovers experienced many hardships and sorrows, each the opposite of the idyllic circumstances of their meeting in the elven land: "stony mountains cold and grey," "halls of iron and darkling door," and "woods of nightshade morrowless" (stanza 9). Tinuviel chose mortality so that she could rejoin Beren.

> The Sundering Seas between them lay,
>> And yet at last they met once more,
> And long ago they passed away
>> In the forest singing sorrowless.

The poem thus moves from the awakening and development of love in the succession of specific scenes to its ultimate fulfillment in the vague and uncertain other-life beyond the Sea. Strider's song, though a translation of an elvish mode "hard to render in our Common Speech," is nevertheless anything but the "rough echo" for which he apologizes. The poem abounds in musical effects. There are twenty instances of alliteration in the short lines, two of them triple alliteration.[5] Tolkien has frequently used consonant sounds especially suitable to the context. The sounds of the many aspirates (*h* and *wh*), voiceless dentals (*f* and *th*), and voiceless sibilants (*s* and *sh* and *ch*) help to create images of the breathlessness of the lovers' chase. Even more prominent are the sonorant sounds of the hums (*n* and *m* and *ng*) and the liquids (*l* and *r*), all of which contribute to the resonance of many of the lines and make the poem the more suitable for chanting. Particularly effective for their sound effects are such phrases as "Elven-river rolled" (1. 11), "woven woods in Elvenhome" (1. 21), and "Immortal maiden elven-wise" (1. 62). The texture of vowel sounds also contributes to the euphonious quality of the poem; meaning is not only stated but enacted, as these lines describing Tinuviel's song illustrate:

> Like rising lark, and falling rain,
> And melting water bubbling.
> (11. 43-44)

The suggestion of the sonorous quality of the song is conveyed by the collocation of long vowels and the initial *l*'s in the first line. The second line contains the onomatopoetic "bubbling" as well as the repetition of the *l*'s.

[5] "Leaves" and "long" and "grass" and "green," 1. 1; "shadow" and "shimmering," 1. 4; "came" and "cold," 1. 9; "lest" and "leaves," 1. 10; "river" and "rolled," 1. 11; "woven" and "woods," 1. 21; "left" and "lonely," 1. 23; "light" and "linden-leaves," 1. 26; "hidden hollows," 1. 28; "sighing sound," 1. 30; "wintry woodland," 1. 32; "mantle" and "moon," 1. 37; "hill-top high," 1. 38; "song" and "sudden," 1. 42; "Immortal maiden," 1. 62; "darkling door," 1. 67; "Sundering Seas," 1. 69; "met" and "more," 1. 70; and "singing sorrowless," 1. 72.

Perhaps the best stanza to examine for the sound effects is the fourth, which concerns sound:

> He heard there oft the flying sound
>   Of feet as light as linden-leaves,
> Or music welling underground,
>   In hidden hollows quavering,
> Now withered lay the hemlock-sheaves,
>   And one by one with sighing sound
> Whispering fell the beechen leaves
>   In the wintry woodland wavering.

The liquid consonants predominate. The *l*-sound, triply alliterating in line two, appears in every line but one (1. 6). Only two lines do not contain an *r*-sound. The soft consonant *w*, which triply alliterates in line eight, appears in four lines (1. 3 "welling," 1. 5 "withered," 1. 6 "one," as well as 1.8). In all these instances the consonant sounds contribute to some degree to the depiction of pleasant sounds. The initial *h*'s and *sh* (1. 1 "heard," 1. 4 "hidden hollows," and 1. 5 "hemlock-sheaves") suggest the panting of the running singer as well as the rustling of fallen leaves. Both "sighing" (1. 6) and "whispering" (1. 7) are onomatopoetic, and their imitative effects, like the other sound effects in the stanza, provide special suggestiveness entirely appropriate in the context of the poem. The sung story of beautiful creatures no longer known to either the primary or secondary audience seems the more remote. Furthermore, the language of the poem retains the most important characteristic of the elvish tongue, noticed by Frodo when Lady Arwen sang of Elbereth: "sweet syllables . . . like clear jewels of blended word and melody" (I, 250).

Other elvish poems contain sound effects which operate in much the same way as in the Tinuviel poem. In general, the noticeable frequency of sibilants, aspirants, and light

vowels—a characteristic common to the elvish poetry—
suggests the light, fading existence of the elves as well as the
particular circumstances of the Tinuviel story. Even Bilbo's
song about the wanderings of the mariner Eärendil during
the Elder Days (I, 246-249), while not as carefully structured as Strider's, nevertheless retains the sound-appeal of
the elvish songs. The irregular rhyme scheme and stanza
pattern and the frequently inverted word order ("Through
Evernight he back was borne" and "his wings him bore")
indicate Bilbo's lack of familiarity with the elvish modes.
His listeners at Rivendell congratulate him on his composition and ask him to repeat the verse, but there is a note of
sarcasm in their praise: " 'You know you are never tired of
reciting your own verses' " (I, 249).

In contrast to Bilbo, Legolas is a master of elvish song-
craft. Just after the ring companions cross the stream Nim-
rodel to enter Lothlórien, he sings to them of the maid who
long ago lived beside the stream (I, 354-355). The thirteen
irregular ballad stanzas contain the usual references to sunlight, starlight, and natural beauty, expressed in words
which reinforce the sense. Although the song is sad, its immediate effect is to refresh the listeners spiritually just as
their draughts from the stream refresh them physically.
Later in the trilogy, while recounting his march with Aragorn on the Paths of the Dead to Merry and Pippin, Legolas
pauses to sing of the plains of Lebennin. They were "dark
. . . grey wastes in the darkness" when Legolas last saw them,
but in the songs of his people they were green. The song,
contrasting with the mood of fearful gloominess of Legolas'
narrative, praises the silver streams, white lilies, and golden
bells, all signs of beauty and prosperity, in fields green with
the promise of life. Again we see the elvish preoccupation
with the days-that-were-once, the time before all things became gray both for the Elves and for all creatures. Legolas'

final song in Middle-earth is sung as he leaves the celebration at Cormallen for the Sea and then for Elvenhome (III, 234-235). The twelve lines of the poem, rhymed in couplets, express his joy in going home to "the voices of my people that have gone before me." Like the end of a melody that has been wound on a music box, the last lines of the song are longer and slower in tempo than the others, appropriately suggesting the gradual failing of the days of Legolas' people:

> In Eressëa, in Elvenhome that no man can discover,
>> Where the leaves fall not: land of my people for ever!

Sad and sweet is the sound of the voice of the elven Lady Galadriel in Lothlórien. Her singing makes Frodo consider the Elves in the way men of later days still at times do: "present and yet remote, a living vision of that which has already been left far behind by the flowing streams of Time" (I, 389). Galadriel's song of fourteen long, seven-foot lines bemoans the approach of winter, signifying both the seasonal winter and the decline of the reign of the Elves. She recalls the former days when she "sang of leaves, of leaves of gold, and leaves of gold there grew" (1. 1). The golden leaves had endured long "upon the branching years" (1. 7) during the summer of the Elves. Now it is fall, and "The leaves are falling in the stream, the River flows away" (1. 10) toward the Sundering Sea. Although Galadriel, like Legolas, longs to be on the far shore, she has almost despaired of reaching it:

> But if of ships I now should sing, what ship would come
>> to me,
> What ship would bear me ever back across so wide a Sea?

As Galadriel appears to be slipping away when the boats of Frodo and his company move onto the Great River, she sings again, this time in elvish (I, 394). The words, which tell of Varda, Queen of the Stars, provide the same kinds of musical effects noted in Strider's "Common Speech" poem. There are frequent alliteration, assonance, and consonance and a preponderance of sonorant consonants in the song.

Thus the songs of the fading Elves repeatedly capture musically the mood of beauty mingled with sadness which yet brings comfort and solace to the hearers. Touching the Phial of Galadriel in Cirith Ungol, Sam's tongue is loosened in the elvish song of Elbereth; he gains new strength to continue the Quest. At the conclusion of the story, the song of Elbereth (III, 308) is heard as if in answer to Frodo's singing the old marching song. Elrond and Galadriel have come to carry the Ring-bearer back with them over the sea to the Havens to join at last the departed Elves in everlasting comfort:

> Gilthoniel, A! Elbereth!
> We still remember, we who dwell
> In this far land beneath the trees
> The starlight on the Western Seas.

IV. THE ENT POETRY

The poems of the Ents are among the most interesting in *The Lord of the Rings* because they are so successfully adapted to Tolkien's fascinating tree-creatures. Treebeard explains to Merry and Pippin the peculiar nature of Ent speech: " ' It is a lovely language, but it takes a very long time to say anything in it, because we do not say anything in it, unless it is worth taking a long time to say, and to listen to' " (II, 68). Long lines and frequent repetition characterize Entish poetry. Often the teller has to curtail his poem or resort to a non-Entish version if he wants to finish it. In trying to recollect the poem of the "List of Living Creatures" (II, 67) to find where hobbits fit, Treebeard interjects many a "hm" and "hoom" before he gives up, saying, " 'It was a long list.' " Later he composes a suitable addition to the list which refers to the hobbits in typical wordiness:

> and hungry as hunters, the Hobbit children,
> the laughing-folk, the little people. (II, 191)

Striding through the woods with the hobbits as passengers, Treebeard bemoans the loss of the former free wandering of the Ents (II, 72). The first part of the well-structured poem contains long anapestic lines about each season's travels, interspersed with short iambic lines conveying Treebeard's former delight (11. 3, 6, 9, and 12). The last six lines, relating his present unhappiness in being confined to his own land, gradually become shorter, suggesting the limiting of the Ents' wanderings. Tree imagery is used throughout the poem, but most effectively in the concluding lines where it serves to combine the sense of ancientness of both trees and land:

> And I walk in Ambarona, in Tauremorna, in Aldalómë,
> In my own land, in the country of Fangorn,
> Where the roots are long,
> And the years lie thicker than the leaves
> In Tauremornalómë.

Bregalad (Quickbeam) sings of the fall of the rowan trees at the hands of the Orcs (II, 87). The eight iambic heptameter lines rhyme aaabbaaa. All but the first and last contain words linked by internal rhyme which compress and emphasize the narrative essence of the respective lines. Thus the rowan, once the bearer of the "fair" "hair" (1. 2) and "bright" rind and "light" leaves (1. 4), has now a "dead" "head" (1. 6), a "spilled" crown and "stilled" voice (1. 7).

Although the Ents do not like to be aroused, when provoked they can be violent, as the song they sing on the way to attack Isengard reveals (II, 88-89). The lines, iambic octameter except for the final two, are typically repetitious. The anticipation of fierce battle is seen in the many allusions to hardness and coldness. In contrast, the Ents themselves are afire with zeal: "For bole and bough are burning now, the furnace roars—we go to war!" (1. 4). The sound of the drumbeat is conveyed by the many plosives (*b*, *d*, *g*, *k*, *p*, *t*). Especially effective in this regard are the repetitive final lines:

> To Isengard with doom we come!
> With doom we come, with doom we come.

The most delightful of the songs sung by the Ents is not really Entish at all. Because, as Treebeard explains, the tale of the Entwives " 'would have been a very long song in Entish' " (II, 80), he sings a translation of an Elvish song (II, 80-81). The poem combines the different kinds of nature imagery associated with each of the two races—the light streams and gold sunlight of the Elves and the fruit, leaves, and boughs of the Ents. The Ents themselves make no songs about Entwives; it is as if their stout hearts are ashamed to indulge in sentimentality. They consequently are content to speak through the mode of the Elves to whom the sad theme of unfulfilled love is most familiar.

V. THE POETRY OF ARAGORN AND THE MEN OF ROHAN

The men who inhabit Middle-earth at the time of the events in *The Lord of the Rings* express themselves in poetry as much as the other creatures do. Aragorn, who eventually becomes king, is also a kingly poet to whom Tolkien has given some of the most strikingly effective songs in the work. Along with Legolas, Aragorn delivers the exquisite funeral song for Boromir (II, 19-20). The body of the son of Denethor, killed by Orcs, has been sent out in a primitive seaburial. Watching the funeral boat disappear over Rauros Falls, Aragorn, Legolas, and Gimli think of Boromir's home. " 'They will look for him from the White Tower,' " says Aragorn, and then he slowly begins to sing. In the poem, unusual for its dramatic structure, the friendly West, South, and North winds are personified as bearers of tidings whom the tower watcher asks for news of Boromir. Each stanza of ten iambic heptameter lines is divided as follows: the first two lines describe the approaching wind; lines three and four state the question of the watcher, representing all Boromir's people; lines five through eight give the wind's reply; and lines nine and ten state the reaction of the watcher. The sound effects here indicate a deliberate attempt to suggest the sound of the winds. There are thirty-one instances of alliteration[6] as well as onomatopoetic words ("wailing" and "moans," 1. 12; "sighing," 1. 13). The "walking" West Wind is depicted in words with predominantly gentle sounds (*w* and *h*), the "flying" South Wind is associated with

[6] "Fen" and "field," and "grass grows," 1. 1; "West Wind," "walking," and "walls," 1. 2; "wandering wind," 1. 3; "saw" and "seven" and "waters wide," 1. 5; "walk" and "away," 1. 6; "heard" and "horn," 1. 8; "walls westward." 1. 9; "Sea" and "South," 1. 11; "South" and "sighing," 1. 13; "doth dwell," 1. 15; "shores" and "shores," 1. 16; "find" and "flowing," 1. 17; "North" and "North," 1. 18; "Boromir! Beyond," and "seaward" and "south," 1. 19; "gulls" and "grey," 1. 20; "rides" and "roaring," 1. 21; "clear," "cold," and "calls," 1. 22; "news" and "North," 1. 23; "Boromir" and "Bold," 1. 24; "foes" and "fought," 1. 25; "broken," and "brought," 1. 26; "face" and "fair" and "limbs" and "laid," 1. 27; "Rauros" and "Rauros" and "bore" and "breast," 1. 28; and "Rauros" and "Rauros," 1. 30.

stronger ones (*s*, *sh*, *f*, and *d*), and the mighty riding North Wind with harsh sounds (*k*, *t*, *br*).

The answers of the first two winds look forward to the news of the North Wind whose answer relates back to the circumstances surrounding the telling of the poem:

> 'Beneath Amon Hen I heard this cry. There many foes he fought.
> His cloven shield, his broken sword, they to the Water brought.
> His head so proud, his face so fair, his limbs they laid to rest;
> And Rauros, golden Rauros, bore him upon its breast.'
>
> (11. 25-28)

The tower guard then promises to look toward Rauros, as the speakers of the poem themselves are doing.

Aragorn recites an old poem of Rohan on the way to that country. Supposedly composed by a forgotten poet "recalling how tall and fair was Eorl the Young, who rode down out of the North" (II, 112), the poem has the classic *ubi sunt* theme. The rhythm, predominantly dactyllic hexameter, is slowed by the spondee in the penultimate foot of lines two, three, four, and seven. The poem depicts the life of the war-like Rohirrim in terms similar to those of Anglo-Saxon poetry. Images of battle are presented in the opening two lines; line three shifts to the scene inside the hall where the scop sings before the fire; line four moves to the natural signs of growth and prosperity. All these have passed "like rain on the mountain" (1. 5) into the shadow. The last two lines vaguely refer to a champion who shall be the agent through which these glories will return, and thus refer to the singer of the poem, Aragorn, and his role in the Ring-Quest.

It is appropriate that the poetry of the men of Rohan, who live in an Anglo-Saxon-type duguth society and whose language is almost a direct translation of Old English (see John Tinkler's essay above, pp. 164-169), has the form of Old English accentual verse. Tolkien has successfully retained the four-stress line, the alliteration, the repetition, and the word order characteristic of Old English poetry. Short examples include Théoden's call to arms of the Men of the Mark (II, 122), his battle cry before Gondor (III, 112), Éomer's exhortation after the death of Théoden (III, 119), his battle cry (III, 122), and Gléowine's song at Théoden's funeral (III, 254-255). Each is a fitting expression of the bold, daring spirit of the Rohan warriors.

In the longer poems of the Rohirrim the imitation of Old English verse applies to style as well as to form. For example, the anonymous song about the muster of Rohan (III, 76-77) contains twenty-one lines of accentual verse. Tolkien has imitated such features as interest in lineage ("Thengel's son," 1. 2); references to the duguth hall ("ancient halls," 1. 3 and "hearth and high-seat," 1. 7); allusions to fate ("fate before him," 1. 10 and "Doom drove them on," 1. 19); periodic sentence structure (11. 1-2); inverted word order ("Farewell he bade," 1.6) and "Fealty kept he," 1. 10); repetition ("Forth rode the king," 1. 9 and "Forth rode Théoden," 1. 12); and the scop formula ("so the songs tell us," 1. 21). The song of the Mounds of Mundburg (III, 124-125) is similarly imitative, and, like the song of the muster of Rohan, serves to heighten the atmosphere of its setting. The impending doom of Théoden's ride and the hard heroic victory on the Pelennor Fields are both impressed more firmly on the mind of the reader because of inclusion of the poems.

VI. MISCELLANEOUS POETRY

There are a number of miscellaneous poems in *The Lord of the Rings* which deserve attention if only for their singularity. Gandalf, though not a poet himself, repeats messages and riddles in verse form. The enigmatic wizard whose actions can never be predicted seems to enjoy teasing his hearers with partial truths and indirect answers. Thus when Théoden asks whether the moving trees are part of Saruman's wizardry, Gandalf answers with this riddle about the Ents:

> Ere iron was found or tree was hewn,
> When young was mountain under moon;
> Ere ring was made, or wrought was woe,
> It walked the forests long ago. (II, 149)

Théoden's inability to determine the solution gives Gandalf an opportunity to urge, " 'If you would learn that, you should come with me to Isengard.' " Théoden soon is persuaded to go.

Gandalf occasionally sings songs of other races. He gives to Aragorn and Legolas Galadriel's dark warnings of the sea (II, 106). Later he sings an elvish song of praise for Galadriel as a reply to Wormtongue's insult before Théoden (II, 118). The song, with its typical elvish images of clarity and brightness, holds that the Elves and their land are "More fair than thoughts of Mortal Men" (1. 10).

Gimli, the dwarf, has only one poem to himself in the trilogy, and that he chants in a deep voice when the Ring companions are beneath Moria (I, 329-330). The echoes of his song about the former splendor and glory of the dwarf kingdom under the mountain make "the darkness seem heavier" to Sam. The iambic tetrameter couplets recount the dwarves' consummate skill in making things and their rapturous delight in the beauty of what they had made. Unlike the Elves, they were not nature-lovers; their realm was under the dark mountain where they had to provide artificial light:

> The light of sun and star and moon
> In shining lamps of crystal hewn

> Undimmed by cloud or shade of night
> There shone for ever fair and bright.
> (11. 21-24)

The final ten lines shift to the present scene where the dwarf world is gray, the fire cold, the hammer silent. Yet the sight of the ancient king's crown gives hope to Gimli for better days:

> There lies his crown in water deep,
> Till Durin wakes again from sleep.
> (11. 45-46)

In the House of Healing at Gondor the herb-master repeats the old folk-rhyme about the legendary virtues of *kingsfoil* or *athelas*, an herb for which he has found no practical use. The verse, although nearly doggerel, is worthy of notice for is potent image of death:

> When the black breath blows
> and death's shadow grows
> and all lights pass,
> come athelas! come athelas!
>   Life to the dying
> In the king's hand lying! (III, 141)

The herb-master himself does not understand that the last two lines refer to the healing power of the king, in whose hands the efficacy of the herb and its name (*king's foil*) become apparent. The song thus foreshadows Aragorn's coronation.

Tolkien effectively depicts in verse the heights of exultation occasioned by the destruction of Mordor. At the feast in Ithilien, he relates, "as the Hobbits approached swords were unsheathed, and spears were shaken, and horns and trumpets sang, and men cried with many voices and in many tongues.

'Long live the Halflings! Praise them with great praise!
Cuio i Pheriain anann! Aglar'ni Pheriannath!
. . .' (III, 231, 11. 1-2).

Five of the ten lines of the song are in an unidentified foreign
tongue, probably elvish. The mixture of the unfamiliar with
the familiar words and the repetition of the glad phrases help
to convey the impression of tumultuous, undisciplined rejoicing.

Another celebration song is sung by the great Eagle who
spreads "tidings beyond hope from the Lords of the West"
(III, 241) to the City of Gondor. The poem is reminiscent
of Psalm 47 in both content and form. Those who favor a
Christian interpretation of the trilogy can note in this poem
significant allusions to the Savior-king which may be appli-
cable to Christ:

> Sing and be glad, all ye children of the West,
> for your King shall come again,
> and he shall dwell among you
>   all the days of your life.

(11. 9-12)

The tree, which functions in the story as a symbol for the
prosperity of Gondor, may be taken to refer to the cross.
The benefits of Christ-worship may thus be inferred from
these lines:

> And the Tree that was withered shall be renewed,
> and he shall plant it in the high places,
>   and the City shall be blessed.

(11. 13-15)

The verses of Gollum should not be overlooked. The evil
creature croaks with pleasure while splashing in the stream:

> But stream and pool
> is wet and cool:

199

> so nice for feet!
> And now we wish—(II, 227)

Before he admits his lust for Frodo's ring, Gollum catches himself and changes his poem to a riddle about fish. Even in composing poetry the perverted creature is crafty. His state of mind is the direct opposite of the childish innocence of his speech.

Finally, the most important poem in the structure of the *Ring* trilogy is that which first appears as an epigraph indicating its relevance to the central theme of the quest:

> Three Rings for the Elven-kings under the sky,
> Seven for the Dwarf-lords in their halls of stone,
> Nine for Mortal Men doomed to die,
> One for the Dark Lord on his dark throne
> In the Land of Mordor where the Shadows lie.
> One Ring to rule them all, One Ring to find them,
> One ring to bring them all and in the darkness bind them
> In the Land of Mordor where the Shadows lie.

Like the riddles of Gandalf, the full meaning of the poem cannot be fathomed unless the listener has special knowledge. Frodo must be told that the ring in his possession was *the* one ring, but only as his Quest progresses does he, and the reader, learn of the full extent of the ring's binding force. The poem refers to all the benevolent races with whom the hobbits associate in the Quest—Elves, dwarves, and men. The ambiguous reference to the "Dark Lord" and the nature of his power adumbrates the ambiguity of Sauron in the story. No one ever is sure in just what his corruption lies, whether it is the deadly sin of pride, Machiavellian power-perversion, or alliance with death-forces. Significantly, the Ring-poem ends where the Quest ends: "In the Land of Mordor where the Shadows lie."

13

THE SHIRE, MORDOR, AND MINAS TIRITH

Charles Moorman

A VAST COMPENDIUM OF ELVES, DWARVES, AND MEN; HIS-
tory, saga, and poetry; philosophy, adventure, and sentiment
—the *Lord of the Rings* is unique in modern fiction. No
contemporary novel, perhaps no work of prose fiction, in
any way rivals its scope and diversity. For while *The Lord
of the Rings* has much in common with and derives a great
deal of its technique from the tradition of the English novel,
its ultimate forebears must be sought elsewhere, in the forests and mountains of the Nordic lands and in the sagas,
lays, eddas, and fairy tales which the inhabitants of those
lands sang and passed on to their progeny.

The Lord of the Rings is essentially a Nordic myth and its
distinctive qualities become clear only when it is approached
as a myth rather than as a novel or as a children's book or
even as a fantasy. In a sense, it defines its own genre, just as
Moby Dick does, and like *Moby Dick*, it is as bewildering
in its variety as it is convincing in its unity. The great difficulty, in fact, in discussing in any organized fashion either
of these two created myths, however different their problems
may appear to be on the surface, lies in losing one's way
among the many diverting sidetracks which intersect the
highway. It is altogether too easy to become diverted by the

lore of whaling or by the geography of Gondor, by the symbolism of the Pequod's gams or by the significance of the twenty Elven rings of Middle-earth.

The reader of the "genreless" work is thus left without the convenient key to itself with which genre usually provides him. Once he has established that a given work is an elegy, or a novel, or a play (or for that matter a sonata or a still life), he can begin to apply principle to particular with at least some good hope of constructing a fair analysis of the book's central issue. With *The Lord of the Rings* this particular device (happily perhaps) is denied the reader and another key must be sought. Here *Moby Dick* again provides a useful comparison. For as both books are myths, both revolve about a journey, and it is by following the progress of the journey, the quest of the mythical hero, whether Ishmael the New Englander or Frodo the Hobbit, that we can see the central pattern of the work emerge, the plain way from which all other paths are merely diversions.

The character and quest of the hero have been charted meticulously by the myth critics. Joseph Campbell's convenient *The Hero with a Thousand Faces* recounts, with references to myths drawn from all ages and countries, how the hero living in a quiet and happy, albeit static, land is darkly challenged by a strange messenger, how he crosses with difficulty the threshold of a country full of trials and dangers, how he wins a token of power or a piece of valuable information, and finally how he returns to his people bringing with him the saving knowledge or token he has gained beyond the boundaries of his own land—"and I only am escaped alone to tell thee." And seemingly this quest represents, symbolizes even, something very basic to the human personality. Heinrich Zimmer in *The King and the Corpse* imagines it to be the quest of the individual into the depths of his own psyche whence, if successful, he emerges bringing self-knowledge. A. J. Toynbee sees this withdrawal and return of the hero as the unifying pattern of all historical process. But for whatever reason, the quest of the myth hero is of absorbing interest and whether it takes place in the vast reaches of the southern Pacific or among the wildernesses of Mordor, it tells a true tale, perhaps the only tale worth telling.

It is just here that the concept of the City is of vital importance in the myth of the quest of the hero. For the journey is undertaken always on behalf of the City; the hero is always the representative of a community. This is why the hero is nearly always a king or prince and why in a princeless society the Pequod with its polyglot crew is itself an image of America seeking its destiny. And the myth is thus, in any and all of its forms, the myth of the founding of the City. Odysseus journeys to Ithaca, Aeneas to Italy, Beowulf to Denmark, and Frodo Baggins to Mount Doom to found a City, to dispel the reign of chaos and old night, and to establish a community, a civility, in the midst of what had been a wilderness of landscape or emotion.

All this is, I warrant, quite general and perhaps even a little fanciful. Yet it is very much to the point. For, as in *Taliessin Through Logres*, the clue to the meaning of *The Lord of the Rings* lies in the maps which accompany each volume. Frodo and his companions journey from the Shire to the dark land of Mordor and then to the City of Minas Tirith and finally home again to the Shire. We are therefore confronted with three stages of the journey, actually three states of man: as he exists in the Shire, in the wilderness of Mordor, and in the City. The Shire, the point from which the Ring journey begins, like the journey in *The Hobbit* or in any fairy tale, is a quiet, comfortable land. Its inhabitants, the small hobbits, live there in snug, warm burrows, happy in their rural surroundings and habits:

> Their faces were as a rule good-natured rather than beautiful,
> broad, bright-eyed, red-cheeked, with mouths apt to laughter,
> and to eating and drinking. And laugh they did, and eat, and
> drink, often and heartily, being fond of simple jests at all
> times, and of six meals a day (when they could get them).
> They were hospitable and delighted in parties, and in presents,
> which they gave away freely and eagerly accepted. (I, 1)

But for all its good humor and simplicity, the Shire is
static, self-satisfied, complacent. It is by no means Eden,
for although the Shire is free from major crimes, there are
the inevitable family feuds and squabbles, the usual nasti-
ness and petty thievery. This static complacency is the cause
of the decision of Bilbo Baggins, Frodo's uncle and the hero
of *The Hobbit*, to leave the comfort of the Shire and return
to the hardships and the glories he had met during his own
remarkable journey, from which he had returned bearing a
dragon's treasure and also a ring which he had won (though
Bilbo tries to disguise the fact) through trickery. And after
Bilbo's departure from the Shire, his nephew also finds the
Shire lacking in some vital ingredient of life: " 'I love the
Shire,' " he says. " 'But I begin to wish, somehow, that I had
gone too' " (I, 50). In spite of his joy at being Master of
Bag End, Bilbo's estate, "half unknown to himself the regret
that he had not gone with Bilbo was steadily growing" (I,
52).

Nor in its complacency does the Shire realize that its innocence must be ceaselessly protected from the growing evil
beyond its borders; Rangers and Wizards constantly patrol
its boundaries. Gildor the Elf tells Frodo that " 'the Shire is
no longer any protection to [the hobbits]' " and that hobbits
can no longer hope to fence out the wide world about them
(I, 93). Strider somewhat bitterly remarks that he is scorned
by Barliman Butterbur, the innkeeper, " 'who lives within a
day's march of foes that would freeze his heart, or lay his

little town in ruins, if he were not guarded ceaselessly' " (I, 261). And another of the Rangers remarks of the hobbits that " 'little do they know of our long labour for the safe-keeping of their borders, and yet I grudge it not' " (III, 53).

I suggest that there is present here a variation of the same theory of knowledge that appears so dominantly in Dorothy L. Sayers' *The Zeal of Thy House*. Knowledge—and this would include, of course, the knowledge of good and evil—is to some degree the source of energy. Lack of knowledge may thus bring contentment, but it must bring, along with contentment, stagnation. A complete return to a perpetual Eden, the course that Miss Sayers' Faustus elects in *The Devil to Pay*, is thus an impossibility in a fallen world. Bilbo and (because of Bilbo) Frodo feel a kind of nagging discontent in the Shire; they "love the Shire," but they feel a desire to escape from its complacency and its minor irritating quarrels.

But Frodo must pay a fearful price for his daring. I can do no better here than to refer the reader to Joseph Campbell's description of the trials of the hero or, better still, to Arnold Toynbee:

> As for the human protagonist's part, suffering is the keynote of it in every presentation of the drama, whether the player of the part is Jesus or Job or Faust or Adam and Eve. . . . The Fall, in response to the temptation to eat of the Tree of the Knowledge of Good and Evil, symbolizes the acceptance of a challenge to abandon this achieved integration and to venture upon a fresh differentiation out of which a fresh integration may—or may not—arise. The expulsion from the Garden into an unfriendly world in which the Woman must bring forth children in sorrow and the Man must eat bread in the sweat of his face, is the ordeal which the acceptance of the Serpent's challenge has entailed.[1]

[1] *A Study of History*, abr. D. C. Somervell (Oxford University Press, 1947), pp. 65-66.

Tolkien and the Critics

Frodo's decision to leave the Shire is prompted by Gandalf the Wizard's report that Sauron the Great, the Dark Lord, has rebuilt his Dark Tower in Mordor and is sending his evil emissaries throughout Middle-earth[2] to seek the Ring that Bilbo found on his journey and which is now in the possession of Frodo. It is the Master Ring of the Elven Rings, capable of uniting its types scattered about the world and by doing so of assuring Sauron complete domination. Frodo's task is that of destroying the Ring and with it Sauron's hope of victory by casting it into Mount Doom deep in Mordor, hundreds of miles away from the Shire. This task is made many times more difficult in that the Ring itself constantly seeks to corrupt the mind of its bearer, to twist his mind to the service of Sauron.

Frodo's journey carries him eastward into the dominions of Sauron and finally into Mordor itself. The pleasant rolling landscape of the Shire hardens into the crags and cliffs of the Black Mountains, and Frodo meets creatures vastly different from the jolly hobbits of his own land: cruel, misshapen Orcs, giant trolls, hideous spiders, and the featureless Ringwraiths, whose very touch freezes.

But Mordor differs from the Shire not only in its external features. As in C. S. Lewis' N.I.C.E., the servants of Sauron

[2] Some mention must be made of the setting of *The Lord of the Rings*. The scene is Middle-earth, our own Earth, but Tolkien's geography is completely his own and while the book has the "feel" of Northern Europe, no equations between Tolkien's lands and our own can be attempted. The time is mythical: the end of the "Third Age" of Middle-earth, a time before the domination of men and the disappearance of other "speaking peoples." It is impossible even to suggest here the detail with which Tolkien has constructed the history, chronology, language, and even customs of the various races of Middle-earth. The reader is invited to consult the appendices contained in *The Return of the King* for discussions of these matters. Tolkien has on hand also a complete history of the "Second Age," the Age of Númenor, which he hopes to see published.

continually bicker with and even attack one another. The Companions of the Ring, Frodo and his eight friends, many times escape the traps of the enemy simply because their foes, particularly the Orcs, become so involved in their own quarrels that Frodo and his companions escape. After the destruction of Sauron's tower, the black forces throughout the world capitulate almost immediately; without the direction of Sauron's evil will, they become easy prey.

Like the N.I.C.E. also, Mordor is industrial and scientific; its black engines and factories contrast with the serene agrarianism of the Shire. Saruman, a corrupt Wizard, is said to have "a mind of metal and wheels; and he does not care for growing things, except as far as they serve him for the moment" (II, 76). The hobbits, on the other hand, "do not and did not understand or like machines more complicated than a forge-bellows, a water-mill, or a hand-loom, though they were skilful with tools" (I, 10). When the forces of Sauron infiltrate the Shire, they characteristically begin to erect factories; "the Old Mill had vanished, and a large red-brick building was being put up where it had stood" (I, 378). It is interesting also that, in epic fashion, the forces of nature themselves are involved in the conflict. Harsh mountain storms willfully hinder the Ring Companions and menacing forests imprison them. On the other hand, the Ents, the great trees which are the oldest of living things, and Tom Bombadil, a thoroughly pagan nature deity, assist the Companions on their journey.

Mordor thus stands opposed to both Shire and City. Under its dark shadow, both Nature and man are perverted; the natural impulses for good are turned to evil purposes. Its power is seen in the Ring which works toward the corruption of all its bearers, even the good-hearted hobbits who have pledged themselves to its destruction.

The City of Minas Tirith, however, portrays a third condition of man, different from both the pastoral innocence of the Shire and the mechanized horror of Mordor. Most of *The Return of the King* is devoted to the establishment of the City, Minas Tirith, under Aragorn, one of the Ring Companions. It is noteworthy that before the destruction of Sauron, Minas Tirith is a place of confusion and terror. Its king, Denethor, cannot cope with, indeed cannot even believe in, the evil which has already infiltrated the defenses of his City. But as Gandalf later tells Denethor's servants: " 'Ill deeds have been done here; but let now all enmity that lies between you be put away, for it was contrived by the Enemy and works his will' " (III, 131). With the destruction of Sauron, however, the City assumes its proper order and glory. Aragorn, no longer Strider the lonely Ranger of the earlier volumes, enters into his true place as King Elessar and marries Arwen, the daughter of Elrond, the Elf King. And in the time of Elessar:

> the City was made more fair than it had ever been, even in the days of its first glory; and it was filled with trees and with fountains, and its gates were wrought of mithril and steel, and its streets paved with white marble; and the Folk of the Mountain laboured in it, and the Folk of the Wood rejoiced to come there; and all was healed and made good, and the houses were filled with men and women and the laughter of children, and no window was blind nor any courtyard empty. (III, 246)

Nor is the establishment of the City a matter of only local concern. The coming of the King heralds the arrival of the Fourth Age of Middle-earth, which, as Gandalf tells the King, is to mark the end of Middle-earth as they know it:

> 'The Third Age of the world is ended, and the new age is begun; and it is your task to order its beginning and to pre-

serve what may be preserved. For though much has been saved, much must now pass away; and the power of the Three Rings also is ended. And all the lands that you see, and those that lie round about them, shall be dwellings of Men. For the time comes of the Dominion of Men, and the Elder Kindred shall fade or depart.' (III, 249)

The effects of Elessar's reign are felt throughout Middle-earth. Dwarves and Elves, traditionally antagonistic, are reconciled:

> After the fall of Sauron, Gimli [the Dwarf] brought south a part of the Dwarf-folk of Erebor, and he became Lord of the Glittering Caves. He and his people did great works in Gondor and Rohan. . . . Legolas his friend also brought south Elves out of Greenwood, and they dwelt in Ithilien, and it became once again the fairest country in all the westlands. (III, 362)

The hobbits are placed under Elessar's special protection. Men are forbidden to enter the Shire, and it is made "a Free Land under the protection of the Northern Sceptre" (III, 377). Even the wastelands, long haunted by Orcs and trolls, are to be made useful:

> 'Then the Greenway will be opened again, and [the King's] messengers will come north, and there will be comings and goings, and the evil things will be driven out of the wastelands. Indeed the waste in time will be waste no longer, and there will be people and fields where once there was wilderness.' (III, 272)

The foundation of the City is thus the natural climax of the destruction of Sauron. Before the War of the Rings there had been only an ancient tradition of kingship. "But there had been no king for nearly a thousand years, and even the ruins of Kings' Norbury were covered with grass" (I, 18). Once the evil of Sauron is stamped out, then all the inhabitants of Middle-earth may join in the ordered social state which is their natural condition. I have little doubt that Tolkien is picturing here something very close to the establishment of the City of God on Earth. If we translate *The Lord of the Rings* into Augustinian terms, then both the Shire and Mordor may be said to mirror the condition of man in the *Civitas Terrena*, the only civilization possible for him in a world where evil still exists. Mordor is, of course, the *Civitas Terrena* seen at its worst, wholly given over to the uses of evil, and the Shire the Earthly City seen at its best, existing however in a false and dangerous innocence, plagued by minor irritations and distractions, threatened by evil (even if it does not realize it) from the outside. However, once the evil is destroyed, the City may descend "in its web of exchanged glory"[3] and its benevolence may extend throughout the Earth.

But Frodo's journey does not end with the establishment of the City. The hero's quest must end where it began, since "a transfiguration [and no one will doubt that the returning Frodo is far from being the simple hobbit who had set forth from the Shire six months before] in solitude can have no purpose and perhaps even no meaning except as a prelude to the return of the transfigured personality into the social milieu out of which he had originally come; a native environment from which the social animal cannot permanently estrange himself without repudiating his humanity and becoming, in Aristotle's phrase, 'either a beast or a god.' "[4]

And so Frodo comes home to "scour" the Shire which during his absence has been infiltrated and corrupted by Saruman. The borders of the Shire are now policed, the

---

[3] The phrase is Charles Williams'. See *He Came Down from Heaven* (London, 1950), p. 100.

[4] Toynbee, p. 217.

mills and farms are owned and operated by outsiders, the best beer and tobacco are exported, most of the older, more responsible citizens are in jail, martial law is everywhere enforced, gangs of ruffians patrol the roads. The point is obvious: this is the price the Shire has had to pay for its innocence. Once Frodo is gone and the guard relaxed, the agents of corruption descend into a defenseless land, defenseless because unprepared. As Sam says, " 'this is worse than Mordor! . . . It comes home to you, as they say; because it is home, and you remember it before it was all ruined' " (III, 297). The Battle of Bywater, "1419, the last battle fought in the Shire, and the only battle since the Green Fields, 1147, away up in the Northfarthing" (III, 295) decides the issue very quickly (the invaders, like all bullies, capitulate without much of a fight), but the cleaning up, the "scouring" takes time. Trees must be planted and gardens restored, but with the help of Nature and the Elves, the work of the hobbits is rewarded, and the Shire is soon more brautiful than ever:

> Altogether 1420 in the Shire was a marvellous year. . . . All the children born or begotten in that year, and there were many, were fair to see and strong, and most of them had a rich golden hair that had before been rare among hobbits. The fruit was so plentiful that young hobbits very nearly bathed in strawberries and cream. . . . And no one was ill, and everyone was pleased, except those who had to mow the grass. (III, 303)

Even the old feuds are patched up, and the Shire enters a new era of prosperity, better and happier than any it had ever known. Now a part of the City, it no longer exists in pastoral ignorance, but ruled by the Ring Companions, it is aware of its place in the world, though it retains its simple pattern of agrarian life.

The framework of the journey from the Shire to Mordor to the City to the Shire thus supports *The Lord of the Rings*, but a discussion of the framework cannot in any way describe adequately the glories of the body that skeleton defines. The great Nordic theme of courage—courage to grapple not only with human foes, but with the monsters of the outer darkness—runs through *The Lord of the Rings* as it does through *Beowulf*.[5] The endless temptations for Frodo to use the Ring wrongly, the innumerable and marvelously-varied dangers and escapes, the sense of urgency which pulls the company forward, at times against its judgment and will, all have their places in the slow transformation of a simple hobbit into an epic hero bound upon a wheel of fire.

The greatest single influence upon Tolkien is the eddas and sagas of the North. The monsters, the landscapes, the battles all have a Nordic feel to them. And one feels that Tolkien has avoided the worst pitfalls of the type of literature he has set out to create: *The Lord of the Rings* is neither "cute" in the fashion of Walt Disney nor bombastic and sentimental in that of Wagner. But there has been at least one other perceptible influence on Tolkien (though I am sure that he would deny it): *The Lord of the Rings* in many places echoes the characteristic ideas and themes of C. S. Lewis. This "echo," as I have called it, is by no means conscious nor does it in any way qualify the originality of Tolkien's work. But that it is there I am convinced.

[5] Tolkien's lecture, "Beowulf: the Monsters and the Critics," is of great interest in its connections with *The Lord of the Rings*. Tolkien's use of monsters in his own work becomes clear in the light of his discussion of the dragons in *Beowulf*. And the frequent references to the past history of Númenor are explained by Tolkien's statement that in *Beowulf* the "impression of depth is an effect and a justification of the use of episodes and allusions to old tales, mostly darker, more pagan, and desperate than the foreground" (p. 80).

Tolkien undertook the composition of *The Lord of the Rings* shortly after the publication of *The Hobbit* in 1937. The trilogy was composed following the course of the narrative line and except for a number of additions and rewritings, particularly the foreshadowing passages in *The Fellowship of the Ring* and the transitional passages needed to insure exact chronological accuracy (a matter of great importance to Tolkien), it stands now as it was orginally composed and set down. During the period of its composition it was read aloud "chapter by chapter" in its entirety to the Oxford Christians by Tolkien and, later, by his son Christopher. But the evidence of *The Hobbit*, as well as the statements of Tolkien and his friends, indicates beyond doubt that much of the structure and general narrative and great chunks of the historical, cultural, and linguistic background of *The Lord of the Rings* existed before the book was composed. One of the members of the group, in fact, believes that Tolkien wrote the narrative of the *The Lord of the Rings* simply as a handy means of presenting his real interest, the manufactured Common Language of Middle-earth, though Tolkien's own statement that the saga had been in him "like a great tumor" for a number of years is probably a more accurate description of its birth.

But if the created milieu, the myth of Middle-earth, had gradually accumulated over the years in Tolkien's brain, the actual detailed narrative of the three volumes was worked out with great struggle during the writing process. The problems of narrative, which were "constantly before our minds,"[6] gave Tolkien considerable trouble; it was no easy task to follow nine heroes through three volumes, especially when for much of the time these heroes are traveling alone or in small groups. And even though Tolkien may have

[6] *Essays Presented to Charles Williams*, p. v.

been (as he doubtless was) totally impervious to "the hard-hitting criticism of the circle," his mind during the period of composition must have been to some degree open to the ideas of the others. One member of the group in fact remarked that he believed that much of the "allegorical significance" of *The Lord of the Rings* came to Tolkien during the actual writing of the book and that he was perhaps influenced, though for the most part unconsciously, by the group in evolving this "allegorical significance."[7]

Whatever the extent of Tolkien's indebtedness to the Oxford Christians, his work makes one point abundantly clear: if he borrowed or absorbed, whether consciously or unconsciously, any ideas from his friends, it was from C. S. Lewis that the ideas came. Evidently Tolkien was somewhat unsympathetic to Charles Williams' general point of view, however much he may have enjoyed the man, and *The Lord of the Rings* has little of Williams in it. Tolkien's strong Nordic clarity will admit none of the tortured, twisted, almost obscene dilemmas of good and evil in which Williams' characters find themselves. But there are echoes of Lewis' characteristic strains, and their presence and particular uses show how closely the minds of the two men are related.

The opposition of the Shire and Mordor is essentially that of Logres and Britain. Both the Shire and Logres are agrarian societies, simply and quietly governed; both value the rights of the individual and preserve the worth-while values and traditions of the past. Mordor and Britain are falsely progressive, both complex, industrial states in which the individual counts for very little and the past for nothing. Saruman in *The Lord of the Rings* could well be a spokesman for the N.I.C.E.:

---

[7] Tolkien himself maintains that he is most certainly indebted to the group, but only for the encouragement of his work.

'A new Power is rising. Against it the old allies and policies will not avail us at all. There is no hope left in Elves or dying Numenor. This then is the one choice before you, before us. We may join with that Power. . . . Its victory is at hand; and there will be rich reward for those that aided it.' (I, 272)

And like the battle of Logres and Britain, that of the Shire and Mordor is never-ending; "always after a defeat and a respite, the Shadow takes another shape and grows again" (I, 60). As in *That Hideous Strength*, the task of waging the battle against evil is put into the hands of ordinary men chosen for the task. When Frodo regrets that all this has happened in his time, Gandalf can only tell him that " 'so do all who live to see such times. But that is not for them to decide. All we have to decide is what to do with the time that is given us' " (I, 60). Later, Gandalf, in reply to Frodo's protests at having fallen heir to the task of destroying the Ring, tells him that he must attempt the mission, that he " 'must . . . use such strength and heart and wits' " (I, 70) as he can muster. In a vision, Frodo sees the war in which he is engaged symbolized by the opposing towers:

Then turning south again he beheld Minas Tirith. Far away it seemed, and beautiful: white-walled, many-towered, proud and fair upon its mountain-seat; its battlements glittered with steel, and its turrets were bright with many banners. . . . But against Minas Tirith was set another fortress, greater and more strong. Thither, eastward, unwilling his eye was drawn. It passed the ruined bridges of Osgiliath, the grinning gates of Minas Morgul and the haunted Mountains, and it looked upon Gorgoroth, the valley of terror in the Land of Mordor. Darkness lay there under the Sun. . . . Then at last his gaze was held: wall upon wall, battlement upon battlement, black, immeasurably strong, mountain of iron, gate of steel, tower of adamant, he saw it: Barad-dûr, Fortress of Sauron. (I, 417)

There are some slight echoes also of some of Lewis' more typical situations and ideas. Frodo's sympathy for Gollum (I, 63), Gandalf's offer of an opportunity for repentance to both Saruman (II, 188) and the hapless Gríma (III, 262), and Frodo's final gestures of mercy to both (III, 299) are reminiscent of the conversations of redeemed and unredeemed spirits in *The Great Divorce*. The Ents and Tom Bombadil, representatives of Nature in *The Lord of the Rings*, are in their rough pagan strength very like the figure of Merlin in *That Hideous Strength*. The battle of Gandalf with the Balrog under the Earth where the "world is gnawed by nameless things" (II, 105) and his recovery upon the mountain recall Ransom's battle with the Un-man in *Perelandra*. And the Frodo of the last days—calm, judicious, harassed by the pain of his shoulder wound, leaving all matters of battle to others—is much like Mr. Fisher-King in *That Hideous Strength*.

But in one final quality the two writers are much alike, though it would be folly to search for influence here. In his essay "On Fairy Stories" Tolkien names as perhaps the distinctive mark of the fairy story the presence of what he calls "eucatastrophe," the final consolation, "the joy of the happy ending," neither "escapist, nor fugitive," denying "universal final defeat and in so far is *evangelium*, giving a fleeting glimpse of Joy, Joy beyond the walls of the world, poignant as grief" (p. 81):

> It is the mark of the good fairy story, of the higher or more complete kind, that however wild its event, however fantastic or terrible the adventures, it can give to child or man that hears it, when the 'turn' comes, a catch of the breath, a beat and lifting of the heart, near to (or indeed accompanied by) tears, as keen as that given by any form of literary art, and having a peculiar quality. (p. 81)

One thinks immediately not only of the glorious final passing of Frodo—accompanied, as always, by Sam—to the sea, but of the Great Dance of the Planets in *Perelandra* and the happy mating of the beasts in *That Hideous Strength*. And this eucatastrophe is marked in both writers by a stateliness of language which bears witness both to the high seriousness of their purpose and to an affirmation of images rare in modern literature:

> Then the King welcomed his guests, and they alighted; and Elrond surrendered the sceptre, and laid the hand of his daughter in the hand of the King, and together they went up into the High City, and all the stars flowered in the sky. And Aragorn the King Elessar wedded Arwen Undomiel in the City of the Kings upon the day of Midsummer, and the tale of their long waiting and labours was come to fulfillment. (III, 251)

14

THE LORD OF THE RINGS
AS LITERATURE

Burton Raffel

MY POSITION IS THIS: THE LORD OF THE RINGS IS A MAGNIFI-cent performance, full of charm, excitement, and affection, but it is not—at least as I am here using the term—litera-ture. Tolkien's three volumes tell an entrancing "good and evil story"[1] and tell it with power and wisdom; he has succeeded in constructing a self-contained world of extraor-dinary reality—and grace. "I have been a lover of fairy-stories since I learned to read," Tolkien has noted,[2] and by his own definition "*Faërie* contains many things besides elves and fays, and besides dwarfs, witches, trolls, giants, or dragons: it holds the seas, the sun, the moon, the sky; and the earth, and all things that are in it: tree and bird, water and stone, wine and bread, and ourselves, mortal men, when we are enchanted. . . . [And] if fairy-story as a kind is worth reading at all it is worthy to be written for and read by adults."[3] Fair enough. But not only that: "The peculiar quality of the 'joy' in successful Fantasy can . . . be explained as a sudden glimpse of the underlying reality or truth. . . . [This is] indeed narrative art, story-making in its primary and most potent mode."[4] Yet I con-

[1] J. R. R. Tolkien, *Tree and Leaf* (London, 1964), p. 14.
[2] Ibid., p. 11.
[3] Ibid., pp. 15-16, 43.
[4] Ibid., pp. 62, 45.

tend that making stories, even wonderful stories, is not the same thing as making literature.

Let me divide what I mean by literature into three parts; without defining the whole under which they are subsumed: style, the way in which language is used, characterization, the way in which human (or human-like) traits are portrayed, and incident, the way in which events are organized and presented. Not all literature can be readily discussed under each of these three headings; *The Lord of the Rings*, however, not only requires examination under all three headings, but the first heading, style, needs to be subdivided to account for both the prose and the poetry. It is I think obvious from Tolkien's remarks in *Tree and Leaf* that the third heading is most important to him.[5] In addition a fourth heading, morality, although not strictly a part of literature, can be briefly examined and will afford some additional insights.

I.   STYLE

A. PROSE

It would be foolish to say that Tolkien does not write well. He does, he writes admirably, whether his prose be discursive, scholarly, or imaginative. His deservedly famous essay "*Beowulf:* The Monsters and the Critics" broke upon the philological walls and released the poetry long hidden behind them. "For it is of their nature that the jabberwocks of historical and antiquarian research burble in the tulgy wood of conjecture, flitting from one tum-tum tree to another. Noble animals, whose burbling is on occasion good

[5] In the Foreword to *The Lord of the Rings*, Tolkien thus explains the triology's origin: "The prime motive was the desire of a tale-teller to try his hand at a really long story that would hold the attention of readers, amuse them, delight them, and at times maybe excite them or deeply move them" (I, 6).

to hear; but though their eyes of flame may sometimes prove searchlights, their range is short."[6] The *Proceedings of the British Academy* cannot often have been graced with such supple prose, nor could Tolkien have virtually forced literary awareness on *Beowulf* scholars had he not been so abundantly possessed of it himself.

But prose is not autotelic, and if Tolkien writes admirably one still must ask, to what purpose? That is, his prose may do admirably just what he wants it to do, and what he wants it to do may be—and in fact is—very much worth doing, but if his objectives are limited and basically exclude what I here term literature, then his prose must be limited similarly. I think it is. I repeat: it does not denigrate Tolkien or his superb book to assert and to try to prove this. I would hope that Tolkien himself would prefer not to be praised for what he has neither tried to do nor succeeded in doing. *The Lord of the Rings* is not only not *The Iliad* or *The Odyssey*, neither is it *Beowulf* or *Paradise Lost*, or *The Great Gatsby*.

Consider simple description. For most purposes Tolkien's prose is brilliantly adequate, straightforward, just starched enough to have body, resilient enough to catch the echoes of speech, not a supercharged instrument, nor one with great range, but very competent. "On this occasion the presents were unusually good. The hobbit-children were so excited that for a while they almost forgot about eating. There were toys the like of which they had never seen before, all beautiful and some obviously magical. Many of them had indeed been ordered a year before, and had come all the way from the Mountain and from Dale, and were of real dwarf-make" (I, 35). There are traces of

---

[6] As reprinted in *An Anthology of Beowulf Criticism*, p. 56. See also pp. 53 and 55. The paper was read as a lecture in 1936 and first printed in that year. *The Lord of the Rings* was begun in 1936.

coyness in the references to "Mountain and Dale" as specific places; there are traces of sentimentality in the references to the hobbit-children. But this is good clean writing; in the narrative it fits neatly into place. So too with most reported conversation: " 'Oh, they're both cracked,' said Ted. 'Leastways old Bilbo *was* cracked, and Frodo's cracking. If that's where you get your news from, you'll never want for moonshine. Well, friends, I'm off home. Your good health!' He drained his mug and went out noisily" (I, 54).

But other sorts of description strain Tolkien's powers. When Bilbo disappears, "he jumped over a low place in the hedge at the bottom, and took to the meadows, passing into the night like a rustle of wind in the grass" (I, 44). Bilbo is to disappear quickly, the language is apt. But is it anything more than that? There is, first of all, virtually no sense impression of the hedge; it is generalized, as is the "low place" through which Bilbo jumps. But more important, to have Bilbo "passing into the night like a rustle of wind in the grass" is to write something perilously close to stereotyped prose. In context this is not a cliché, nor is it notable for anything more than the bare transmission of information: Bilbo left, fast, quietly. I would argue that the language of literature must do more than this, must transmit information as well as sense impressions of some sort, and to effect this the language must be both more deeply felt and more deeply worked.

A larger sample will perhaps make my point more clearly:

> Next morning after a late breakfast, the wizard was sitting with Frodo by the open window of the study. A bright fire was on the hearth, but the sun was warm, and the wind was in the South. Everything looked fresh, and the new green of

> Spring was shimmering in the fields and on the tips of the trees' fingers. (I, 55)

Can one *feel* that fire? It is "bright"; we know that and know all we are meant to know. "Everything looked fresh": we know exactly what that means, and it is not much. "The new green of Spring" is surely *not* fresh; to have it "shimmering in the fields" is to rely on the essentially stale diction of the nineteenth century; "the tips of the trees' fingers" is outright cliché. And yet the paragraph is in context more than adequate. What we are to know is that the wizard (Gandalf) and Frodo were sitting peacefully at talk, having breakfasted, and that the world too was (or seemed to be) at peace. Except for the final barefaced cliché there is no real attempt to explore sensory realities; only narrative realities matter to Tolkien, and so adept is he that nothing more matters to us.

Tolkien's nature descriptions are frequently somewhat overwrought. (This is, as I shall show, especially true of the poetry.) It is as though Tolkien in person, not Tolkien as author, feels both more than he can express and things which are irrelevant to his tale. "In the morning Frodo woke refreshed. He was lying in a bower made by a living tree with branches laced and drooping to the ground; his bed was of fern and grass, deep and soft and strangely fragrant. The sun was shining through the fluttering leaves, which were still green upon the tree. He jumped up and went out" (I, 95). Frodo has been with elves the night before; the elves are wood people; when Frodo wakes he quite properly wakes "refreshed"—the word is totally generalized, a state, an idea, rather than a specifically felt and explored sensory reality—and he quite properly wakes in bright woody greenness. This is however two-dimensional surface description: whatever Tolkien may have imagined he was conveying by "fluttering leaves," for example, it seems plain that he in fact conveys nothing more than that the leaves were in motion. There is no further depth to the words.

> Christmas passed, the wet, drenched, cold days of January recurred monotonously, with now and then a brilliance of blue flashing in, when Brangwen went out into a morning like crystal, when every sound rang again, and the birds were many and sudden and brusque in the hedges. Then an elation came over him in spite of everything, whether his wife were strange or sad, or whether he craved for her to be with him, it did not matter, the air rang with clear noises, the sky was like crystal, like a bell, and the earth was hard. Then he worked and was happy, his eyes shining, his cheeks flushed. And the zest of life was strong in him.[7]

This passage, which is not by Tolkien, is description of a very different order. It is not that the scene is more visual: Tolkien is capable of great accuracy and detail. Rather, this is much more fully felt: D. H. Lawrence has a story to tell, but he is interested in more than the story and the stark facts of good and evil. This deals with matter just as primeval as that Tolkien writes of, but Lawrence sees complexities, complications, subtleties, which Tolkien does not admit. It would destroy *The Lord of the Rings* if Tolkien wrote as D. H. Lawrence did, and vice versa. But Lawrence was writing literature, his style suited his aim. Tolkien is working in a separate genre.

When Gandalf tells Frodo that the Enemy, universally feared and hated, knows that the Ring has survived, Tolkien breaks into the text with a space—and there follows this paragraph:

[7] D. H. Lawrence, *The Rainbow* (New York, n.d.), p. 65.

>A heavy silence fell in the room. Frodo could hear his heart beating. Even outside everything seemed still. No sound of Sam's shears could now be heard. (I, 68)

It is just right, in context. The ominous quality is what we are to feel, and we feel it. Frodo has the Ring, the Enemy is after it, knows it is somewhere but not exactly where—oh Lord, oh Lord. We make sure the room is not too dark and go on reading, entranced. But out of context it is easy to see how distinct from literature this language is. "A *heavy* silence" is a silence in capital letters; if it "falls" we do not notice, because falling is what heavy silences regularly and invariably do. We expect the word, it comes, and we read rapidly on. "Frodo could hear his heart beating": to be sure, the little hobbit is frightened, yes, what else, quick, quick, tell us more. The narrative drives ahead—but all the same, to have the frightened hero "hear his heart beating" is not, as language, very communicative.

Here is Tolkien's account of the hobbits' arrival at the Prancing Pony Inn, in Bree, proprietor Barliman Butterbur:

>Off he went at last, and left them feeling rather breathless. He seemed capable of an endless stream of talk, however busy he might be. They found themselves in a small and cosy room. There was a bit of bright fire burning on the hearth, and in front of it were some low and comfortable chairs. There was a round table, already spread with a white cloth, and on it was a large hand-bell. But Nob, the hobbit servant, came bustling in long before they thought of ringing. He brought candles and a tray full of plates. (I, 166)

Disregarding aspects of characterization, the basic impression is that of a rural Old English inn. The operant words are *small and cosy*, *bit of bright fire*, *low and comfortable*, *white cloth*, *bustling*. The picture is clearly painted; one cannot mistake either the setting itself or the things about it of which Tolkien approves. And in the narrative these are the notes Tolkien needs to sound: the party of hobbits has just come to Bree, after a series of harrowing adventures and, in particular, after leaving the sanctuary provided by Tom Bombadil. They wanted "only to find a fire, and a door between them and the night" (I, 160) and what they found was the Prancing Pony Inn. But to tell us, for example, that a room is "small and cosy," is to tell us only that the feeling Tolkien wants us to have about the room is one of comfortableness and modest size. "Low and comfortable chairs" tells us, again, what we are to feel about the chairs, not very much of the chairs themselves.

> She replaced the disreputable furniture of the house by new shiny Grand Rapids chairs and tables. There was a varnished bookcase, forever locked, stored with stiff sets of unread books—*The Harvard Classics*, and a cheap encyclopaedia.[8]

Even to say that the furniture is "new shiny" is to describe it in a way very unlike Tolkien's. The information we are given is slanted, to be sure; Thomas Wolfe has a point to make, and he bangs it home relentlessly. But he also allows the reader to experience the chairs and tables for himself. We can see the "varnished bookcase," the rows of "unread books" in "stiff sets": "Grand Rapids" furniture is mass-produced, factory-made furniture—but what is a "low and comfortable" chair? Wolfe is not I think as durable a writer as Tolkien; I would far rather read *The Lord of the Rings* than *Look Homeward Angel*, and nothing could persuade me to reread the others of Wolfe's repetitious, sprawling, adolescent novels. But for all that Wolfe's style belongs to literature and Tolkien's does not. When Tolkien tells us

---

[8] Thomas Wolfe, *Look Homeward Angel* (New York, n.d.), p. 147.

about "small and cosy" rooms or "low and comfortable chairs" he is writing as a narrative moralist. The social and esthetic virtues of the room and the chairs are basic to his tale, but neither have independent existence, neither are experienced for us or by us. They are no more than Faërie props.

Tolkien has argued, in a lecture written about 1938, that "true literature . . . works from mind to mind," rather than from object to mind.[9] The specific contrast he intends is that of the writer, on the one hand, the illustrator and the man of the theater on the other; the comparison shows a good deal about his own conception of what language is intended to do:

> Should the story say 'he ate bread,' the dramatic producer or painter can only show 'a piece of bread' according to his taste or fancy, but the hearer of the story will think of bread in general and picture it in some form of his own. If a story says 'he climbed a hill and saw a river in the valley below,' the illustrator may catch, or nearly catch, his own vision of such a scene; but every hearer of the words will have his own picture, and it will be made out of all the hills and rivers and dales he has ever seen, but especially out of The Hill, The River, The Valley which were for him the first embodiment of the word.[10]

"He climbed a hill and saw a river in the valley below" does not, I suggest, evoke any kind of scene at all. It is a cog in some narrative machine: there was some reason for this person to climb a hill, there was some reason for him to see a river, and some consequences perhaps flowed therefrom. What were they, these reasons and these possible consequences? Read on and discover. None of this has anything

[9] *Tree and Leaf*, p. 67.
[10] Idem.

o do with what words as words can communicate; the question of style is simply not at issue.

A piece of writing which is part of literature, but which is bad literature and bad style, may show the distinction more clearly:

> He watched a tomcat slink along the fence ledge; he stared at the spot he had newly boarded so that his old man wouldn't yelp about loose boards; he looked about at the patches in the grass that Martin and his gang had worn down playing their cowboy and Indian games. There was something about the things he watched that seemed to enter Studs as sun entered a field of grass; and as he watched, he felt that the things he saw were part of himself, and he felt as good as if he were warm sunlight; he was all glad to be living, and to be Studs Lonigan.[11]

This has not got Tolkien's stately, nicely old-fashioned cadences; it does not have the extraordinary, detailed luminescence of D. H. Lawrence; it does not have even the whipped-up intensity of Thomas Wolfe. But there is no need to train an elephant gun on the 1930's prose of James T. Farrell: it is bad prose, and Tolkien's is relatively good prose—and once again it needs to be said that Farrell is trying (in good part unsuccessfully) to do something quite beyond Tolkien's purpose. The fence is not a prop, neither are Studs' father and younger brother Martin. The fence is decaying, as the discarded furniture in the Thomas Wolfe paragraph was "disreputable," because these are particular objects in particular relationships with the characters in Farrell's and Wolfe's books. But for Tolkien a hill is the generality of hill-ness, a chair is "low and comfortable"— that is, the generality of comfortableness. They are, in his

---

[1] James T. Farrell, *Studs Lonigan* (New York, 1938), I, 67.

terms, "at once more universal and more poignantly particular."[12] Indeed, if we knew about them what literature would be apt to tell us, we might no longer be interested.[13]

> . . . it looked like a dark black bundle left behind. But as they looked it seemed to move and sway this way and that, as if searching the ground. It then crawled, or went crouching, back into the gloom. . . . (I, 109)

"Crawled, or went crouching": the uncertainty, the ambiguity, are what Tolkien's style aims to create. "The realm of fairy-story is wide and deep and high . . . but its very richness and strangeness tie the tongue of a traveler who would report them. And while he is there it is dangerous for him to ask too many questions, lest the gates should be shut and the keys be lost.[14]

B. POETRY

I do not want to discuss the poetry of *The Lord of the Rings* at any length. A very few examples will suffice.

> Hey! Come merry dol! derry dol! My darling!
> Light goes the weather-wind and the feathered starling.
> Down along under Hill, shining in the sunlight,
> Waiting on the doorstep for the cold starlight,
> There my pretty lady is, River-woman's daughter,
> Slender as the willow-wand, clearer than the water.
> Old Tom Bombadil water-lilies bringing
> Comes hopping home again. Can you hear him singing?

[12] *Tree and Leaf*, p. 67.
[13] Austin Tappan Wright's *Islandia*, first published in 1942 and very recently republished as an inexpensive paperback, shows many of the same stylistic traits. Wright's book is far less elegant than Tolkien's in imaginative projection and in the ability to articulate and sustain self-contained world it is, however, very similar.
[14] *Tree and Leaf*, p. 11.

Hey! Come merry dol! derry dol! and merry-o,
Goldberry, Goldberry, merry yellow berry-o!
Poor old Willow-man, you tuck your roots away!
Tom's in a hurry now. Evening will follow day.
Tom's going home again water-lilies bringing.
Hey! come derry dol! Can you hear me singing? (i, 129-130)

Tolkien notes that the hobbit listeners to this song, Frodo and Sam, "stood as if enchanted." My two oldest sons, when I read them the trilogy aloud, were equally fascinated; they considered Tolkien a fine poet, as do, apparently, other serious observers.[15] I find almost all of Tolkien's verse embarrassingly bad. The "kind of balladry" in the Tom Bombadil song I have reproduced is a tissue of ill-digested borrowings from Shakespeare's plays, Longfellow, Browning, and I-know-not-what-else. The very first line, intended to be hearty, is to my ear thumpingly dull. The starling is "feathered," in line two for prosodic reasons: it might be more interesting if a starling were not feathered. "Shining in the sunlight," "the cold starlight," "slender as the willow-wand": this is all stale and virtually meaningless. Tom Bombadil is an earth-figure: his song typifies what I have called the overwrought quality of Tolkien's nature verse.

Bilbo sings an elven song. I cannot quote it at full length, but the long fifth stanza will do it justice:

> The winds of wrath came driving him,
> and blindly in the foam he fled
> from west to east and errandless,
> unheralded he homeward sped.

---

[15] The back pages of *Tree and Leaf* quote Mr. Anthony Thwaite as follows: "Professor Tolkien revealed . . . that he had a talent for songs, riddling rhymes, and a kind of balladry. In *The Adventures of Tom Bombadil* [verse largely from *The Lord of the Rings*] the talent can be seen to be something close to genius. . . ."

There flying Elwing came to him,
and flame was in the darkness lit;
more bright than light of diamond
the fire upon her carcanet.
The Silmaril she bound on him
and crowned him with the living light,
and dauntless then with burning brow
he turned his prow; and in the night
from otherworld beyond the Sea
there strong and free a storm arose,
a wind of power in Tarmenel;
by paths that seldom mortal goes
his boat it bore with biting breath
as might of death across the grey
and long-forsaken seas distressed:
from east to west he passed away. (I, 247)

"The winds of wrath," "the living light," "and dauntless
then": one begins to wonder if Tolkien is not pretty clearly
more poetaster than poet?

The poetry is at its best in relatively simple forms like
that of Bilbo's "farewell":

The Road goes ever on and on
    Down from the door where it began.
Now far ahead the Road has gone,
    And I must follow, if I can,
Pursuing it with eager feet,
    Until it joins some larger way
Where many paths and errands meet.
    And whither then? I cannot say. (I, 44)

This has at least the virtues of directness. The general use
of enjambement, followed by the striking caesura of the
final line, varies the rhythm pleasantly. It is bland, in-
offensive verse, and it fits the story, it communicates some-

230

thing about Bilbo. But is it poetry? Even the introductory poem to the trilogy succeeds, as it definitely does succeed, in good part by extrapoetic means:

> Three Rings for the Elven-kings under the sky,
>   Seven for the Dwarf-lords in their halls of stone,
> Nine for mortal men doomed to die,
>   One for the Dark Lord on his dark throne
> In the Land of Mordor where the Shadows lie.
>   One Ring to rule them all, One Ring to find them,
>   One Ring to bring them all and in the darkness bind them
> In the Land of Mordor where the Shadows lie.[16]

This is far more skillful than most of the poetry. It has unusual restraint, for Tolkien: words are used as magical incantations, and the magic is not marred by inversions, frantic adjectives, and the like. The rhyming and the repetitions are deft: this is, in my view, the one unforgettable verse in the trilogy. But for all that, the poem is a charm which works only within the tale. Not, that is, that only those who know the tale can understand the poem: rather, that without the magical intensity of the tale the poem is slight, trivial. It lacks—and is meant to lack—poetic existence in its own right.

I concede the trilogy's poetry almost no independent literary merit. Why then did Tolkien include it, and what purpose does it serve? It does serve a purpose: the song within a tale is a recognized convention, breaking into a narrative where a break is needed, providing lyric (or comic) relief, expounding on a character's feelings more succinctly (or at least differently) than prose might do. In context, too, the poetry is less conspicuous than naked on the critical page. It is interesting, often, even when it is

---

[16] This introductory verse is a kind of epigraph to each volume of the trilogy.

bad—and the narrative is so powerful that one easily condones its badness. But why did Tolkien include it, in spite of its badness? The question is perhaps best answered with another question: if he knew how bad the poetry was, would he have published it as a separate volume, *The Adventures of Tom Bombadil?* Clearly not. There is relatively little poetry in *The Lord of the Rings:* it does not get in the way, and when it does it can be skipped with no loss to the tale. I think it should also be kept in mind that there is much more, and much better (because less pretentious) poetry in Tolkien's earlier tale, *The Hobbit.* Since Tolkien had gotten into the habit of poeticizing, and indeed having carried over many of the same characters who indulged in verse-making, it surely would have been difficult for him to be objective about the later and much less good poetry. But isn't it time—like the emperor in the famous fairy-story about the nonexistent new clothes—that he was told?

II. CHARACTERIZATION

What we are entitled to ask of characterization is that it portray for us, meaningfully, significant aspects of human reality. The four or five chief characterizations in *The Lord of the Rings* are the hobbits Bilbo, Frodo, and Sam, the wizard Gandalf, and Aragorn. It will surely put both my approach and *The Lord of the Rings* to the severest test to consider these major characterizations rather than any of the numerous lesser ones.

Bilbo, who first encounters the Ring, is abundantly characterized in *The Hobbit,* of which he and Gandalf are the two principal figures. It is a cheerful, amiable characterization: Bilbo is full of vitality, courageous, generous, honest—in short, a kind of small-sized exemplar for the small-

sized readership for whom Tolkien intended the book.[17]
Bilbo has moments of laziness, moments of fear, but in a
crisis regularly rises to the occasion, whether with mercy (as
with Gollum), truthfulness (as with Thorin), or varieties
of imaginative resourcefulness (decoying the huge spiders,
riddling with Gollum, bringing the Arkenstone to Bard,
and the like). Bilbo as child-exemplar ages in *The Lord of
the Rings:* the trilogy is in all respects a more mature tale.
He is still full of fun and poetry, but he dozes more—and
under the Ring's long-continued influence he whines and
snivels a bit, too, rather like Gollum, but in a milder way.
It takes Gandalf's insistence to make him give up the Ring;
however, true to his virtuous origins, Bilbo is, as Gandalf
explains, the first in the Ring's history to surrender it
voluntarily. Nor is Bilbo *the* hobbit in *The Lord of the
Rings.* Frodo has taken that position; Bilbo is slightly off
to the side, a little like the old man dozing by the chimney
corner. He is still amiable, courageous, generous: he volun-
teers to become the Ring-bearer again; without being asked
he gives Frodo Sting, his elven sword, and the fabulous
mithril shirt. When Bilbo offers to take up the Quest, Boromir, knowing nothing of hobbits, is about to laugh, "but

[17] However, see above, p. 218 and n. 3. There is notably more child-
like tone to *The Hobbit.* Gandalf is a wizard of distinctly minor and
magicianly proportions; no Quest of any great significance is involved;
and most importantly the good and evil involved are parochial and in
all ways limited. To call *The Hobbit* an "enchanting prelude to *The
Lord of the Rings*"—a publisher's blurb—is therefore both accurate
and inaccurate. Enchanting it is, and it does precede the great trilogy,
but it gives no real hint of the intensity and fervor to be encountered
later on. I suspect that Tolkien himself had no idea. Speaking of the
years 1938-1939, he has written, in the introductory note to *Tree and
Leaf:* "At about that time we had reached Bree, and I had then no more
notion than they had of what had become of Gandalf or who Strider
was; and I had begun to despair of ever finding out." As Tolkien also
says, in the Foreword to *The Fellowship of the Ring*, "This tale grew in
the telling."

the laughter died on his lips when he saw that all the others regarded the old hobbit with grave respect" (I, 283). For as Gandalf says frequently, " 'Hobbits really are amazing creatures, as I have said before. You can learn all that there is to know about their ways in a month, and yet after a hundred years they can still surprise you at a pinch' " (I, 72).

What "significant aspects of human reality" (the phraseology is horribly academic and would surely offend Tolkien) are portrayed for us by the hobbit Bilbo? We are made to feel that small things can be very good things; that generosity is heartwarming in both the giving and the receiving, and is furthermore not very difficult to accomplish if only the heart is willing; that one can be courageous even if afraid, bold even if uncertain, decent even if provoked. These are surely significant aspects of human reality; to be made to feel these things is salutary. But how "meaningfully" are we offered these lessons? The morality is fine: how subtle is it, how aware of the true complexities of existence? There is no inherent virtue in being small, especially in a world where most things are larger. There is no universal joy in gift-giving and receiving, as there is no universal sense of honor in men: I think of the scene in Nathaniel West's *A Cool Million*, where the naive hero defends a young lady from a bully, beats the bully fair and square, holds out his hand to the bully afterwards, and is promptly hauled into oblivion (the young lady, who faints at this sight, is promptly raped by the bully). West did not intend anything but an exaggeration of traits usually somewhat less rank; Tolkien does, I think, intend his portrayal as Truth.

It is almost a religious teaching, rather than a literary one: it should not surprise us that Tolkien has said that "The Gospels contain a fairy-story, or a story of a larger

kind which embraces all the essence of fairy-stories. . . .
There is no tale ever told that men would rather find was
true. . . . To reject it leads either to sadness or to wrath."[18]
This too is Noble, this is Good, this is plainly one way to
happiness. It would be good, too, if it were in fact Truth
which *The Lord of the Rings* offers us—and there is the
difficulty. This is Faërie, not reality, and in response to
the question, "Is it true?" Tolkien has proferred the answer,
"If you have built your little world well, yes: it is true in
that world."[19] It is, I am afraid, not a sufficient answer,
for "in that world" the artist controls everything. If Bilbo
is to be rewarded for his virtue, Tolkien is the executive
force which sees to it that he is rewarded. Outside that
"little world," however, nothing better illustrates Tolkien's
own awareness of human impotence than the introductory
note to *Tree and Leaf*. After explaining that the story, "Leaf
by Niggle," was influenced by "a great-limbed poplar tree
that I could see even lying in bed," he adds: "It was suddenly lopped and mutilated by its owner, I do not know
why. It is cut down now, a less barbarous punishment for
any crimes it may have been accused of, such as being large
and alive. I do not think it had any friends, or any mourners,
except myself and a pair of owls." It is a very short step to
Tolkien's convictions about the Escape function of Faërie:

> I have claimed that Escape is one of the main functions of
> fairy-stories, and since I do not disapprove of them, it is plain
> that I do not accept the tone of scorn or pity with which
> 'Escape' is now so often used. . . . Why should a man be
> scorned, if, finding himself in prison, he tries to get out and
> go home? Or if, when he cannot do so, he thinks and talks
> about other topics than jailers and prison-walls? . . . The

[18] *Tree and Leaf*, pp. 62-63.
[19] Ibid., p. 62.

critics have chosen the wrong word, and, what is more, they are confusing, not always by sincere error, the Escape of the Prisoner with the Flight of the Deserter.[20]

Tolkien adds:

> I do not think that the reader or the maker of fairy-stories need even be ashamed of the 'escape' of archaism: of preferring not dragons, but horses, castles, sailing-ships, bows and arrows; not only elves, but knights and kings and priests. For it is after all possible for a rational man, after reflection (quite unconnected with fairy-story or romance), to arrive at the condemnation . . . of progressive things like factories, or the machineguns and bombs that appear to be their most natural and inevitable, dare we say 'inexorable', products. . . . The maddest castle that ever came out of a giant's bag in a wild Gaelic story is not only very much less ugly than a robot-factory, it is also (to use a very modern phrase) 'in a very real sense' a great deal more real. . . . It is indeed an age of 'improved means to deteriorated ends.'[21]

Let me be clear: I am not concerned, here, with Tolkien's social views. As T. S. Eliot said of another writer of epic narrative, "You cannot afford to *ignore* Dante's philosophical and theological beliefs, or to skip the passages which express them most clearly; but . . . on the other hand you are not called upon to believe them yourself."[22] I am however concerned with what Tolkien is able, by means of characterization, to tell us, "meaningfully," about our own existences. He props up Faith: I think that is a fair summary of the maximum effect which can legitimately be claimed for him in this line. And this is not, I think, an achievement for which one need go, or for which one usually does go, to literary characterization.

[20] Ibid., pp. 53-54.
[21] Ibid., pp. 56-57.
[22] "Dante" in *Selected Essays, 1917-1932*, (New York, 1932), p. 218.

It would be dull stuff to march doggedly through the four other characterizations I have named, making the same (or similar) points. Summary discussion will do. Sam is, I maintain, pure stock character—lovable, useful *ficelle* (in Henry James' terms[23]), but as a characterization virtually meaningless. Sam grows a bit, in the course of the trilogy; he learns to compose verse, he sobers and matures, and these are tributes to Tolkien's organizing genius. It was not only the tale which "grew in the telling."[24]

We are made suspicious of Aragorn, at first meeting. He is "a strange-looking weather-beaten man, sitting in the shadows near the wall . . . listening intently to the hobbit-talk. . . . The gleam of his eyes could be seen as he watched the hobbits (I, 168). But as Frodo and the others quickly discover, Aragorn is all gold and a yard wide. He is brave, loyal, honest, faithful—everything in Faërie one would expect of a king (which is what he becomes, at the end). Gandalf too is everything one might expect of a wizard, and for much of the way he is rather more than that. Gandalf is mercurial, in the sense that he adjusts to his setting, to his environment, human, hobbit, elf, or wizard, not becoming all things to all persons, but not presuming, either, on the knowledge or capacities of anyone. He is flexible, and he is also limited: this is not a wizard who can do anything he likes, but a "real" wizard, who makes mistakes, who exceeds his own capacity—and who, as far as we know, dies in the tunnels of Moria, pulled to his death by a Balrog, "a great shadow, in the middle of which was a dark form, of man-shape maybe, yet greater; and a power and terror seemed to be in it and to go before it" (I, 344). At the end of the first volume of the trilogy, Gandalf is a heroic memory, a

---

[23] See, e.g., Henry James, *The Art of the Novel* (New York, n.d.), pp. 323 ff.
[24] See note 17.

beloved memory. Less than two hundred pages later, in the second volume, he has returned, "passed through fire and deep water," (ii, 98) resurrected after his—one is tempted to say, after His Passion, though "Sacrifice" will do. And Aragorn says to him " 'You are our captain and our banner. The Dark Lord has Nine: But we have One, mightier than they: the White Rider. He has passed through the fire and the abyss, and they shall fear him. We will go where he leads' " (ii, 104). The biblical tone is no accident. Not that Gandalf is to be taken as a Christ-figure pure and simple: " 'I am Gandalf, Gandalf the White, but Black [the Enemy] is mightier still ' " (ii, 103). It is an impressive transformation, and for the forces of Good a necessary resurrection. One is delighted to have Gandalf back, even if he has mutated from Grey to White and has become distinctly otherworldly. But one is also disappointed: the limited wizard, the less than omnipotent wizard, the "real" wizard, has become a figure of impressive magic. As a characterization Gandalf is necessarily less meaningful from that point on: he is a force more than he is a personage.

I have saved Frodo, the Ring-bearer, for last. He is the hardest case to deal with. Frodo has something of Bilbo in him, and something of Sam, and something almost like Aragorn—but something more, too, which is very much himself. It is in Frodo, and in Frodo only, that I think Tolkien achieves something of what one can call the characterization of literature. It is not the keen sharp portrayal of, say, Jay Gatsby, "with his hands plunged like weights in his coat pockets, . . . standing in a puddle of water glaring tragically into my eyes,"[25] stepping outside so he can step inside and meet, again, Daisy Buchanan, for whom he has waited and schemed. It is not simply that Tolkien has not Fitz-

---

[25] F. Scott Fitzgerald, *The Great Gatsby* (London, 1954), p. 92.

gerald's style, that he cannot do with a single sentence what Fitzgerald can. The slow subtlety of Gatsby's portrayal is I think considerably more meaningful than the portrait of Frodo. " 'Why, my God! they used to go there [Gatsby's mansion] by the hundreds'," a casual, once-drunken guest has just been saying, at Gatsby's lonely funeral. "He took off his glasses and wiped them again [it is raining hard], outside and in. 'The poor son-of-a-bitch', he said."[26] This is a sparse epitaph beyond Tolkien's stylistic powers. When Sam, Merry, and Pippin see Frodo and the others off on their journey out of life, the testimonial is more elaborate but much less eloquent: "At last the three companions turned away, and never again looking back they rode slowly home-wards; and they spoke no word to one another until they came back to the Shire, but each had great comfort in his friends on the long grey road" (III, 311). Fitzgerald has shown us, through Gatsby, something we did not know, or knew only vaguely or partially: the pathos of Gatsby's love for Daisy, and the bitterness of "society's" use of him. Tol-kien has demonstrated to us, again, that Friendship is a Good Thing.

But Frodo throughout is something more than this. He grows in stature much more impressively than his servant and friend, Sam: open, jolly, in many ways like Bilbo at the start, Frodo also has a reflective, almost a worldly-wise side. His long series of incredible experiences, his hardships, pain, the friends he meets, loses, the enemies he must confront— all temper his openness, all deepen and broaden his reflec-tiveness. His mission succeeds, but though it has not been too much for him in any literal sense it proves, afterwards, too much to have lived through. "Saruman [a fallen wizard] . . . stared at Frodo. There was a strange look in his eyes of

26 Ibid., p. 182.

mingled wonder and respect and hatred. 'You have grown, Halfling,' he said. 'Yes, you have grown very much' " (III, 299). But as Frodo soon after tells Sam, who finds him "very pale and his eyes [seeming] to see things far away, . . . 'I am wounded . . . wounded; it will never really heal' " (III, 305). And when Frodo decides it is time to take the final journey he again tells Sam: " 'I have been too deeply hurt, Sam. I tried to save the Shire, and it has been saved, but not for me. It must often be so, Sam, when things are in danger: some one has to give them up, lose them, so that others may keep them' " (III, 309). The message is true but not remarkable; what gives it power is that we have by this point seen Frodo living it, seen him pass from unknowing hobbit to something larger and wiser and sadder. The strength of Tolkien's faith supports this renunciation: there do have to be heroes, and if Frodo has not been one, no one ever has. Nor are heroes a notably happy breed. Frodo goes, life goes on; Sam weeps, but he goes back to the Shire—and the trilogy ends, in perhaps the highest tribute to the just-departed Frodo that one could imagine, with Sam returning home, sitting down with his new daughter in his lap, and drawing "a deep breath. 'Well, I'm back', he said" (III, 311).

III. INCIDENT

Little needs to be discussed, I think, under this heading. *The Lord of the Rings* is a genuine epic, with all the vast sweep and complex dovetailing necessary to sustain a large and powerful tale. Narrative art is, as I said at the start, Tolkien's primary concern; it is also and quite obviously his forte. The trilogy almost never flags. Tolkien's inventiveness carries off variation after variation; his story-telling virtuosity is wonderful, and I do not want to deny this talent its worth.

All the same, there is a certain amount of what comes close to the trickery, the mechanical plot manipulation of the lesser tale-teller. After the first appearance of the Black Riders (we are still in the Shire), Frodo is being taken to the ferry by Farmer Maggot.

> *Clop-clop, clop-clop.* The rider was nearly on them.
>
> 'Hallo there!' called Farmer Maggot. The advancing hoofs stopped short. They thought they could dimly guess a dark cloaked shape in the mist, a yard or two ahead.
>
> 'Now then!' said the farmer, throwing the reins to Sam and striding forward. 'Don't you come a step nearer! What do you want and where are you going?'
>
> 'I want Mr. Baggins. Have you seen him?' said a muffled voice—but the voice was the voice of Merry Brandybuck. A dark lantern was uncovered, and its light fell on the astonished face of the farmer.
>
> 'Mr. Merry!' he cried.
>
> 'Yes, of course! Who did you think it was?' said Merry coming forward. As he came out of the mist and their fears subsided, he seemed suddenly to diminish to ordinary hobbit size. He was riding a pony, and a scarf was swathed around his neck and over his chin to keep out the fog. (I, 106)

It cannot reasonably be argued, I think, that this is tongue-in-cheek. Tolkien has a sense of humor, but not about Black Riders and the Quest.

There are other, essentially similar manipulatory incidents. I have mentioned the resurrection of Gandalf; there is throughout something of a propensity for last-minute, *deus ex machina* rescues, for what can be called "O. Henry" endings. This is part of the delight which we take in the story, and surely part of the delight Tolkien takes in it— discovering for us, and for himself, how Good is to prevail over Evil. These ironical confrontations of Evil with sudden-appearing Good rest on Faith; they do not harm the narrative per se but certainly they lessen the stature of the trilogy.[27]

IV. MORALITY

Tolkien's foreword to the trilogy declares, flatly:

> As for any inner meaning or 'message', it has in the intention of the author none. It is neither allegorical nor topical. . . . I cordially dislike allegory in all its manifestations, and always have done so since I grew old and wary enough to detect its presence. I much prefer history, true or feigned. (I, 6-7)

C. S. Lewis has said something very similar: "Some published fantasies of my own have had foisted on them (often by the kindliest critics) so many admirable allegorical meanings that I never dreamed of as to throw me into doubt whether it is possible for the wit of man to devise anything in which the wit of some other man cannot find, and plausibly find, an allegory."[28] If it is hard to quarrel with an author on a subject as to which he has so peculiarly excellent a source of information, it is perhaps harder to ignore the contrary evidence of the stories themselves.

Consider, first, a tale called "Leaf by Niggle." Written in 1938-1939, "when *The Lord of the Rings* was beginning to unroll itself,"[29] it is from beginning to end an allegory of salvation. "There was once a little man called Niggle," the

---

[27] I must confess—and it seems to me relevant—that one of my chief pleasures, while writing this essay, has been the opportunity for rereading much of the trilogy. It stands up beautifully.

[28] Quoted in Roger Sherman Loomis, *The Development of Arthurian Romance* (New York, 1964), p. 10. The back cover of *The Two Towers*, in the Ballantine edition, quotes C. S. Lewis: "No imaginary world has been projected . . . so relevant to the actual human situation yet so free from allegory. . . ."

[29] *Tree and Leaf*, introductory note. "Leaf by Niggle" forms the second part of the book, being reprinted from the *Dublin Review* of 1947.

tale begins, "who had a long journey to make." The "long journey" is physical death—this is a distinctly Christian allegory, in which life after death, and redemption through purgatory, play a large role—and Niggle is a failed artist. He, and also his neighbor (called Parish!), meet with success (i.e., redemption), finally, by dint of concern for others rather than with themselves. It is all very sentimental, with a style to match: questioned, in purgatory, by a pair of Judging Voices, all Niggle can talk about is his poor neighbor, at rather nauseating length. When shortly thereafter he and his neighbor meet, in the afterlife, "They did not speak, just nodded as they used to do, passing in the lane; but now they walked about together, arm in arm."[30] When Parish decides to wait for his wife, Niggle declares, as he moves to higher ground, " 'Things might have been different, but they could not have been better. . . . Good-bye!' He shook Parish's hand warmly: a good, firm, honest hand it seemed. He turned and looked back for a moment. The blossom on the Great Tree was shining like flame. All the birds were flying in the air and singing. Then he smiled, and nodded to Parish, and went off. . . ."[31] The story is slight, uninteresting even as narrative: in spite of his concern with small things and small people, Tolkien is distinctly not a miniaturist. He requires the vast machinery of plot complexity, a challenge to which he rises with apparent ease. But as an indication of Tolkien's frame of mind, "Leaf by Niggle" is fascinating. It underlies the basically moral purpose of his work, and emphasizes, too, some of the things of which his morality approves: kindness, friendship, artistic devotion and single-mindedness, trees and birds and mountains. A train finds its way into the story, but it is "a very pleasant little local train," it has a "little engine [which] puffed along," and when the

[30] *Tree and Leaf*, p. 87.
[31] Ibid., p. 90.

train arrives at its destination "There was no station, and no signboard, only a flight of steps up the green embankment."[32]

Taking allegory in its very loosest sense, I think *The Lord of the Rings* is indisputably allegorical. I do not mean that Frodo, or even Gandalf (as we first meet him), is a symbolic representation of Good—though surely the Nazgûl, not to mention the Lord of Mordor, are symbols of Evil. Nor do I mean that Frodo's journey is a neat representation of, say, the kind of journey undertaken by Niggle. Rather, so much Faith underlies the trilogy, so much strong feeling about the world (the so-called real world, as Tolkien might say), that representational elements are unavoidable: this is, again, a "good and evil story." When Frodo has reached Rivendell, for example, and Gandalf is telling him about "the Dark Lord in Mordor," Gandalf exclaims: " 'Not all his servants and chattels are wraiths! There are orcs and trolls, there are wargs and werewolves; and there have been and still are many Men, warriors and kings, that walk alive under the Sun, and yet are under his sway. And their number is growing daily.' "[33] It can be argued that the reference to men is essential, since they too are part of Middle-earth. It must however be clear that Men are singled out by Gandalf-Tolkien, receiving very special and detailed attention beyond the needs of the story proper. One does not need to claim any precise allegory, or even any particular topical reference, to see what C. S. Lewis has called the trilogy's relevance "to the actual human situation."[34] In loose terms this is allegorical enough.

---

[32] Ibid, pp. 84, 85.

[33] I, 234. In *The Two Towers*, after the destruction of Saruman's factory-like fortress, the orc-allies of Saruman are obliterated but "the Ents let the Men go, after they had questioned them" (p. 173).

[34] See note 28.

Tolkien's strong Christian beliefs underly the ultimate frailty of *all* the personages in *The Lord of the Rings*, not excluding the greatest of them, Sauron, the Dark Lord, the Enemy. Man needs God (or whatever the unnamed Force ought to be termed), and God needs Man's goodness to carry out His will. It is Gandalf once more who phrases it; again he is speaking to Frodo, rather earlier in the story, and discussing Bilbo's finding of the Ring:

> 'Behind that there was something else at work, beyond any design of the Ring-maker. I can put it no plainer than by saying that Bilbo was *meant* to find the Ring, and *not* by its maker [its maker is Sauron, the Enemy]. In which case you also were *meant* to have it. And that may be an encouraging thought.' (I, 65)

Tolkien never becomes more specific than this; he hardly needs to. When Frodo tries to make matters clearer, demanding "Why was I chosen?", Gandalf replies:

> 'Such questions cannot be answered. . . . You may be sure that it was not for any merit that others do not possess: not for power or wisdom, at any rate. But you have been chosen, and you must therefore use such strength and heart and wits as you have.' (I, 70)

And Gandalf assures Frodo, " 'It may be your task to find the Cracks of Doom; but that quest may be for others: I do not know. At any rate you are not ready for that long road yet' "(I, 75). Frodo's Quest is, in these terms, the education of the soul, the striving for salvation. There is no need to push the representational element, or to force it into a consistently Christian-like mould. It is there, it conditions Tolkien's whole approach to the "good and evil" of his long tale, and its importance in any literary estimate of the trilogy seems unmistakable.

My position, from the start, has been that *The Lord of the Rings* is magnificent but that it is not literature. I have taken a deliberately narrow view of literature, and pursued my analysis in rather narrow fashion. And I have omitted, also deliberately, what is of course the primary requirement of any literary work: imagination. That Tolkien has it, and that *The Lord of the Rings* abundantly displays it, is so obvious as to need no discussion. In broader terms than I have here employed, accordingly, there is small doubt that the trilogy is literature and very fine literature. I have meant this paper as a corrective, as a curb on some of the irresponsible adulation currently being extended to Tolkien. He deserves high praise, even adulation, but there is little sense in praising Milton as a writer on domestic science, Wordsworth as a botanist, or T. S. Eliot as a teacher of Sanskrit.

15

TOLKIEN AND FRODO BAGGINS

Roger Sale

IN ANY STUDY OF MODERN HEROISM, IF J.R.R. TOLKIEN'S
The Lord of the Rings did not exist it would have to be invented. For at one place or another in this massive trilogy
all the heroic issues of the western world, from *Beowulf* to
D. H. Lawrence, are enacted, and the matter of these many
heroisms is also the matter of the work's worth and ability to
outlast its cults. Just why Tolkien has established himself so
strongly among the eager young is not yet clear, and his
popularity there is probably much more significant than his
gradual acceptance into those academic realms that are
loyal to the likes of C. S. Lewis and Chesterton. For the
young show no signs of admiring Anglo-Oxford as such and
generally have no positive response to the Old and the old
heroic ways. What they see, then, in *The Lord of the Rings*
may be a good part of what is really there, but because the
enthusiasts as yet are more excited than articulate they have
not really been able to say what makes Tolkien such an exciting author for them. As a result, literary assessment of
the achievement is in its infancy and liable to remain so as
long as elvish runes and details discussed in the appendices
are still lively issues. The middle position—the position that
firmly believes that *The Lord of the Rings* is a great work

but refuses to become entangled in hunts after fascinating trivia—remains fairly open, and the historian of modern heroism can at least attempt to assume this position without fear of a horde of rivals.

The prospect, it must be confessed, is terribly exciting. For in Tolkien's Middle-earth lie the riders of Rohan, Beowulf-like in their love of lore, their simple and great strength, and their belief that brave men die well in defense of their lord and their honor; Aragorn, half-elven figure of romance, the wandering ranger who becomes King Elessar of Gondor; gigantic Wordsworthian tree-like Ents who swoop down in revenge on the man who treated them wantonly; Sam Gamgee, the namesake of Pickwick's servant, staunch in his servility and love of domesticity; Sam's master, Frodo Baggins, the real hero in this book where all must be heroic, who acts like any modern alienated man but who also is Tolkien's affirmation of possibility in a world where all old and other heroic types are by themselves inadequate. It is, thus, epic and romance and novel by turns, held together by a central myth that manages to partake of all the myths of all the heroes of the past without ever ceasing to be a myth of Tolkien's own devising. Those who start but do not finish *The Lord of the Rings* complain of its literariness, its air of deriving from countless earlier works, but this quality, though apparent in very sentence and often indeed embarrassing, is also the source of its greatest strength. Just why this should be so must be the central concern for those for whom the work is both a marvel and a curse, the masterpiece of a crank and also a central document in modern literature.

Tolkien's biographer will someday be able to say just when the myth of the Ring and the idea of heroism attendant upon it came into being. For an outsider only a few things are clear. *The Lord of the Rings* was published as separate volumes in the middle fifties—*The Fellowship of the Ring* (1954), *The Two Towers* (1955), *The Return of the King* (1956)—but the work had been in the making for more than fifteen years. Tolkien had published *The Hobbit* in 1938, and the end of that book clearly foreshadows the later trilogy; he may have had the work in mind before then. It looks, strictly on the basis of internal literary evidence, as though Tolkien had been musing about Middle-earth for a long time but did not discover until he was finishing *The Hobbit* just how his vastly inventive genius could be used to make a story. For most of its length *The Hobbit* is the sort of book—*The Wind in the Willows* and the Pooh books are other examples—that appeals to a particular sort of reader, be he child or adult, whose sense of wit is near his sense of fun and whose willingness to pretend is akin to his ability to remember. The hobbits are not strictly human, but, like Mole and Toad in Kenneth Grahame or Pooh and Rabbit in Milne, they are based on recognizable English types. Hobbits are smaller and longer-lived than men, fond of living in houses without windows, fond of beer and good conversation, always in need of tobacco and able to live without the usual restraints of police or unfriendly women—indeed, C. S. Lewis' reminiscences of life at Oxford with Tolkien and others are often descriptive of hobbit life. In *The Hobbit* and in parts of *The Lord of the Rings* Tolkien writes of the hobbits with a satisfaction about their life that, for all his clarity about what is deficient in them, reflects a personal well-being:

> They went round the hole, and evicted three young hobbits (two Boffins and a Bolger) who were knocking holes in the walls of one of the cellars. Frodo also had a tussle with young Sancho Proudfoot (old Odo Proudfoot's grandson), who had begun an excavation in the larger pantry, where he thought

there was an echo. The legend of Bilbo's gold excited both curiosity and hope, for legendary gold (mysteriously obtained, if not positively ill-gotten) is, as every one knows, any one's for the finding—unless the search is interrupted. (I, 48)

In *The Hobbit* this search for legendary gold might take up a whole chapter, and so delight a kind of reader and disgust another kind. But here, at the opening of the trilogy, Tolkien is, as the parenthetical remarks show best, too fond of this kind of fooling really to repudiate it and yet too much concerned with other and larger matters to dwell on such things. We know, as we read this, that no one would try to make a whole trilogy of such stuff, and yet we can sense also that its author rather enjoys the game of giving names and making asides and spinning out details of the lore of curious creatures.

This lore, this love of naming and of dwelling on ritual details, is the ground bass of Tolkien's imagination, and it is therefore that to which he returns whenever he is in doubt about where to go next. But the myth of the Ring consistently transforms this realm into a larger and sterner world where describing something is a matter of making clear and not a matter of spinning delightful bits of closely detailed decorations. His writing does not change—the literariness is always there, as is the love of lore and the reliance on naming, but when he is telling his story of the Ring none of these things is done for its own sake.

But everywhere he looked he saw the signs of war. The Misty Mountains were crawling like ant hills: Orcs were issuing out of a thousand holes. Under the boughs of Mirkwood there was deadly strife of Elves and Men and fell beasts. The land of the Beornings was aflame; a cloud was over Moria; smoke rose on the borders of Lórien. Horsemen were galloping on the grass of Rohan; wolves poured from Isengard. From the havens of Harad ships of war put out to sea; and out of the East Men were moving endlessly: swordsmen, spearmen, bowmen upon horses, chariots of chieftains and laden wains. All the power of the Dark Lord was in motion. (I, 416-417).

From a distance this passage is only a more portentous version of the first, war instead of games. But to say this is only to say that Tolkien makes the matter of his great doings out of the same material as he makes his minor tricks, and, as it is hoped will become clear, what the second passage does that the first does not is to transform lore from subject into activity, not just by being serious but by being about something that matters. The Ring forces Tolkien to be an author rather than a collector, to choose his names and his details with an eye to their relevance rather than to their mere attractiveness. It does this, furthermore, by showing Tolkien (almost against his will, it sometimes seems) that the heroism about which he writes best and therefore most cares about is of a distinctively modern cast—a heroism based upon the refusal to yield to despair rather than on any clear sense of goal or achievement, a heroism that accepts the facts of history and yet refuses to give in to the tempting despair that those facts offer.

The Ring was forged long before the story opens by Sauron, the Dark Lord, and was created as a master ring, one that could bind the rings of power fashioned by the elves for themselves, dwarves, and men. The Ring was lost by Sauron in an earlier war and passed by a series of accidents and deceits into the hands of a hobbit, Bilbo Baggins, who had no notion of its power beyond knowing it could make him invisible when he wore it. Sauron gradually became powerful once again and returned to his stronghold of Mordor, from whence he began a long search to find his lost Ring. As *The Fellowship of the Ring* opens Bilbo hands the

Ring over to his nephew and heir, Frodo. Bilbo leaves the Shire, home of the hobbits, and Frodo keeps the Ring while knowing nothing of its power until he is visited by the wizard Gandalf. Gandalf tells Frodo the history of the Ring, shows him the inscription on it, and recites its power:

> Three Rings for the Elven-kings under the sky,
>   Seven for the Dwarf-lords in their halls of stone,
> Nine for Mortal Men doomed to die,
>   One for the Dark Lord on his dark throne
> In the Land of Mordor where the Shadows lie.
> One Ring to rule them all, One Ring to find them,
>   One Ring to bring them all and in the darkness bind them
> In the Land of Mordor where the Shadows lie.

In a work filled with riddles and songs this is the only one about the Ring and is much the most important and best. Here, at the beginning, it is both an explanation and an evocation of mystery. Gandalf tells Frodo about the three elven rings and the seven dwarf rings, but all this means little to Frodo. Bilbo got the One Ring from a small nasty hobbit-like creature named Sméagol, the Gollum, and now Frodo has it; Sauron, furthermore, has gradually pieced together the history of the Ring and is at that moment searching for a hobbit by the name of Baggins. Frodo asks Gandalf why they do not merely destroy the Ring to keep it from Sauron. Gandalf asks him to do so:

> It was an admirable thing and altogether precious. When he took it out he had intended to fling it from him into the very hottest part of the fire. But he found now that he could not do so, not without a great struggle. He weighed the Ring in his hand, hesitating, and forcing himself to remember all that Gandalf had told him; and then with an effort of will he made a movement, as if to cast it away—but he found that he had put it back in his pocket.

Gandalf laughed grimly. 'You see? Already you too, Frodo, cannot easily let it go, nor will to damage it. And I could not "make you"—except by force, which would break your mind. . . . There is only one way: to find the Cracks of Doom in the depths of Orodruin, the Firemountain, and cast the Ring in there, if you really wish to destroy it, to put it beyond the grasp of the Enemy for ever.' (I, 70)

Frodo then wants to know why Gandalf himself cannot take the Ring since he knows so much more about it and is more powerful than Frodo:

'No,' cried Gandalf, springing to his feet. 'With that power I should have power too great and terrible. And over me the Ring would gain a power still greater and more deadly.' His eyes flashed and his face was lit as by a fire within. (I, 70-71)

The Ring must be destroyed because its only use is to bind the power of others, but to destroy it means taking it to the land of Mordor where the shadows lie. It is a very simple conception, really, and all its ramifications will not become clear either to Frodo or the reader until much later, but even here it is possible to see how much the idea of the Ring does for Tolkien. The stronger the Ring-bearer the stronger his power and temptation to use the Ring himself, and this means that the whole machinery of ancient fairy tales can be employed with someone not at all heroic (in the ancient sense) as the central figure. Frodo knows he is "not made for perilous quests," and yet he can see that no one else is better suited.

So Frodo sells his home and sends out word he is retiring to his childhood home farther east in the Shire. But even before he leaves the need for haste becomes clear, as mysterious black riders appear, sniffing and asking for a hobbit named Baggins. Frodo moves stealthily, keeping away from the high road as much as possible, accompanied by his servant Sam Gamgee and eventually two other young hobbits, Pippin Took and Merry Brandybuck. All the others know is that Frodo is in some danger and must go on a long journey, and that they, therefore, must go with him. New people and new dangers keep appearing—first it is a group of friendly elves, then an old eccentric in an ancient forest named Tom Bombadil, then more riders, then a Ranger named Strider who rescues them from the town of Bree when Frodo has given himself away by putting on the Ring in a tavern show. Because the highway is constantly being watched, they must move circuitously and slowly; one night the black riders approach their fire, and Frodo desperately tries to hide by becoming invisible. But the riders are servants of the Ring and Frodo only becomes more visible to them when he puts the Ring on, and so he is seriously wounded in the shoulder. Finally, after a dash along the highway, the hobbits and Strider get the wounded Frodo to Rivendell, ancient home of the half-elven and the original destination given Frodo by Gandalf.

Up to this point the scale of the story is easily comprehensible by hobbit and reader alike—it is a dangerous journey classifiable as "adventure." The black riders seem more than men, to be sure, but the sort of thing the hobbits expected, and Strider's silent strength is exactly what they imagined a Ranger would be. But at Rivendell the half-elven lord Elrond has called a council (Gandalf, Bilbo, and many others are there) and the hobbits begin to glimpse how much is at stake in their journey with the Ring. They learn from the dwarf Gimli of Sauron's effort to use the dwarf-lord to regain the Ring and of the revenge that is threatened when the offer is refused. They learn from a man from Gondor named Boromir that Sauron has moved out of Mordor and has reoccupied some land taken from him in his last defeat. Boromir tells also of a prophecy he heard in a dream:

Seek for the Sword that was broken;
In Imladris it dwells;
There shall be counsels taken
Stronger than Morgul-spells.
There shall be shown a token
   That Doom is near at hand,
For Isildur's bane shall waken,
    And the halfling forth shall stand. (I, 259)

Boromir and his friends had understood none of this, so Strider rises with the sword that was broken and Elrond tells them that Strider is Aragorn, heir to the kingdom of Gondor. Then Gandalf introduces Frodo with the Ring, Isildur's bane, and the halfling stands forth. Here lore and action meet, but not really in a way that any of the hobbits can quite understand—Frodo is fitting into some ancient pattern, but he himself does not know how or why.

Gandalf then describes the treachery of Saruman the White Wizard who had once been the greatest in the councils of the West but who has since sought to capture Gandalf and to gain the Ring for himself. Bilbo tells of his part in the history of the Ring—it had passed from Sauron to Isildur to the waters of the Anduin where it was found by the Gollum from whom Bilbo won it. All this does fill in many details and as this happens the tireless stress on strange names, runes, and lore begins to mean more than it had earlier. Here, for instance, is part of Gandalf's conversation with the eagle Gwaihir who rescues him after his capture by Saruman:

'. . . I will bear you to Edoras, where the Lord of Rohan sits in his hall,' he said; 'for that is not very far off.' And I was glad, for in the Riddermark of Rohan the Rohirrim, the Horse-Lords dwell, and there are no horses like those that are bred in the great vale between the Misty Mountains and the White.

> 'Are the Men of Rohan still to be trusted, do you think?'
> I said to Gwaihir, for the treason of Saruman had shaken my
> faith.
>
> 'They pay a tribute of horses,' he answered, 'and send many
> yearly to Mordor, or so it is said; but they are not yet under
> the yoke. But if Saruman has become evil, as you say, then
> their doom cannot be long delayed.' (I, 275)

Under the pressure of Sauron's rise to power all Tolkien's
manners are taking on clearer lights, and the lore about the
Rohirrim and the portentous naming of places—"that great
vale between the Misty Mountains and the White"—begins
to seem the language of one who seeks to know what the
world is now like and who needs to discover what, in the
world that once was, is still outside the grasp of the Dark
Lord. The effect of the council in Rivendell is to begin to
show that what is involved here is not merely a perilous
journey but also a war.

The old warriors, furthermore, cannot fight this one, for
the elven lords, glorious though they seem to the hobbits,
are faded now, rulers of small lands, unable to stir abroad.
They seek only to hide the Ring, perhaps in the sea, but
Gandalf knows better:

> 'It is not our part here to take thought only for a season, or
> for a few lives of Men, or for a passing age of this world. We
> should seek a final end of this menace, even if we do not hope
> to make one.' (I, 280)

The prose is beginning to ring, yet to accept all the heavy
weight of this sort of speech would be, perhaps, to accept
rather blindly the value of Middle-earth at something like
Gandalf's price. Tolkien is just beginning to argue this way
during the long recitations of Gandalf, Strider-Aragorn, and
Elrond, but for the most part he sticks to the hobbits and to
using their discoveries as the means for our discoveries.

The hobbits, here, listen assiduously, and they see people and maps everwhere which could tell much about the lands they are about to move in, but they ask few questions. " 'I will take the Ring,' " Frodo tells the Council, " 'though I do not know the way.' " Gandalf may seek a final end to the menace but Frodo goes only because he knows that is his task, and the other hobbits go because Frodo is going.

So a fellowship is formed to move south with the Ring: the four hobbits, Gandalf, Aragorn (who is going to Gondor with the sword that was broken), Boromir, Legolas the elf, and Gimli the dwarf. There is no need or use for a powerful army, for that would only attract attention to an even more powerful army of Sauron; the fellowship is best armed in the knowledge that Sauron could not understand the desire of anyone to destroy the Ring and so will not be looking for them to move south from Rivendell, toward Mordor and apparent suicide. The company moves through Moria, ancient underground mountain kingdom of the dwarves, and in a fierce fight there, at the bridge of Khazad-Dûm, Gandalf is lost in a fight with a Balrog and Aragorn assumes command. They then move out of the mountains and into Lothlórien, home of the elven-queen Galadriel, where time seems not to exist and "all that Frodo saw was shapely, but the shapes seemed at once clear-cut, as if they had been first conceived and drawn at the uncovering of his eyes, and ancient as if they had endured for ever" (I, 365). In these places, in Moria and Lothlórien, the hobbits and the readers begin to understand the hugeness of the world in which they move and to see for themselves the ancientness of life that had hitherto been only the lore of others. They meet creatures, some merely ferocious and others really malicious, who have neither knowledge nor care of their mission, the Ring, or Sauron: wargs, orcs, the Balrog. When Boromir casually throws a stone in a pool outside Moria, Frodo says,

" 'I am afraid of the pool. Don't disturb it' "; suddenly the pool "comes to life" and "out from the water a long sinuous tentacle had crawled; it was pale-green and luminous and wet" (I, 321, 322). In Lothlórien there is momentary respite from struggle, but also discovery:

> In Rivendell there was memory of ancient things; in Lórien the ancient things still lived on in the waking world. Evil had been seen and heard there, sorrow had been known; the Elves feared and distrusted the world outside: wolves were howling on the wood's borders: but on the land of Lórien no shadow lay. (I, 364)

The rampant and threatening vitality of Moria, the preserved stillness of Lórien—"in winters here no heart could mourn for summer or for spring"—these are in one sense only places on the journey south, but in another sense they begin to show what the journey is all about. The hobbits cannot quite understand Gandalf when he says that the Shire is in danger, and they are so overwhelmed by Rivendell that they cannot understand that Elrond too is depending on them. But in Moria an ancient kingdom has fallen, and in Lórien another such kingdom is fading, and slowly it becomes clear that these worlds simply *are*, rising and falling in the flux of history, following their natural course. The fellowship is of supreme importance at one moment in history, for if Sauron gains the Ring the whole process of history would be transformed. The Ring can find and bind—that is evil because it is unnatural, because life is being oneself and following one's own nature; war, then, is the struggle to be alive, unbound.

Such a formulation is not, to be sure, made by any hobbit here or by anyone in the trilogy even, but it is one that Tolkien's way of unfolding his narrative and its implications forces upon his reader. The word "natural," in the sense used above, is unknown in *The Lord of the Rings*, but it is the simplest way of beginning to indicate what the book is all about. Here is the way, or one of the ways, Tolkien does it:

'There lies the fastness of Mirkwood,' said Haldir. 'It is clad in a forest of dark fir, where the trees strive one against another and their branches rot and wither. In the midst upon a stony height stands Dol Goldur, where long the hidden enemy had his dwelling. We fear now it is inhabited again, and with power sevenfold. A black cloud lies often over it of late. In this high place you may see the two powers that are opposed one to another; and ever strive now in thought, but whereas the light perceives the very heart of the darkness, its own secret has not been discovered. Not yet.' He turned and climbed swiftly down, and they followed him. (I, 366)

Tolkien here makes a metaphor by repeating a verb—the trees strive and the two powers strive, so that as tree against tree leads to rotting and withering, so light against dark leads to war. We understand that "light" and "dark" are symbolic names, but the effect of the metaphor is to insist they are natural powers as well, warring naturally and fatefully the way tree strives against tree.

But "light" still has the effect here of being a name for the moral power of goodness, and so this paragraph is followed by one much more stunning:

At the hill's foot Frodo found Aragorn, standing still and *silent as a tree;* but in his hand was a small golden bloom of elanor, and a *light was in his eyes.* He was *wrapped in some fair memory:* and as Frodo looked at him he knew that he beheld things as they once had been in this same place. For the grim *years were removed* from the face of Aragorn, and he seemed clothed in white, a young lord tall and fair; and he spoke words in the Elvish tongue to one whom Frodo could not see. (I, 366-367, italics mine)

The italicized phrases here can be seen as "literally true." In Lothlórien the trees are now silent but once were not, so that "silent as a tree" does not mean "quiet" or "dumb" but something like "deliberately silent." The light of Lothlórien shines from a vanished world, and the light which Aragorn once saw when all Lothlórien was alive shines now only as a memory. Yet he was there so he now is wrapped in the memory that shines in his eyes. This sense of past illuminating present is clinched with a simple ambiguity: in "as Frodo looked at him he knew that he beheld things as they once had been," the second "he" can refer either to Aragorn or Frodo, so that the light that wraps Aragorn in memory also is seen by Frodo in Aragorn's eyes.

The whole idea of "light," thus, is given resonance as a natural force and a historical motion of living things— Aragorn becomes indeed "clothed in white, a young lord tall and fair," and the word *elven* loses any sense it may have had of being embarrassingly literary and derivative. Song and lore are brought to life, and as they are the war is no longer a struggle of "light" and "dark" seen as names for good and evil, but is now a struggle to "be natural" and to be alive and preserve life when it is threatened. So too the One Ring begins to seem less a lovely idea to animate a tale and more the threat to life that Gandalf and others have insisted it is all along.

Just before they leave Lothlórien, Frodo and Sam are offered a look in Galadriel's mirror, an elven pool, and here the threats begin to become explicit for them. Sam looks and sees the Shire with trees chopped down, the Old Mill destroyed, and Bagshot Row torn up. Elrond had warned them that all was not safe in the Shire, but none had ever dreamed anything like this could really happen. Frodo has glimpses of a wizard that may be Gandalf or Saruman, of the sea and a river, of a city with seven towers, and then "the Mirror went altogether dark, as dark as if a hole had opened in the world of sight," and in the emptiness Frodo sees an eye, single, terrible, intent, "a window into nothing," and the eye is looking among other things, for Frodo (I, 379). The Ring suddenly becomes heavy and Frodo is drawn toward the eye, but Galadriel stops him and shows him her ring, one of the three for the elven-kings under the sky. She tells him that her ring is worthless if Sauron gains the One, and that even if he does not her power will diminsh because it must, naturally. Frodo offers her the Ring and for a moment she thinks of the Queen of the Night it could help her become, but the thought passes and she chooses to remain herself, Galadriel, and so Frodo too must remain himself, the Ring-bearer. From here on, though the Ring becomes increasingly heavy and Frodo seldom knows where he is going, he never again tries to give up his task, valiant and hopeless and absurd though it be.

The Company moves down the river Anduin, the dividing line between Mordor and Gondor miles to the south. Boromir tries to persuade Frodo to stay to the western side and go with him to Gondor, but Frodo knows his destination can only be Mordor. Boromir has never understood what Frodo now understands about the Ring and so he seeks to have it for Gondor in the coming war, not realizing that to use the Ring in the name of anything is to be defeated by the urge to find and bind powerfully. Boromir finally tries to force the Ring from Frodo and Frodo flees, slipping on the Ring and crossing the river. Of the others only Sam can figure out what has happened and so he follows Frodo across while the others remain on the west bank and soon find themselves attacked by a band of orcs. So the fellowship is broken, and the first volume ends.

It is a very good book, *The Fellowship of the Ring*—it has some slow places near the beginning with Bilbo's birthday party and Tom Bombadil, and perhaps nothing in it matches the greatest things in the next two volumes, but it is the one that most consistently improves with each re-reading. Tolkien has serious limitations as a writer about battles and the heroism it demands, but as a writer about danger he hardly has an equal. What makes the first volume so strong is Tolkien's ability to make the sense of danger, the sense of immediate place, and the sense of expanding horizons almost coequal. At the beginning, for instance, we have the black riders, but by the end these riders have taken more ominous form as the Nazgûl, the Ringwraiths of the nine mortal men doomed to die, the very definition of shadow—"a dark shape, like a cloud and yet not a cloud, for it moved far more swiftly, came out of the blackness in the South, and sped towards the Company, blotting out all light as it approached" (I, 403). The quiet of Rivendell and the quiet of Lothlórien are perhaps different, but what is really different is the way Frodo sees them, having had the terrors of Moria and the loss of Gandalf come between. As Frodo understands more there is always more to understand, and as a result the story here seems, really, majestically even and unrelenting for all its changes of pace and tone.

In the last two volumes Tolkien splits the narrative in two: the first part of each volume describes the coming of the war to the lands west of the Anduin—to the forest of Fangorn, the plains of Rohan and Helm's Deep, to Saruman's castle Isengard, and finally to Gondor—and the adventures gain their focus through the members of the fellowship who move west—Aragorn, Pippin, Merry, Legolas and Gimli, and Gandalf who returns from his fight with the Balrog; the second half of each volume covers the trip of Sam and Frodo to Mordor. This journey, where the trilogy rises to its greatest heights, is so much superior to the account of the war in the west that the gap in quality forces one to ask why the heroism of Frodo and Sam should strike such resonant chords in Tolkien while that of the others, gravely and firmly though Tolkien believes in it, should remain so unable to stir his genius. First let us turn to the failures, and then to the success.

Probably everyone who enjoys reading Tolkien has asked at least himself why it is that the hobbits work so well for their author. He fumbles with them and fails, too, but everyone knows that without them the trilogy would not stand a chance. When Tolkien is "good with the hobbits" then everything else seems to go well, and when he is either cute or solemn about the hobbits, everything else becomes cute or solemn too. They are the one rein he is really interested in drawing on his endless inventiveness. Tolkien is no Henry James, and he has no interest in maintaining the point of view of a single consciousness, but he does seem to realize that he needs the hobbits always present to do their learning as the reader does his learning. The external world is far too real and far too glorious for Tolkien to tie himself only to what someone saw or felt, but he also knows that all he cares most for—the Ring, the war, the lore of Middle-earth—needs characters like the hobbits to explore and learn of their dimensions and worth. The war, we have said, is the story of the fight of the world in all its variousness to stay alive when the shadows lengthen and the darkness threatens to obliterate the natural separateness of living things. But the key word there is "alive." As a simple matter of arranging words Tolkien can make the world "live" just by taking all the dead metaphors he knows and writing them as though they were not dead—"the sun climbed the sky," "the wind fell still," "now a star had descended into the very earth." It is a simple enough trick. But its success is totally dependent on someone being there to see the dead metaphor and the lore "come to life." Over and over in the last two volumes Tolkien describes the sun blocked or faded by the shadows over Mordor, but it is only when these facts can be felt as a horror by Frodo or Sam that the passage has the effect Tolkien seeks for it—at other times it is mere ornament, and when it does the writing seems symbolic in the bad sense because the tie with the natural world is lost.

In his essay "On Fairy-Stories" Tolkien has a passage which reflects the importance of having the aliveness of the world being perceived:

> Recovery (which includes return and renewal of health) is a re-gaining—regaining of a clear view. I do not say 'seeing things as they are' and involve myself with the philosophers, though I might venture to say 'seeing things as we are (or were) meant to see them'—as things apart from ourselves. We need, in any case, to clean our windows; so that the things seen clearly may be freed from the drab blur of triteness or familiarity—from possessiveness. (p. 74)

Merely saying that there is a kind of vision that sees things as we are meant to see them is to state only a belief, and the outlining of this belief as a belief requires nothing more than using dead metaphors and insisting they are literally alive and true. But "recovery" demands a recoverer, someone for whom the world was drab and trite and for whom the metaphors about the aliveness of the natural world were dead indeed. This person is then "returned" to a sense that he is seeing things as he is meant to see them. This, in *The Lord of the Rings*, is where the hobbits come in. They come from the extremely comfortable and familiar Shire, possessed by their way of life there, and they are forced on their journey into gaining or regaining a quite different sense of their world. The Ring is the ultimate danger because it embodies the final possessiveness, the ultimate in power that binds things apart from ourselves to ourselves.

Sauron's weakness is that he cannot imagine others seeing the world differently from the way he sees it—as Gandalf says at one point, "That we should try to destroy the Ring itself has not yet entered into his darkest dream." Sauron sees the world possessively, tritely, while the hobbits are Tolkien's instruments of showing other ways in which the world can be seen. He needs, thus, a peculiar double way with the hobbits—they must be there to do the seeing, but what they must see is a world of things apart from themselves. That is why Tolkien can neither do without the hobbits on the one hand nor work strictly within their consciousnesses on the other—he must constantly mediate between the world as seen apart from any vision and the renewed sense of vision that the hobbits come to.

Pippin's description of the eyes of the Ent Treebeard as he first saw them is a good instance of a perception by a hobbit:

> One felt as though there was an enormous well behind them, filled up with ages of memory and long, slow, steady thinking; but their surface was sparkling with the present; like sun shimmering on the outer leaves of a vast tree, or on the ripples of a very deep lake. I don't know, but it felt as if something that grew in the ground—asleep, you might say, or just feeling itself as something between root-tip and leaf-tip, between deep earth and sky, had suddenly waked up, and was considering you with the same slow care that it had given to its own affairs for endless years. (II, 66-67)

The renewal here, the escape from ordinary vision, comes from Pippin's "seeing" that plant and animal are alike—at this moment they are indeed indistinguishable—Treebeard *is* like a tree, but he is like a lake too, and a well, and a man. With writing this good, every inflated gesture—"age of memory," "between deep earth and sky," "endless"—is

immediately shown up by the surrounding context. The last
clause is perhaps the best—". . . and it was considering
you with the same slow care it had given to its own inside
affairs for . . . years"—if you believe the world is alive and
you can write a phrase like that, nothing can be denied
you for long.

But such passages are very rare in the parts of the last
two volumes that deal with the war in the west. Much more
often we have something like this, Merry's meeting with
Théoden, King of the Mark of Rohan, outside Saruman's
castle:

> 'But there are not legends of their [the hobbits'] deeds, for it is
> said they do little, and avoid the sight of men, being able to
> vanish in a twinkling; and they can change their voices to
> resemble the piping of birds. But it seems that more could
> be said.'
>
> 'It could indeed, lord,' said Merry.
>
> 'For one thing,' said Théoden, 'I had not heard that they
> spouted smoke from their mouths.'
>
> 'That is not surprising,' answered Merry, 'for it is an art
> which we have not practised for more than a few generations.
> It was Tobold Hornblower, of Longbottom in the South-
> farthing, who first grew the true pipe-weed in his gardens,
> about the year 1070 according to our reckoning. How old
> Toby came by that plant. . . .'
>
> 'You do not know your danger, Théoden,' interrupted
> Gandalf. 'These hobbits will sit on the edge of ruin and discuss
> the pleasures of the table, or the small doings of their fathers,
> grandfathers, and great-grandfathers, and remoter cousins to
> the ninth degree, if you encourage them with undue patience.'
> (II, 163)

It is not Théoden who is unduly patient, really, but Tolkien,
and he loves to indulge himself by having the hobbits
discuss the pleasures of the table while sitting on the edge

of ruin. The hobbits are being used here, sported with patronizingly for the amazement of the solemn men and the amusement of those readers who like hobbits. Nothing is seen here, or recovered or renewed, and Merry is allowed to become a performer rather than a perceiver. This is in itself annoying, but it is accompanied by something graver, and more disappointing than irritating.

The men in Tolkien's world are all cast in rather ancient molds—the riders of Rohan are very much like Dark Age germanic tribes and the citizens of Gondor are residents of a decaying Alexandria or Constantinople. So their heroism is also ancient—stern, solemn, and filled with belief in portents and absolute loyalty to tribe and city:

> 'It is not strong,' said Faramir, 'I have sent the company of Ithilien to strengthen it, as I have said.'
>
> 'Not enough,I deem,' said Denethor. 'It is there that the first blow will fall. They will have need of some stout captain there.'
>
> 'There and elsewhere in many places,' said Faramir, and sighed. 'Alas for my brother, whom I too loved!' He rose. 'May I have your leave, father?' And then he swayed and leaned upon his father's chair.
>
> 'You are weary, I see,' said Denethor. 'You have ridden fast and far, and under shadows of evil in the air, I am told.'
>
> 'Let us not speak of that!' said Faramir.
>
> 'Then we will not,' said Denethor. 'Go now and rest as you may. Tomorrow's need will be sterner.' (III, 88)

This is not seeing things as they were meant to be seen. It is only trying to write in this century the way men wrote over a thousand years ago; it has all the solemnity of *Beowulf* or an early romance but with nothing of their dignity. There is nothing here for a hobbit to discover, nothing to see and by seeing to return to. Into such a world and such inflated ways of speaking and acting the hobbits can move in only one of two ways. They can either be clowns or else versions themselves of these heroes, either silly folk or plucky warriors, and in either case the reason for the hobbits is missing and so the result is false language, false manner, page after page of weary writing. This old world of men is almost certainly very important to Tolkien in one sense, and much effort in the trilogy is put into having it seem important and its fate impressive. But it turns out that Tolkien does so well with other creatures—either the traditional ones like dwarves and elves, or the fully invented ones like hobbits and Ents—because they are part of what for him is the natural world, the world of things waiting to be seen as we are meant to see. Men, though, Tolkien knows only through books and so with them he is truly derivative in the limiting sense of the word; he copies down their manners as he has read of them, but he does not see them "as they are meant to be seen."

Nor does it really help to reply that all this fits in with the whole story, though of course it does. We do see, to be sure, that the war in the west is necessary, and for two reasons, and though both are important neither is strong enough to bring it to life. The first reason for the war is strategic, as Gandalf makes clear:

'His Eye is now straining towards us, blind almost to all else that is moving. So we must keep it. Therein lies all our hope. This, then, is my counsel. We have not the Ring. In wisdom or great folly it has been sent away to be destroyed, lest it destroy us. Without it we cannot by force defeat his force. But we must at all costs keep his Eye from his true peril. We cannot achieve victory by arms, but by arms we can give the Ring-bearer his only chance, frail though it be.' (III, 156)

Tolkien's conception of his story is strong, and he shows that the war in the west, though subordinate, is essential.

But there is another and more important reason. Tolkien's whole intuition tells him that when Sauron resumed his ancient seat in Mordor and the shadows lengthened it was not only in Mordor that they fell. Saruman wrestled with Sauron and was defeated, and in his defeat set himself up as conqueror and hunter of the Ring; he enlisted orcs, he subverted Théoden with a despairing counselor; he and his workers cut trees wantonly in Fangorn and so woke Treebeard's anger; he corrupted some small folk in Bree and in the Shire and had them destroy willfully and pettily. Like Saruman, Denethor Steward of Gondor wrestled with Sauron and was defeated and despaired, but in his case despair led not to dreams of conquest but to fatalism and suicide. What all this shows us is that if evil is the refusal to live and let others live, then evil cannot be localized. Tolkien does need all Middle-earth to show when and how evil invades, corrupts, makes small and clutching and possessive, because for him evil is not merely Satanic.

That is why the scenes with Treebeard work so well. He is roused not just because Pippin and Merry appear in Fangorn but because Saruman's orcs have chopped down trees and Treebeard can see he has let himself "care" only about his "own inside affairs" much too long. Treebeard is something to be seen as well as a thing in himself while with almost everyone else in the west there is far too little there of interest for the hobbits to discover. The men of Rohan and Gondor are exactly the way the hobbits thought heroes were, the way we all thought they were, and for all his knowledge of their ways Tolkien has little to add. So while the conception remains strong throughout, the reason for having the conception—the moment-to-moment sense of discovery and return—is not acted upon for long stretches in these last two volumes. It turns out that Tolkien is no more interested in the old heroism than we are—for all his claims to the contrary he is betrayed by his imagination which becomes sterile when it can only repeat what the imaginations of others have told him.

Heavy though the weight of all this material is, however, no one has ever rejected Tolkien's book because of it. In the first place the worst parts come in the beginning of *The Return of the King* and by that time the grand expansiveness of the design is so clearly felt by most readers that the dullness of the writing page by page matters less than it would have before the design became clear. In the second place, there are some fine things here: the end of the battle of Helm's Deep when the Ents appear to surround Saruman's forces; the appearance of the Lord of the Nazgûl before the gates of Gondor; the last council in Gondor which is Gandalf's finest hour. In addition there are other moments where Tolkien tries valiantly to do something worth doing which he simply cannot bring off: Aragorn's ride through the Paths of the Dead and Gandalf's talk with Saruman after the fall of Isengard. In the third place, one knows while reading these sections that they will end and the story will move across the Anduin to Frodo and Sam where a much different kind of heroism and a vastly more impressive role for the hobbits are found. Here *The Lord of the Rings* has its central justification, and all that the first volume promised and all that the war in the west cannot offer are delivered with a pressure and stateliness that belongs to great literature.

After Frodo and Sam cross the river they find themselves in the Emyn Muil, a wasteland of crags and gullies:

> The hobbits stood now on the brink of a tall cliff, bare and bleak, its feet wrapped in mist; and behind them rose the broken highlands crowned with drifting cloud. A chill wind blew from the East. Night was gathering over the shapeless lands before them; the sickly green of them was fading

into a sullen brown. Far away to the right the Anduin, that had gleamed fitfully in sun-breaks during the day, was now hidden in shadow. But their eyes did not look beyond the River, back to Gondor, to their friends, to the lands of Men. South and east they stared to where, at the edge of the on-coming night, a dark line hung, like distant mountains of motionless smoke. (II, 209)

The moment we move across the river we find landscapes, and here Tolkien, because he has no real predecessors in these landscapes, is forced to invent carefully and keep the hobbits in the scene. The moment he can do that all goes well, and most of the job of his critic is quoting. Sam looks at the dark line and comments wryly:

'That's the one place in all the lands we've ever heard of that we don't want to see any closer; and that's the one place we're trying to get to! And that's just where we can't get, nohow.' (II, 209)

As the dangers increase and the route must be discovered rather than followed, Sam moves closer to a position equal to Frodo's, as his "we" here shows. In *The Fellowship of the Ring* Sam is very much the servant or slave of the last century, thinking only of Master Frodo, translating all problems into domestic logistics, speaking in a crude and ill-written slang designed to keep him in a class lower than Frodo and the others. But beginning here in the Emyn Muil all that gives way to a sense of mutual dependency forced upon them by the wilderness and the brittleness of their hopes.

Even before this, though, they are aware that Sméagol, the Gollum, is following them. Legolas had said at the Council of Elrond that Sméagol had escaped from the elves who had been guarding him after his capture by Gandalf. Earlier still, after losing the Ring to Bilbo, Sméagol had gone to Mordor, been broken by Sauron, and let go to try to find the Ring. He has tracked the fellowship south from his prison in the Mirkwood and now he has caught up with Frodo and Sam, only to be caught by them and "tamed." Sam is all for getting rid of him somehow, but Frodo had heard Gandalf say long before, back in the Shire:

> 'I have not much hope that Gollum can be cured before he dies, but there is a chance of it. And he is bound up with the fate of the Ring. My heart tells me that he has some part to play yet, for good or ill, before the end; and when that time comes, the pity of Bilbo [in not destroying Gollum] may rule the fate of many—yours not least.' (I, 69)

There are many such warnings and prophecies in the trilogy, and most are only shabby devices for framing the story. But here we have more than a device, for Frodo has his own feelings to act upon as well as Gandalf's musings. Sam can see in Sméagol only a dangerous nuisance because Sméagol is slithery and cunning and obviously given to lying. But Frodo has begun to feel the weight of the Ring quite heavily, and he can see—in a way that Sam cannot understand and Gandalf could only guess—why Gollum is more an object of pity than of scorn or anger. Here the natural kinship of similar creatures and the mythical kinship of the Ring-bearers becomes one:

> 'And what would you swear?' asked Frodo.
> 'To be very, very good," said Gollum. Then crawling to Frodo's feet he grovelled before him. . . . 'Sméagol will swear never, never to let Him [Sauron] have it. Never! Sméagol will save it. But he must swear on the Precious.'
> 'No, not on it,' said Frodo, looking down on him with stern pity. 'All you wish is to see it and touch it, if you can, though you know it would drive you mad. Not on it. Swear by it, if

you will. For you know where it is. Yes, you know, Sméagol. It is before you.'

For a moment it appeared to Sam that his master had grown and Gollum had shrunk: a tall, stern, shadow, a mighty lord who hid his brightness in grey cloud, and at his feet a little whining dog. Yet the two were in some way akin and not alien: they could reach one another's minds. (II, 225)

One can only hope that Tolkien himself knew that this relationship of Frodo and Sméagol, as seen by Sam, was his masterstroke. Here, in the instinctive wish to tame rather than to destroy Sméagol (it can hardly be called a decision), is the seed of Frodo's heroism. Just as he could see the light in Aragorn's eyes and so discover a young but ancient lord, so he can look at the Gollum at his feet and see "himself," struggling to stay alive against powers insuperably great. He cannot see what Sméagol can have in mind, but he knows this. Duty and need have become action, and here Frodo can understand who he is, what he must at least in part become, what he must struggle not to become. Gollum tells of his first trip to Mordor:

'Once, by accident it was, wasn't it, precious? Yes, by accident. But we won't go back, no, no!' Then suddenly his voice and language changed, and he sobbed in his throat, and spoke but not to them. 'Leave me alone, *gollum!* You hurt me, O my poor hands, *gollum!* I, we, I don't want to come back. I can't find it. I am tired. I, we can't find it, *gollum, gollum*, no, nowhere. They're always awake. Dwarves, Men, and Elves, terrible Elves with bright eyes. I can't find it. Ach!' (II, 222)

Sméagol is the expert on the journey, the one who knows where they are going because he has been there, and so Frodo, still against Sam's will, makes him their guide. They travel by night and sleep by day; Gollum leads them out of the gullies of the Emyn Muil and into the Dead Marshes, where lights like candles flicker in stagnant pools. Their guide gives them the information about the past here as Gandalf and Strider and Galadriel had done earlier; Sméagol knows about the Marshes just as Gandalf knew the way through Moria:

> 'Yes, yes,' said Gollum. 'All dead, all rotten. Elves and men and orcs. The Dead Marshes. There was a great battle long ago, so they told him when Sméagol was young, when I was young before the Precious came. It was a great battle. Tall men with long swords, and terrible Elves, and Orcses shrieking. They fought on the plain for days and months at the Black Gates. But the Marshes have grown since then, swallowed up the grave; always creeping, creeping.' (II, 235)

This is still a play of light and dark—"You should not look in it when the candles are lit"—and the act of seeing is an act of understanding the landscape by understanding history. But all else has changed from the silent wonder of Lórien and the open menaces of Moria. Then "a black shadow loosed from Mordor, a vast shaped winged and ominous," a Nazgûl comes, "sweeping the fen-reek with its ghastly wings." Finally, "Frodo and Sam got up, rubbing their eyes, like children wakened from an evil dream to find the familiar night still over the world" (II, 237). But when day comes, "Frodo looked round in horror":

> Dreadful as the Dead Marshes had been, and the arid moors of the Noman-lands, more loathsome far was the country that the crawling day now slowly unvieled to his shrinking eyes. Even to the Mere of Dead Faces some haggard phantom of green spring would come, but here neither spring nor summer would ever come again. Here nothing lived, not even the leprous growths that feed on rottenness. The gasping pools were choked with ash and crawling muds, sickly white and grey, as if the mountains had vomited the filth of their entrails upon

the lands about. High mounds of crushed and powdered rock, great cones of earth fire-blasted and poison-stained, stood like an obscene graveyard in endless rows, slowly revealed in the reluctant light. (II, 239)

Children, lost on the way to the mountain of their doom, led by a wretched snivelling Wight—in this bleakest of modern landscapes Tolkien makes every act an heroic perception. This is the legacy of the Lord of the Rings; it was a brilliant stroke to use another of those repetitions that makes a metaphor here: the day crawls, the mud crawls, and the "light" is thus indeed "reluctant." This is no world for the old heroes but rather the landscape of a journey made by one who knows no more of heroism than Joyce's Bloom. With each step into this country the old terms for the struggle of good against evil—courage, hope, despair— seem increasingly irrelevant:

One Ring to rule them all, One Ring to find them,
One Ring to bring them all, and in the darkness bind them.

The work is called *The Lord of the Rings* and though Frodo never fully becomes Sauron's servant he does bring the Ring to Mordor and he is bound to what he sees there. In the Marshes, on the foul plains before Mordor, down the dark road to Minas Morgul, and up the stairs into the mountains to Cirith Ungol, we see no fight of good and evil but only the effects of being alive and the consequences of giving in to death.

Frodo, because he bears the Ring, becomes less and less able to do more than merely walk, and so Sam must assume command more and more. Frodo's last great effort comes after the stairs have been climbed and the hobbits discover that Sméagol has reached his destination. For he keeps his promise, and hideously, not to deliver them into Sauron's hands. Instead he takes them to Shelob, a giant spider-like creature who lives in the caves and the top of the mountains:

> There agelong she had dwelt, an evil thing in spider-form, even such as once of old had lived in the Land of the Elves in the West that is now under the Sea, such as Beren fought in the Mountains of Terror in Doriath, and so came to Lúthien upon the green sward amid the hemlocks in the moonlight long ago. (II, 332)

Here is lore pouring forth wantonly, but by this time Tolkien is so strongly in control of his present that almost any news of the past can help describe it. One needs to know nothing of elves and Beren and Doriath in order to read rightly the age and power of Shelob:

> Already, years before, Gollum had beheld her, Sméagol who pried into all dark holes, and in past days he had bowed and worshipped her, and the darkness of her evil will walked through all the days of his weariness beside him, cutting him off from light and from regret. And he had promised to bring her food. Little she knew of or cared for towers, or rings, or anything devised by mind or hand, who only desired death for all others, mind and body, and for herself a glut of life, alone, swollen till the mountains could no longer hold her up and the darkness could not contain her. (II, 332-333)

Tolkien has filled his world so full that he can easily distinguish Shelob from the rest by saying "little she knew of or cared for towers, or rings, or anything devised by mind or hand"—all her age and filth is right there, and for a moment even Sauron becomes a kin of the hobbit and, by comparison with Shelob, lofty in his aims and lusts. Also, as we see what has happened to Gollum, and why he has brought the hobbits here—"it may well be, O yes, it may well be that when She throws away the bones and the empty garments, we shall find it, we shall get it, the Precious"—we can also see how alike he is to Frodo now, for Frodo too is almost cut off from light and from regret in all the days of *his* weariness. But it is still "almost"—he fights and wounds Shelob with the help of Sting, Bilbo's sword, and of a vial of light given him by Galadriel. But he falls too, and suddenly Sam is left with a bitter choice: he can stay by his fallen master, or he can take the Ring and go on.

There follow two chapters where Sam is entirely the focus of the story, and though there are some discrepancies of fact and some awkwardnesses that come from Sam's determinedly domestic habit of mind, they show how well Tolkien can overcome even some of his worst faults when the pressure of his tale is fully upon him. At first Sam chooses to go on with the Ring, but when he discovers that a cohort of orcs has dragged Frodo's body away, he finds he cannot continue. He stops outside the huge tower of Cirith Ungol, built long before by men of Gondor to keep Sauron in Mordor and now used by Sauron to keep his slaves from escaping, and looks toward Mount Doom, where the Ring was forged:

> . . . he felt himself enlarged, as if he were robed in a huge distorted shadow of himself, a vast and ominous threat halted upon the walls of Mordor. . . . Already the Ring tempted him, gnawing at his will and reason. Wild fantasies arose in his mind; and he saw Samwise the Strong, Hero of the Age, striding with a flaming sword across the darkened land, and armies flocking to his call as he marched to the overthrow of Barad-dûr. (III, 177)

Tolkien knows, to be sure, of the vulgarity of Sam's fantasies, yet for a moment he can do no more than patronize him:

> In that hour of trial it was the love of his master that helped
> most to hold him firm; but also deep down in him lived still
> unconquered his plain hobbit-sense: he knew in the core of
> his heart that he was not large enough to bear such a burden,
> even if such visions were not a mere cheat to betray him. The
> one small garden of a free gardener was all his need and due,
> not a garden swollen to a realm; his own hands to use, not
> the hands of others to command. (III, 177)

It is awful, in the midst of the grandeur of the surrounding
pages, to realize Tolkien is not above such writing, for here
the snobbery that could create Sam in the first place is still
able to say that Sam really did not wish to be uppity after
all, and "hobbit-sense" is only a synonym of rigid class
consciousness. But then all is saved, because Sam himself
speaks and puts the matter rightly:

> 'And anyway all these notions are only a trick,' he said to
> himself. 'He'd spot me and cow me, before I could so much
> as shout out. He'd spot me, pretty quick, if I put the Ring on
> now, in Mordor.' (III, 177)

This *is* hobbit sense, and even though the whole matter of
the trilogy is here reduced to a question of getting caught,
the scale is the right one and Sam faces his task in the act
of knowing who his enemy is. He moves into the tower to
find Frodo, a version of a hero himself, amused now as he
overhears an orc-captain describe him as "a great fighter,
one of those bloody-handed Elves." He climbs the tower and
comes out in a large chamber where an orc stands with
a whip over a bundle:

> With a cry Sam leapt across the floor, Sting in hand. The orc
> wheeled around, but before it could make a move Sam slashed
> its whip-hand from its arm. . . . Sam's next blow went wide,
> and thrown off his balance he fell backwards, clutching at the

orc as it stumbled over him. Before he could scramble up he heard a cry and a thud. The orc in its wild haste had tripped on the ladder-head and fallen through the open trap-door. Sam gave no more thought to it. He ran to the figure huddled on the floor. It was Frodo. (III, 186)

Sam's heroism, then, has nothing to do with the Ring, really, and the closer Tolkien tries to bring Sam to that kind of stature the more he stumbles on the old problem of Sam's servility. But Frodo has fallen here, and he is now unable to get any farther with his burden—as Sméagol had guided the hobbits down to Mordor, so now must guide while they are in this dark country. Frodo's greatness lies in his ability to know this, to gain and seek the help of others because he cannot move alone. But the price has been awful and great; when he discovers that Sam now has the Ring he almost falls to pieces:

> 'Give it to me!' he cried, standing up, holding out a trembling hand. 'Give it to me at once! You can't have it.'
> 'All right, Mr. Frodo,' said Sam, rather startled. 'Here it is!' Slowly he drew the Ring out and passed the chain over his head. 'But you're in the land of Mordor now, sir; and when you get out you'll see the Fiery Mountain and all. You'll find the Ring very dangerous now, and very hard to bear. If it's too hard a job, I could share it with you, maybe.' (III, 188)

Tolkien has caught Sam's position beautifully—he both knows how terrible the burden is going to be for Frodo, and he wants the Ring, if only in some small way, for himself. But Frodo, for a moment totally lost, can only see Sam's want as a reflection of his own much greater want, cut off as he is from light and from regret, bound as he is in the shadows:

'No, no!' cried Frodo, snatching the Ring, and chain from Sam's hands. 'No you won't, you thief!' He panted, staring at Sam with eyes wide with fear and enmity.

For a moment Frodo is himself Sméagol, but then:

A mist seemed to clear from his eyes, and he passed a hand over his aching brow. The hideous vision had seemed so real to him, half bemused as he was still with wound and fear. Sam had changed before his very eyes into an orc again, leering and pawing at his treasure, a foul little creature with greedy eyes and slobbering mouth. But now the vision had passed. There was Sam kneeling before him, his face wrung with pain, as if he had been stabbed in the heart. (III, 188)

Frodo has "bound" Sam by seeing him as an orc, by placing him under his feet as he had placed Gollum, by seeking the Ring as his own, but then he is still Frodo, and Sam is still Sam, and Sméagol is nowhere to be seen.

The hideous moment passed, Sam helps Frodo on with an orc uniform and they descend the mountain to the plains of Mordor. Frodo is almost helpless now as they move along the high road to Barad-Dûr that is now deserted because Gandalf's lure has captured Sauron's attention. Sam has to pull and carry Frodo up Mount Doom, but when they reach the brink of the chasm where the Ring was forged, he suddenly hears Frodo, and in a voice "clearer and more powerful than Sam had ever heard him use":

'I have come. But I do not choose now to do what I came to do. I will not do this deed. The Ring is mine!' And suddenly, as he set it on his finger, he vanished from Sam's sight. (III, 223)

Suddenly Sméagol is there, and he knocks Sam down and pursues the Ring-bearer; Sauron too leaps in response:

From all his policies and webs of fear and treachery, from all his stratagems and wars his mind shook free; and throughout his realm a tremor ran, his slaves quailed, and his armies halted, and his captains suddenly steerless, bereft of will, wavered and despaired. . . . At his summons, wheeling with a rending cry, in a last desperate race there flew, faster than the winds, the Nazgûl, the Ringwraiths, and with a storm of wings they hurtled southwards to Mount Doom. (III, 223)

But too late, for at the edge Gollum struggles with the invisible Frodo. Years before Sauron had lost the Ring when Isildur cut it from his hand, and so now Frodo, Lord of the Ring for a moment, is attacked:

Suddenly Sam saw Gollum's long hands draw upwards to his mouth; his white fangs gleamed, and snapped as they bit. Frodo gave a cry, and there he was, fallen upon his knees at the chasm's edge.

Sméagol shouts that the prize is his, "and with that, even as his eyes were lifted up to gloat on his prize, he stepped too far, toppled, wavered for a moment on the brink, and then with a shriek he fell." As the Ring falls to its doom the mountain shakes and throbs. Sam runs and picks up Frodo:

And there upon the dark threshold of the Sammath Naur, high above the plains of Mordor, such wonder and terror came on him that he stood still forgetting all else, and gazed as one turned to stone . . . . Towers fell and mountains slid; walls crumbled and melted, crashing down; vast spires of smoke and spouting steams went billowing up, up, until they toppled like an overwhelming wave, and its wild crest curled and came foaming down upon the land. . . . Down like lashing whips fell a torrent of black rain. And into the heart of the storm, with a cry that pierced all other sounds, tearing the clouds asunder, the Nazgûl came, shooting like flaming bolts, as caught in the fiery ruin of hill and sky they crackled, withered, and went out. (III, 224)

With power great enough to bind everything, Sauron's world can only be destroyed with a bang. But the instrument of destruction was the Gollum and Frodo, neither grand at all, especially at the climax. So Sauron is defeated, and Sam and Frodo are left:

'Well, this is the end, Sam Gamgee,' said a voice by his side. And there was Frodo, pale and worn, and yet himself again; and in his eyes there was peace now, neither strain of will, nor madness, nor any fear. His burden was taken away. (III, 224)

But as Frodo says almost immediately, he never destroyed the Ring; rather, "his burden was taken away" by the only one whose need to make the Ring his own was greater than Frodo's. This is what Frodo first thinks of. Peaceful though he is, he is bound too, and he seeks solace and compassion for his bound companion the Gollum.

In the end they are rescued and returned, first to Gondor where Aragorn is crowned, then to the Shire where Saruman and his cronies have destroyed so much. But trees that have been destroyed can be replaced, food can be grown and children born, while Frodo finds his wounds cannot heal, his ties cannot be cut, and he must leave. He does so, however, knowing that this too in its way is natural, and that he must go to the Grey Havens and over the sea to the west with Gandalf and the faded elves because he too was part of their age, the instrument of its end and of the world's living still to have more cycles and more ages. There is a bang, then, in the destruction of Mordor, and a whimper too in Frodo's discovery that he will never be well again. But more than either of these there is merely a passing away of the heaviness that is beyond nostalgia and pain, a passing away through the search for peace in another world, across the sea.

For it is Tolkien's lot, just as it has been that of all great writers, to be an historian of his own imagination and to describe the history of his world as he traced his imaginative boundaries. His world, furthermore, is not entirely his own but belongs to us as well, not just because we read him but because we are of his time and his century. Personally perhaps Tolkien would have wished it differently for in much he has written is a great sense of distaste for his own times, and when he has spoken in his own voice (and not as an historian) he can be very harsh:

> Not long ago—incredible though it may seem—I heard a clerk of Oxenford declare that he 'welcomed' the proximity of mass-production robot factories, and the roar of self-obstructive mechanical traffic, because it brought his university into 'contact with real life.' He may have meant that the way men were living and working in the twentieth century was increasing in barbarity at an alarming rate, and that the loud demonstrations of this in the streets of Oxford might serve as a warning that it is not possible to preserve for long an oasis of sanity in a desert of unreason by mere fences, without actual offensive action (practical and intellectual). I fear he did not. In any case the expression 'real life' in this context seems to fall short of academic standards. The notion that motor-cars are more 'alive' than, say, centaurs or dragons is curious; that they are more 'real' than, say, horses is pathetically absurd. ("On Fairy-Stories," p. 77)

But fortunately we need not trust the artist when we have such a magnificent tale to trust instead. For Tolkien is not of Middle-earth any more than he is of the germanic dark ages that are his special area of scholastic competence. Willy nilly he belongs to our time, and the more he attempts to ignore or escape this fact the worse he becomes as a writer.

William Empson finishes his *Some Versions of Pastoral* with the statement that virtue, intelligence, and good manners are alike lonely and absurd confessions of human limitations. They are, he adds, all the more necessary in our world. That is the idea of modern heroism perhaps most congenial to the liberal spirit, for it accepts the facts of modern life at something like Tolkien's private evaluation of them, and then simply refuses to knuckle under. Empson is a cheerful man, however, and a consistently graceful one, and Tolkien is neither. He is a Christian, not a skeptic, and he believes that the taproot to the past is not yet dried or withered. It would be difficult, therefore, to expect that Tolkien would warm to the idea that his imagination is vastly superior to his theology and that his imagination is of his own time. There are many heroisms in *The Lord of the Rings*, and some are staunch in their commitment to what Empson and many others would consider laughably out of date. Tolkien knows how he wants to reply to their derision, and his defense of his view of the world is careful and polished. But it is, finally, worth rather little because the heroism he writes of best is very modern and even very Empsonian; imagination betrays belief here, as it does so often, yet opens us onto larger worlds too.

For Frodo must try to survive and to win by surviving, and in that case not only valor and physical prowess but the very idea of battles against enemies is not particularly germane. Tolkien has arranged his story so that Sauron cannot openly affect Frodo at all. He binds Frodo only as Frodo binds himself, and Frodo is heroic because he recognizes there is something more important than the question of whether or not he is bound. The landscape of Frodo's great deeds is Sauron's weapon, and for that reason one can call the book Christian and Frodo a pilgrim. But it is a landscape fashioned by the imagination of this century; the wasteland, the valley of ashes, the nightmare cities of Rupert Birkin and Joseph K. What these other authors have tended to think of as the human condition Tolkien finds the grounds for heroic quest, but the circumstances and the atmosphere are the same. He differs from the others primarily because he believes and shows that loneliness, though necessary and unavoidable, is partly a chosen state, the result as much of despair as of the facts of life.

It is for this reason that Sam and Sméagol are so important. In their different ways they are better equipped than Frodo to carry the Ring to Mordor. But they are antagonists because imaginatively they are Frodo's inferiors; they cannot trust or sympathize with each other and they cannot understand Frodo's trust and sympathy for them both. Sam feels the power of the Ring only momentarily, and childishly even then, while Sméagol has been totally corrupted by it, and in each case they are protected in a way Frodo cannot be. Sam serves Frodo and Sméagol serves the Ring, but only Frodo serves the heroic idea of the Ring's destruction. If neither is of anything like Frodo's stature, however, he is lost without them. But Frodo knows this and because he knows it can "find" himself in his love for Sam and his compassion for Sméagol and his dependence on them. As long as he is thus dependent, and willingly so, the urge to possessiveness that lies at the heart of the Ring's power to destroy can be combatted. Frodo's virtue lies in his good manners, and his good manners are his recognition of the blessed and cursed otherness of his servant and his wretched guide.

In a moment of respite on the stairs of Cirith Ungol, before Sméagol takes them to Shelob, Frodo and Sam have a conversation about the songs that will be sung of them after this is all over. Sam does most of the talking, but Frodo makes the key points: 1) "You may know, or guess, what kind of tale it is, happy-ending or sad-ending, but the people in it don't know. And you don't want them to." 2) "No, they never end as tales . . . but the people in them come, and go, when their parts ended." 3) "Why Sam, to hear you somehow makes me as merry as if the story was already written. But you've left out one of the chief characters: Samwise the stouthearted . . . and Frodo wouldn't have got far without Sam, would he. . . ." 4) "It's not good to worry about him [Sméagol] now. We couldn't have gotten so far, not even within sight of the pass, without him, and so we'll have to put up with his ways. If he's false, he's false" (II, 321-322). Sam can begin to understand what Frodo is saying, but he cannot by himself rise to the grim and yet almost sublime equipoise of Frodo's weary generosity. But he knows that quality is there in Frodo, as indeed, for a moment, does the Gollum. For after this conversation Frodo and Sam fall asleep and Sméagol discovers them thus, peaceful in each other's arms:

> A strange expression passed over his lean hungry face. The gleam faded from his eyes, and they went dim and grey, old and tired. A spasm of pain seemed to twist him, and he turned away, peering back up towards the pass, shaking his head, as if engaged in some interior debate. Then he came back, and slowly putting out a trembling hand, very cautiously he touched Frodo's knee—but almost the touch was a caress. For a fleeting moment, could one of the sleepers have seen him, they would have thought that they beheld an old weary hobbit, shrunken by the years that carried him far beyond his time, beyond friends and kin, and the fields and streams of youth, an old starved pitiable thing. (II, 324)

This is Sméagol's finest moment, and so, by implication, it is Frodo's finest moment too. Beyond friends and kin, old and tired, Sméagol loves the specialness that is Frodo's care of him. The love is almost without parallel in our modern literature, because it is neither filial nor sexual but the tentative unbelieving response to a caring so unlikely it seems heroic even to the Gollum. Whatever might have come afterwards because of this moment is destroyed when Sam wakes up first. He accuses Gollum of being a sneak, and by the time Frodo wakes Sméagol is back to his old whining and sniveling self, ready to lead the hobbits to Shelob.

So in a book about hobbits and their return to a world made new, Frodo is the one who can be returned to himself as he sees the light shine in others. Perhaps in Tolkien's official scheme of things this need not seem as important as the original turning out from self to see the world as it is meant to be seen. But still, Frodo finds in this turning out a means to self-knowledge, and in his scarred and beautiful relationship with Sméagol he finds himself and lives by the light of the self he finds. He is saved from the worst ravages of the Ring because he binds himself to others rather than to love of power, and that is his heroism. That is what most profoundly arouses Tolkien's imagination and sympathy too—it may not be what *The Lord of the Rings* is all about and it certainly is not all that it is good for, but it is the cornerstone of its greatness. Over and over in the trilogy we are told of the prices that must be paid when one is called upon to pay them, and with Gandalf, Aragorn, Merry, Pippin, Faramir, the faded elven Kings, and many others we see that such prices are being demanded and paid. But these are ancient heroisms, ancient prices and payments, known and felt to be old and therefore always a trifle artificial, derived, and decorative.

But this very artificiality is our guide to the genuineness of Frodo's heroism and to our understanding that Tolkien is an historian of heroic acts. For in his Middle-earth, as all the other "great deeds" are chronicled, we respond to that which is most like ourselves because our author so responds too. We see, without in the least needing to make the seeing into a formulation, what the heroism of our time is and can be: lonely, lost, scared, loving, willing, and compassionate—to bind oneself to the otherness of others by recognizing our common livingness. History may create the conditions of chaos, but man's nature is to reply to history as well as to acknowledge it.

INDEX

The Index is divided into three sections: names from Middle-earth, names of Tolkien's critics, and points of reference used by the critics. The last section, where possible, groups the references by categories, so that for Nebuchadnezzar or Othello the reader will be referred to Bible or Shakespeare.

I. NAMES FROM MIDDLE-EARTH

II. TOLKIEN'S CRITICS

III. POINTS OF REFERENCE

Tolkien and the Critics

Tolkien and the Critics

DE(